THE MAGIC OF SHAPESHIFTING

THE MAGIC OF

Shape*shifting*

ROSALYN GREENE

WEISERBOOKS
Boston, MA/York Beach, ME

First published in 2000 by
Red Wheel/Weiser, LLC
York Beach, ME
With editorial offices at:
368 Congress Street
Boston, MA 02210
www.redwheelweiser.com

Library of Congress Cataloging-in-Publication Data

Greene, Rosalyn.
    The magic of shapeshifting / Rosalyn Greene.
      p. cm.
    Includes bibliographical references and index.
    ISBN 1-57863-171-8 (pbk. : alk. paper)
    1. Metamorphosis—Miscellanea. 2. Animals—
Miscellanea. 3. Magic. I. Title: Magic of shapeshifting. II.
Title.
BF1623.M47 G74 2000
133—dc21   00-026121

EB

Typeset in 11/15 Adobe Garamond

Cover and text design by Kathryn Sky-Peck

PRINTED IN THE UNITED STATES OF AMERICA

09 08 07 06 05 04
10 9 8 7 6 5 4 3

*The paper used in this publication meets the minimum requirements of the American National Standard
for Information Sciences—Permanence of Paper for Printed Library Materials Z39.48-1992 (R1997).*

Dedicated to

Moria, Brownie, Laura, Becky, Chris, and all the others I wish I could thank here. To those who've taught me everything, and labored, questioned, and wondered along with me at the strange and wondrous things life brings us. Thank you, for without all of you, there could be no book.

Table of Contents

Prologue

This book is about people who possess animal medicine—people who can draw on animal power. Certain animal people are often called "shifters" because of their ability to "shift" into their power animal or totem, astrally, mentally, or in some other way. This ranges from those shifters who practice shifting spirit journeys and those who work with familiars and animal spirit guides, to berserkers, mental shifters, and even, some say, physical shifters. All of these types of animal-people would probably have been called "werewolves" or something comparable if they had lived in more primitive times. In fact, the phenomena associated with them is probably what started many of these legends.

In this sense, werewolves, as well as werebears, werecats, werefoxes, and many other "were-species" do still exist in modern times. They are certainly not the type of "werewolves" depicted in modern novels and movies. In fact, they are not quite the kind of "werewolves" depicted in most folklore either, because the folklore is warped by misunderstandings of the basic phenomena.

I have had the good fortune to know quite a number of shifters in this life. I, myself, am a mental and astral shifter, and I believe that I was a physical shifter in a former life. By drawing on these sources of information, as well as on studies of the paranormal and of shapeshifting folklore, I have produced this book. I cannot guarantee that it is accurate in every particular, but it certainly presents an accurate view both of what shifters believe about themselves and of modern shifter culture.

I have done my best to present the evidence for every type of shifting, and to explain why shifters themselves believe it. The curious reader can easily research many of the same sources that I have used, for I've made an effort to show how all shifting phenomena is rather closely related to other esoteric phenomena, phenomena that is well-documented, and that is believed by many people.

In this book, I have described different kinds of shifters, where they come from, how ordinary people can become shifters, and how weak shapeshifters can become stronger, more regular shapeshifters. I show how to get in touch with your own animal side and your animal spirit guide, and how to produce shifts. I show what magic and techniques are related to shapeshifting, how to choose and train a familiar, and what your familiar can do for you. I tell you what to expect if you do become a shifter, the most common problems you may encounter, and their solutions. I show you how to find a "pack," or organize one yourself, and tell you about modern shifting society. I also show you how to distinguish powerful visions, anxiety attacks, and your own imagination from real shifting and the warning signs of an immanent shift.

There are very few comprehensive and reliable sources of information on shapeshifting, although there are many people in need of this information. With the back-to-nature movement and other trends, more and more people are discovering their dormant animal side awakening, but don't know what is happening to them or what to do about it. I hope that this book is a guide and a blessing for shifters everywhere, helping them to understand themselves and helping the world to better understand shifters.

A WORD OF WARNING

This book is meant to be a compilation of the beliefs and practices of modern shifters. It goes into detail on these beliefs and practices, but it should not be viewed as a source of expert advice for those who wish to follow such practices. It should only be viewed as a source of information and as a collection of rough introductory guidelines, insights, and questions for those who follow such practices.

There are dangers and risks, both mundane and psychic, associated with some of these practices, especially with salves or poisonous herbs. Those who intend to follow the path of a shifter, or who are already on it and wish to go farther, should assess these risks wisely and know that, if they choose to take these risks, they themselves are responsible for any bad effects. At no point in this book do I advise anyone to undertake any practice that may be risky. I merely compile information on these practices and introduce guidelines for those who already intend to pursue these practices.

Concerning those practices that are risky, I have done my best to outline the dangers involved, but the reader should keep in mind that my primary purpose has been to record the beliefs and practices of the shifter movement. There may easily be risks of which I am not aware. Those who decide to follow any of the practices outlined in this book, whether I warn of risks or not, are themselves responsible for any trouble in which they might find themselves.

If you are of unstable physical or mental health, you should not engage in these practices. Again and again throughout this book, I have emphasized that strong physical health is a baseline requirement for following the path of a shifter, and that strong mental health is necessary to successfully navigate the depths of your animal self and subconscious, and of integrating these with your conscious self. Only certain people are ready to follow the path of the shifter, and even these have no guarantee that they will not find themselves in trouble.

—ROSALYN GREENE

1

Beginning the
Shapeshifter's Journey

Did werewolves ever exist? If so, were they anything like what we "know" about them from the main source of the modern werewolf stereotype: movies and novels? The answer, I believe, is "yes" to the first question, and "not exactly, but sort of" to the second.

Consider these events: In the recent past, a young anthropologist named Carlos Castaneda agreed to become apprenticed to an American Indian shaman. In the course of his apprenticeship, he experienced many "impossible" things, including transforming into a crow.[1] And, according to many of the locals to whom he talked, the "diablero," or were-animal, still exists among the Hispanic and Indian populations of the American Southwest.[2] Carlos Castaneda wrote a number of books about his experiences with shamanic magic, and became quite famous among New Agers.

---

[1] Carlos Castaneda, *The Teachings of Don Juan* (Berkeley: University of California Press, 1968), pp. 121–127.
[2] Carlos Castaneda, *The Teachings of Don Juan*, pp. 2–3.

How many others have experienced transformations like Castaneda's? How many similar events have occurred about which no books were written? Judging from the similarity of Carlos' account to the shapeshifting folklore of the region, I would say that quite a few people may have had similar experiences.

Consider another example: A young man had constant vivid, realistic dreams of being a wolf, and of turning into a wolf.[3] In these dreams, he was always himself, but his mind was entirely the mind of a wolf. All his life, he constantly felt as if he were somehow a werewolf, but he did not identify at all with the type of werewolf depicted in movies and novels. Later in life, he happened to go to a ritual meditation held by Native Americans. During the meditation, he felt himself change into a wolf, even though he was awake, and, for the first time, he experienced a mixture of human and wolf mentality while "transformed." After the meditation, one of the Indians said he had seen him turn into a wolf. Others said he had remained human the whole time, but turned into a wolf in their visions. Some also saw his wolf spirit guide, and described the guide in detail, completely accurately. Is this young man a werewolf?

A young woman I know was meowing soon after her birth. Later in life, she found she had a very special relationship with cats. She developed the ability to project her consciousness into animals. She could see what they saw, feel what they felt, and could even sometimes move their bodies as if they were her own. This all occurred without her ousting the original resident mind, which was in there with her and also seeing, feeling, and walking. She could even find out secrets this way, seeing places only cats could get into. Was this young woman a werecat? In more superstitious times, she would certainly have been considered one.

Another young woman had all the typical signs of being a "shifter" her whole life.[4] As a girl, she started having mental shifts. Later in life, she began having very vivid, realistic experiences of running as a wolf at night,

---

[3] I originally heard this story from others, but tracked down the man to get the details straight. Throughout this book, when I relate an anecdote, if it came from a book I will footnote the book. If it happened to someone I've actually talked with or know, I'll say that. In some cases, I never talked to the person, and I'll let you know that I heard story second- or third-hand.

[4] I personally know her very well, and was able to see some evidence of this occurrence.

and her clothes were often muddy in the morning. She considered this as dreaming, combined with sleepwalking. One night, during one of these experiences, a dog she knew ran with her and kept bothering her. She growled at him, but he wouldn't leave. She bit him hard on a front foot, and he yelped and limped away. The next morning, the dog had a front paw split open to the bone and was very afraid of her, but had never been afraid before. Is she a werewolf?

A man I knew, who is a shifter, once felt lonely for some friends who lived far away. He had a vision of going there as a wolf, and trying to play with them. His friends later reported that, at the same time as his vision, a ghostly wolf with glowing eyes had appeared in their apartment and scared them to death by trying to "get" them. Both agreed on all particulars of this visit. In his wolf mind, the man had been puzzled by their fear and kept trying to play with them.

In another relatively modern account, the famous occultist Dion Fortune had some skirmishes with another woman occultist who was a rather unsavory character. Once, this woman sent a ghostly form resembling a giant house cat.[5] Another time, Dion herself was under psychic attack while in a trance, and awoke with many cat scratches on her body.[6] On questioning, she found that this woman was well-known for these scratch marks. If this woman had lived in the Middle Ages, would she have been called a werecat?

These are all modern examples of the phenomenon of shifting. I chose more modern examples, including some that have happened to friends, partly because I wanted to show that these things do still happen. They have not all died out, as some believe. And the older legends, even some that aren't that old, are extremely numerous, existing in every culture and every era (see figure 1, page 4). We know that "30,000 cases of lycanthropy were reported to secular and church officials between 1520 and 1630" in Europe.[7] Thirty thousand in just about a century! And 1520 is after many of the educated people in Europe decided that shapeshifters

5 Dion Fortune, *Psychic Self-Defense* (York Beach, ME: Samuel Weiser, 1992), p. 156.
6 Fortune, *Psychic Self-Defense,* p. 158.
7 Paul Katzeff, *Full Moons* (Secaucus, NJ: Citadel Press, 1981), p. 58.

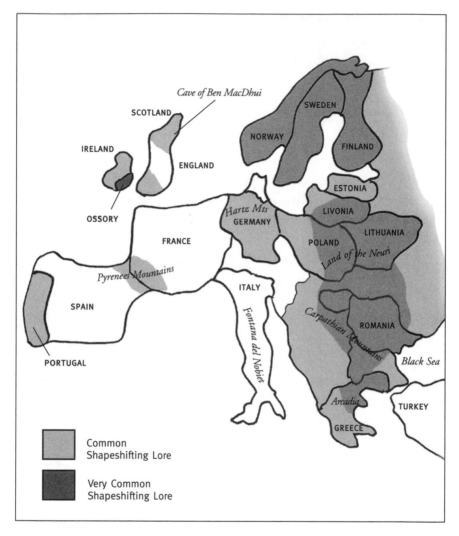

Figure 1. Distribution of werewolf and shapeshifting folklore in Europe. This map shows where werewolf and shapeshifting lore are most common. Note the "werewolf belt" along Eastern Europe, from Greece in the south to Scandinavia in the north. This belt includes the land of the Neuri and the famous Carpathian mountains, known in former times as Transylvania. Some other features of interest are the haunted werewolf cave of Ben MacDhui, and the Fontana del Nobiet near Cimapiasole in Italy, which is reputed to be a lycanthropic stream. (Map is approximate only.)

didn't exist. In even earlier times, especially before 1000, missionaries and clergy found it nearly impossible to get people to give up beliefs in shapeshifting. In 970, Baianus, a prince of Bulgaria, was said to be able to turn himself into both a wolf and a bird.[8] He was said to transform frequently *in public,* in front of all the people, who were amazed at his transformations.

This just scratches the surface of the tradition in Europe, where, historically, shapeshifting folklore has been least common. By reading books about werewolves, which mostly concentrate on the later famous French trials of individual werewolves, many people are led to believe that shapeshifters were rare, solitary, and unusual cases. On the contrary, hordes of shapeshifters are reported in much of the folklore.

Take, for instance, the time when hundreds of werewolves overran Constantinople. This happened in the year 1542, when Constantinople was a major city. It was reported that packs of werewolves roamed the streets and alleys of the city. Things got so bad that Süleyman II, with his Janizaries, hunted many down, killing at least 150 of them.[9] Can you imagine that? Hundreds of werewolves, roaming about a large, major city, in front of countless witnesses, after educated people declared they didn't exist!

And this is not the only case of numerous witnesses reporting large masses of shapeshifters. The Neuri were a nomadic people living in the area that is now Poland and Lithuania who were reported to be hereditary shapeshifters and sorcerers.[10] Whole clans of the Irish were also supposed to be hereditary shapeshifters.[11]

Consider the legend of the leaping wall. This wall was the last remaining portion of an old castle that stood between Lithuania, Livonia, and Courland. It was said that thousands of shapeshifters used to come together at a certain time each year to celebrate at this old castle. They held

---

[8] Montague Summers, *The Werewolf* (Secaucus, NJ: Citadel Press, 1973), p. 245.

[9] Montague Summers, *The Werewolf,* p. 146.

[10] Montague Summers, *The Werewolf,* p. 133.

[11] One of the Irish names that is intrinsically associated with lycanthropy is Fáelad, supposed to be derived from Laignech Fáelad, the founder of a famous line of hereditary Irish werewolves. See Montague Summers, *The Werewolf,* p. 205.

contests such as leaping over this wall. It was also said that many of these werewolves were rich nobles.[12]

From old-time Prussia, Livonia, and Lithuania come reports of packs of werewolves that gathered each Christmas in many villages, breaking into people's beer cellars and having drunken celebrations.[13] This may sound ridiculous, but there were far too many people seriously reporting it, and even complaining to the authorities for something to be done, for it to be simply a "tall tale" or a children's fairy tale. Modern werewolf books that discuss these cases attribute these events to gangs of thugs in werewolf costumes, but the people who made these claims certainly believed otherwise—especially since the werewolves were said to be in full wolf form when they did this, indistinguishable from natural wolves except by their behavior of breaking into beer cellars and getting drunk. It is hard to believe that ordinary wolves would do this, let alone on a particular holiday and never at any other time. It is also hard to imagine that anyone could create "real wolf" (not "wolfman") costumes that could fool people into thinking they were normal wolves.

These cases are just a small sampling of the enormous body of shapeshifting folklore out there, a fair amount of which is substantiated by multiple witnesses, with impeccable reputations.[14] Moreover, there are similarities across different cultures that couldn't have influenced each other's legends. Shapeshifters certainly existed in former times, and still do, albeit weakened and in much smaller numbers.

There is even a fairly significant belief in shapeshifters today. Beliefs in shapeshifters are not just found among superstitious hunter-gatherers. "Walton Brooks McDaniel found that many people of modern Italy believe lycanthropy can be induced by a full moon, witchcraft, or a birth at precisely midnight on particular holy days, including Christmas."[15] Nor are the only witnesses of shapeshifting superstitious and uneducated people. On the contrary, many of the witnesses in the last centuries were

---

[12] Sabine Baring-Gould, *The Book of Were-Wolves* (London: Senate, 1995), p. 54.
[13] Sabine Baring-Gould, *The Book of Were-Wolves*, pp. 53 and 54.
[14] Walter Williams Skeat, *Malay Magic* (London: Frank Cass & Co. Ltd., 1973), p. 161.
[15] Paul Katzeff, *Full Moons*, p. 64.

respected, truthful, down-to-earth people, which is why people took them so seriously when they claimed they saw shapeshifting. Even in this century, educated people have claimed to witness physical shapeshifting, as in the case of Dr. Gerald Kirkland, a government medical officer who saw two were-jackal transformations while stationed in Zimbabwe on March 23, 1933.[16] In the USA, people are still reporting sightings, and still believe in shapeshifters.[17]

I will discuss some of the basic facts of esoteric study first, so that the rest of the book will make more sense. For those of you who are already familiar with the study of esoteric phenomena, I will present my particular perspective and the terminology that I will be using, for perspective and terminology can vary widely from one student of esoteric study to another. Where, you may ask, did I get my information? It's all well and good for me to say that I have detailed information on modern-day shapeshifters, but I don't expect anyone to believe me unless I show them how to prove to themselves that many people who follow such beliefs actually exist. The answer to this question can be found in the epilogue.

THE PARANORMAL AND SUPERNATURAL

The paranormal comprises those things that science does not explain, such as the powers of the psychic, the telepath, and the telekinetic. It also comprises sightings of ghosts, monsters, angels, spirits, the "fairy" folk, poltergeists, and other quasi-physical beings. It is the entire collection of things that are beyond the natural—thus the word "supernatural." The paranormal is in operation when the normal rules of this world seem to be superseded by the rules of some other type of reality.

Esoteric students believe that they know what these other realities are like and how they operate. The basic teachings about the paranormal have arisen again and again, in basically the same form, in every culture. They appear to have very little connection to either culture or religion. The basic facts of the paranormal are notions arrived at by studying the most

---

[16] Paul Katzeff, *Full Moons*, pp. 65–66.
[17] Daniel Cohen, *Werewolves* (New York: Penguin, 1996), p. 12.

basic of phenomena. Because the basic facts are true (that is, founded in basic phenomena), the cultural beliefs and interpretations of observers have little to do with how the phenomena happen. For example, ghosts have had similar characteristics through all time and cultures, even though many cultures have different doctrines about why people become ghosts, or how theology relates to ghosts. The interpretations may be different, but the reported phenomena are always astonishingly similar.

Paranormal teachings say that the physical world is only one of many worlds. Most of these worlds, such as the "fairy realm," have very little to do with our world. Two of these "worlds," however, have a lot to do with our world, albeit in subtle ways most of the time. These are called the *astral plane* and the *etheric plane*. Our physical universe is called the *physical plane*. These realities, including our own, are visualized as planes, one atop another. This is not truly how they are, of course. In the physical direction of up, there is nothing but sky and the endless expanses of outer space. Yet the planes operate almost as if they were stacked like this, and they have been traditionally visualized this way. Our physical plane is on the bottom. Just on top of it is the etheric plane. The etheric plane consists of "matter" that is like a shadow of physical matter. Etheric matter is not physical, yet it is not as "refined" as astral matter. There is something of the physical about it. The etheric plane "overlaps" with this plane. Many physical "objects" of this plane, especially living things, have a counterpart in etheric matter, a counterpart that looks much like a carbon copy of the physical object. The etheric plane is the entire "universe" of these etheric objects, plus etheric objects that do not correspond directly to things in this plane, as well as other "stray" etheric matter. Etheric matter is of a much "finer" substance than physical matter. It almost never breaks. If put under some sort of stress, it deforms and then reforms. Stray etheric matter tends to flow and stretch and form itself as if it were living water or living clay. Etheric matter has an almost infinite ability, at least in comparison with physical matter, to condense or diffuse. Unlike physical matter, etheric matter can also occupy the same three-dimensional space as other etheric matter.

The astral plane is visualized as the plane directly on top of the etheric plane. It also corresponds to the physical plane in many ways, particularly in that many objects, especially living beings, have astral counterparts. However, the astral plane has many more objects and "stray" astral matter that directly corresponds to nothing in this plane. The astral plane also has a bewildering array of "spirits" and "entities" that are native to it— many more than exist in the etheric plane. Moreover, the astral plane has one characteristic that the etheric plane does not: there seem to be entire regions of the astral plane that do not share the same three-dimensional space as our physical plane. They are regions unto themselves. Astral matter is of a much "finer" consistency than etheric matter. The astral plane resembles a great sea of astral substance, with its own features and cycles, slowly changing all the time.

There is one more plane that bears mention here, though it generally has little to do with supernatural phenomena directly. This is called the *mental plane,* found directly on top of the astral plane. This plane does not share the same three-dimensional reality as our physical plane at all. Indeed, direction and distance and dimension are largely meaningless in the mental plane. It, in fact, contains very few "objects" that correspond to anything in the physical world. Living things do have an aspect of themselves on this plane, but it is a high, lofty aspect, often (at least in non-saints) seeming to have little in common with the ego and the normal waking self and its desires. Yet this is the one part of us that is eternal—our soul, our true self. In modern New Age terminology, this is the "higher self," above the astral and etheric bodies, even above the world of the mind and ideas, which are, after all, very much a product of our species and culture, not of our true self. Many believe that there are more planes above the mental plane, but very little is known or even guessed about them.

One of the most basic and universal teachings about the supernatural is that living things, particularly human beings, are comprised of more than the merely physical. Even the modern forms of Christianity have preserved a garbled part of this teaching in their teachings that humans have a soul and spirit. Esoteric study teaches us that we live, simultaneously, on at least four different planes of existence. For the most part, we only perceive the physical plane and our physical body that is resident on it. But we also have an etheric body, an astral body, and a pure form on the so-called "mental" plane of existence. The etheric and astral bodies, and their interactions with the etheric plane and the astral plane, have much to do with certain forms of paranormal phenomena.

The etheric body looks almost exactly like our physical body. It overlaps the physical body and normally occupies exactly the same three-dimensional space. Thus, it is difficult for even psychics to see. There are two conditions, however, under which psychics, and sometimes even ordinary people, can see the etheric body. When people lose an arm or a leg, they do not lose that same part of their etheric body. People who have lost a physical leg still have both etheric legs. More often than not, the etheric leg still sends sensations, still feels as if it were there, even itches or develops pains! Because this etheric part is not shrouded by any physical part, those who are psychic enough might see it.

Another condition under which the etheric body can sometimes be seen is during etheric travel. There are two basic types of out-of-body experiences, astral travel and etheric travel. Etheric travel occurs when a person leaves the physical body, but still occupies the etheric and astral bodies. Astral travel occurs when a person leaves the physical and etheric body, but still occupies the astral body. The etheric body, being closer to the physical, is more likely to be visible during out-of-body travel, sometimes even by non-psychics. The etheric body is also much more likely to be able to affect physical reality in some way, such as leaving footprints.

The astral body is of much "finer" substance than the etheric body. It is generally believed to be smaller than the etheric body, but not everyone agrees on this. It often looks much like the physical body, but it is more changeable, both in size and shape, than the etheric body. When it is separated from the physical body, it sometimes takes on an egg-like or spherical shape. If it is visible to others in this form, it sometimes appears to be a ball of light. Many astral travelers report that the astral body does not hear well, unlike the etheric body. Many also report that it sees in all directions at once, unlike the etheric body which generally can only see from its etheric eyes.

As you may already have guessed, death is simply an out-of-body experience from which there is no return (at least until reincarnation). The "phantoms" of people who are engaging in astral or etheric travel look like (and have the same qualities as) ghosts. When an etheric or astral body is visible, it does not matter if it can return to a body, or whether its body has died. It still has much the same characteristics and properties.

The phenomena of out-of-body travelers being glimpsed as ghostly forms (or, in rare cases, very clear forms) is called "phantasms of the living" in most New Age books. There are many cases where a phantasm of the living, ghostlike, appeared to a family member in a time of great need to convey an urgent message. The family may have believed the person to be dead, but he or she turned up alive later. Some paranormal investigators have taken this as proof that ghosts don't exist, and are only products of the imagination—after all, *how can a living person be a ghost?* This only shows, however, how those who know little about the paranormal can easily misunderstand it, for where do ghosts come from in the first place? Ghosts are simply the leftover "stuff" that did not die when the physical body died. We have that same "stuff" while we are still alive.

There are also more subtle aspects of our non-physical self that are important to an understanding of the supernatural. Nowadays, virtually everyone has heard of chakras and auras, and many have heard of *chi*. Chakras, auras, and *chi* are all characteristics of our subtle bodies, linked very dynamically with both the higher planes and with our own physical bodies.

The aura is visible to some psychics and other people with special perceptions. Many people can train themselves to see the aura by following the directions found in many New Age books. The aura, superimposed on the physical body, is roughly egg-shaped, and huge. It has many layers, the innermost being brighter and easier to see. In fact, aura readers say that the fainter outer layers probably continue outward indefinitely. Some of the best can see an aura thirty feet out from a person quite well.

The various parts and layers of the aura tend to have different colors. These colors correspond to various qualities and emotions. These colors are somewhat subjective and can vary from one aura reader to another. This may be because readers have to peer through the colors of their own aura to see another's, or it may be because the aura is not truly "colored" as we know it. Aura readers may simply see their own impressions and interpret them as color. The colors and patterns of the aura change very quickly in response to emotion in the person, and also contain indications of the person's general health and spiritual inclinations. For some reason that is not entirely understood, the aura generally disappears and fades away altogether before death. This generally happens anywhere from several hours to a day before death, even when the death is accidental and not caused by failing health.

The aura is not so much a thing as it is energy, although, on the higher planes, there is less of a difference between matter and energy. The aura is a shining radiance of energy pouring forth from the subtle body of the living being, fading and thinning as it moves farther from the source, much as light seems to fade as it travels from its source.

There are seven major chakras and numerous minor ones, although some authorities claim that one (or sometimes more) of the minor chakras is also a major chakra. Most of the chakras are located inside the body, although there is one important minor chakra above the head, and another, less important one located outside the body between the feet. There may also be other minor chakras outside the body.

The seven major chakras are much more important than any of the minor ones. In fact, most people do not concern themselves with any but the seven major chakras. Each chakra is an energy structure much like a miniature whirlpool. The major chakras are lined up along a vertical line, corresponding for most of its length to the spinal column. Except for the seventh chakra, which points upward, and the first, which points somewhat downward, every major chakra has the open end of its whirlpool pointing forward. The chakras are more patterns of energy than they are "things," but they do have something of an etheric substance about them. Those who engage in etheric travel often report that they still have chakras in this body, while astral travelers often report that they do not have chakras, or that the lower chakras are missing. The chakras are great processors of energy, sucking in stray energy and matter from the higher planes and assimilating it into our being. They are also bridges, of a sort,

between the etheric and astral bodies and our physical bodies. Peopl
more likely to be aware of their subtle bodies through their chakras tha
in any other way. The seven major chakras correspond roughly, in location, to the major glands: the first to the sexual organs, the fourth to the
heart, and the sixth, or "third eye," to the pituitary gland.

Another characteristic is *chi,* an Eastern term that has become common in New Age circles and in Western esoteric study. This characteristic
has also been known as *orgone, mana, prana, animal magnetism,* and many
other terms.[18] *Chi* is a kind of esoteric energy, a bodily energy associated
almost exclusively with living beings. *Chi* exists throughout the body, and
the *chi* field extends about half an inch outside the skin. *Chi* tends to gather in certain places inside the body and run along certain paths within it.
These paths intersect at the traditional acupuncture points. Traditional
Chinese medicine is almost entirely concerned with ways to make the
body healthier through manipulating *chi* and improving and directing its
circulation.

There are three major "balls" of *chi* gathered within the body. One of
these is in the stomach and lower abdominal area, another is in the upper
chest, roughly in the area of the heart, and the third is in the head. People
are much less likely to be aware of these balls of *chi* than they are of their
chakras. In fact, when people first become aware of their *chi,* they often
mistake the sensation for that of a nearby chakra.

People are much more likely to be aware of abdominal *chi* than any
other, and they often mistake this for the third chakra, which is located in
roughly the same area. *Chi* is different from chakras, however. For one
thing, the chakras are fixed, while *chi* moves around, and can even be
moved around at will by an expert. The balls of *chi* do not have a
whirlpool structure or a rotation to them, as chakras do. Abdominal *chi* is
often associated with physical manifestations. *Chi* in the chest, and especially the head, is associated with saints, holy men, and visionaries. It is

---

18 "Animal magnetism" has, in modern slang, come to have yet another meaning: sexual attraction.
It was originally coined, however, by esoteric students to describe the effects of *chi* in conjunction with
supernatural events.

th manifestations of the paranormal that have to do

mmunication with the highest powers that be.

by various practices, particularly by being healthy, by

id by practicing martial arts. There is an Oriental dis-

g (sometimes spelled *qigong* or *kigong*) which builds

chi dramatically, and also helps people learn to control *chi* consciously. Those who follow practices of purposefully creating paranormal events (in other words, those who work magic) often use *chi* as "fuel" for what they do, particularly for the more "spectacular" effects and for those that affect physical reality more.

So, we know that this world, our world, is made of more than meets the eye. Other planes of reality exist and subtly pervade every aspect of this world. Indeed, we ourselves are made partly of "otherworldly" stuff. We could not live if we were nothing more than physical bodies. The stuff of the paranormal is a part of us. It surrounds us and flows through us every moment of our lives, and even afterward.

Using the Paranormal

There are people who happen to have talents that let them interact with, or even influence, the paranormal. In some cases, these talents are hereditary. Those who have specific talents—those who have prophetic visions, who can move objects with their minds, who can communicate with telepathy, or can start fires by the force of their will—often discover their talents by chance. In many cases, that talent, or similar talents, ran in the person's family. In other cases, the talent may have been awakened by a single dramatic event. This is often true in the case of the "general" psychic, one who has several psychic talents or simply a sensitivity to events that happen on other planes.

There are also ways to deliberately develop these talents, to enhance rudimentary abilities into noticeable skills. The easiest way is to turn ourselves into general psychics by simply being more sensitive and aware of the paranormal currents around us. Deliberately seeking and cultivating our own talents, even trying deliberately to produce paranormal events—this is the path to magic.

Magic is the *force* behind the supernatural. It is an all-inclusive term that includes all the "stuff" I've been discussing—other realities, the etheric and astral, *chi,* subtle matter, energy associated with subtle matter, and even finer and higher forces that we know little about. Many people speak of magic being all around us and flowing through us. In this sense, they mean the entirety of the supernatural, the other worlds and their currents and channels and energy. Magic is also used to describe an action—a witch or sorcerer or shaman is said to "do" magic or "practice" magic. In this sense, magic is the act of creating supernatural events or interacting with the supernatural in some other way.

Magic has often been associated with religion—both are ways of interacting with the supernatural. In the past, when magic was more openly practiced and more common, many of the religions were pagan, and so magic was often associated with paganism. The pagan deities were later demonized by the Christians. The magic-working associated with them was also demonized. Magic-working, in certain circumstances, does attract strange spirits, but the magic-worker does not need to have any dealings with them, let alone make pacts. Magic, in fact, does not have any religious affiliation. It is a part of each person, and of the world in which we live. Like science, it is simply there to be used, available, for good purposes and bad.

WEREBEASTS AND SHAPESHIFTERS

What is a werewolf or other werebeast? And what is a modern shifter? How are modern shifters related to the legends of werewolves and other werebeasts? First, a shifter is not exactly what most people think of when they think of a werewolf or shapeshifter. There are many ways of becoming an animal, and most of these ways are not the type of physical transformation that most people think of as the defining characteristic of shapeshifters.

Physical transformation is only the most dramatic possible symptom of the life-encompassing fact of being a shifter. Shapeshifting is something that is there all the time, something that we live and breathe and deal with every day, something that consists of a thousand subtle characteristics woven into all that we do. People can be werewolves, truly be werewolves in every fiber of their being, and never experience a physical transformation into a wolf. This is one reason why many of us call ourselves "shifters" and not "shapeshifters." We don't want to imply that we shift our physical shape. Also, we like to get away from the term "werewolf," because many of us are of species other than wolf, and we need a name that doesn't exclude any other species. Another reason we do not like to use "werewolf" is because shifters are nothing like what the term "werewolf" has come to mean. We are nothing like the "werewolves" generally depicted in movies and novels, and we don't want to be associated with such a horrible stereotype.

A shifter is a person with "animal medicine." This animal medicine is stronger than other animal medicines. It is also different. I have known people with incredibly strong animal medicine who were not shifters. It is not merely the strength of the animal connection that matters. The magic of "shapeshifting" is a type of animal magic, a type of connection with the animal that is quite different from ordinary animal medicine.

Outwardly and in public, a shifter may appear to be no more than simply just another person with strong "animal medicine." But shifters have an additional, very important, characteristic. Shifters "shapeshift" into their power animal or totem animal. This shapeshifting may happen in a number of different ways, but all of these are ways of somehow "becoming" the animal. The most common type of shifting is called "mental shifting."

Mental shifting is a kind of opening up to the inner animal self that normally dwells within the subconscious, and letting it pervade more of the conscious, waking mind. All shifters have an inner animal self (much like the inner child) that is simply a mind-set, a way of looking at the world and reacting as an animal would. It is not (as many werewolf novels would have us believe) some kind of evil "other," someone with multiple-personality disorder. Most shifters have the animal self in the background at all times, but it can be brought into the foreground to a greater or lesser degree, pushing human habits into the background. This often leads to enhanced alertness, a feeling of being more comfortable and "in tune" with the body, heightened sens s, and a temporary change in mind-set to a sort of pure "wordless" awareness, free of the human mental habit.

The second most common type of shift is often called an "astral shift." This is the "shamanic shapeshifting" (sometimes incorrectly called just "shapeshifting") that is featured in so many New Age books. Astral shifting is a spirit journey that involves the shapeshifting of the astral body into animal form. This usually involves astral travel and occurs during meditation, trance, or sleep, although some shifters use the term "astral shifting" to refer to experiences during mental shifting when they feel that their astral body has shapeshifted, but when there is no out-of-body travel involved.

Sometimes mental shifts are accompanied by minor paranormal effects, and sometimes these effects happen independently of any mental shifts. These are effects that are reminiscent of the berserker of Norse legend. This would include such things as more-than-human strength, speed, senses, stamina, or agility. Many shifters have experiences of "phantom limbs," extremities such as a muzzle, wolf ears, paws, or a tail, extremities that can be felt in great detail (much as an amputee feels a missing leg), but are invisible and insubstantial.

Other abilities of shifters resemble those commonly found in werebeast folklore. In rare cases, shifters experience "possession shifting," in which they possess a real animal's body. In other rare cases, shifters experience "apparition shifting." Apparition shifting is very like astral shifting except that the spirit-body appears as a ghostly apparition that others can see, and that, like real ghosts and apparitions, can sometimes affect physical reality in some small way.

The rarest abilities of shifters are physical shifting and bilocation shifting. Physical shifting occurs when the inner animal becomes powerful enough and substantial enough to periodically, for a short time only, take the physical matter of the shifter's human body and change it to conform to an animal body in every way. Physical shifting is true shapeshifting, the shifting of the physical shape. I myself have never seen this kind of shift. Many shifters believe that it doesn't exist, or they believe that other, more minor paranormal effects create a convincing illusion that it has happened, an illusion shared by the werewolf and any observers. Physical shifting is quite rare, but I believe that it does exist. The endless stream of accounts of it from all cultures and from credible witnesses can not be entirely mistaken.

Bilocation shifting is the ultimate manifestation of what is seen in lesser form in astral and apparition shifting. In werewolf legends, bilocation shifting is actually more common than physical shifting. In bilocation shifting, the person becomes unconscious and leaves his or her body in etheric travel. However, this person is in an animal-shaped etheric body, and this body is not invisible or ghostly, as in astral shifting and apparition shifting. As in normal bilocation, where the materialized body is a "carbon copy" of the human body, the etheric body materializes to a fair degree and becomes apparently entirely real. Although there may be a few differences between this materialized body and a truly physical one, they are usually minor and of little importance.

To be a shifter is something much wider, deeper, and more significant than just the act of physical transformation. There are many ways to shift, many ways to manifest the inner reality of what a shifter is. Humans tend to place the most emphasis on the act of physical transformation, but shifters tend to feel that spiritual reality is more important. After all, even those few who physically shift or bilocation shift get to spend only a tiny percentage of their time in the physical form of an animal.

Western esoteric tradition has emphasized the attainment of enlightenment through the sun-self, male aspect, or ego. Other magical paths, particularly those of pre-Christian Europe and the Eastern traditions, have tended to put more emphasis on working with the subconscious, the instinctual self, and female energies. They are more connected to the body and the rhythms of the Moon and the seasons.

Western esoteric schools have largely ignored totemism and animal-based nature magic. They have also distanced themselves from the female aspects of nature magic, preferring systems like astrology and qabbalah over systems like shamanism, weather-working, even herb magic. No wonder, then, that shapeshifting has been little known and less understood in the Western esoteric world.

Western tradition has often considered animal magic to be a lower form of magic, below the lofty art of human-based consciousness raising. Shapeshifting has been seen as a regression to a lower animal order, a step backward in evolution and spiritual advancement. Human beings have viewed animals as unimportant lower beings, and female qualities have been seen as lower aspects of the human self in our patriarchal society. We have seen the path to enlightenment as man reaching upward toward God, purging his own female and animal qualities, and freeing himself from the "taint" of Earth and earthly things. The idea that animals are "lower" beings and shapeshifting is a step backward on the path to enlightenment is false. The world of earthly things is part of the whole, infused with the divine, and a part of many of the paths that lead to enlightenment. We are not here, in this earthly realm, merely to try to escape. We are here for a reason.

It is true that animals are generally inhabited by lower souls. As souls move from lifetime to lifetime in the cycle of reincarnation, they tend to start out in animal incarnations. Once a soul has experienced its first human incarnation, it tends to remain human for its remaining lifetimes. Shapeshifting is a way to connect to animal power, to regain those valuable aspects that animals possess and humans lack, without actually taking a step backward in our evolution or having to reincarnate as an animal. Animals have souls, but they are usually very young, undeveloped souls, unevolved and unrefined. These are traditionally called "lower souls." This does not mean that they are evil or unimportant souls, or that they don't deserve respect and dignity. In fact, lower souls of this kind tend to have a kind of pure innocence and goodness about them, as young children have.

These souls are not irrelevant or useless to higher souls on the path to enlightenment. Many things can be learned from lower souls; some of life's hardest and most poignant lessons come from lower souls. Humankind is imperfect, because it has neither the harmony of animals nor the harmony of angels. It is a species caught in awkward mid-evolution. Lower animal souls have a deeper, more primitive, yet more complete connection to the highest powers—a childlike perfection, a learning connection we can use.

Jesus spoke truly when he said, "Whoever does not receive the Kingdom of God like a child will never enter it" (Luke 18:17). He was speaking of the path to enlightenment, and of the fact that the so-called "lower" aspects are also a part of that path, an important part.

Shapeshifting lets us connect our whole being. Not only does it link us with important powers that animals possess and humans have largely lost, it also helps us connect with the higher self, our true being, the soul. There is a larger spiritual purpose to shapeshifting. This purpose is knowing, truly knowing, the real self. This is a very noble spiritual accomplishment, similar in some ways to enlightenment. Being a shifter and integrating your selves teaches you things about yourself that most humans never know. You discover that you are not your body, you are not your species, you are not your habits, your career, your likes and dislikes. You are not your culture, nor a person made in the image of your parents. When you discover who you are not, you learn more about who you really are. You discover who you really are as a divine, eternal soul. It is sacred, wonderful knowledge.

You become more aware of your subconscious, because your animal side is closer to it and part of it. You learn to know all your true self, and appreciate your merits. By acknowledging, dealing with, and learning the true value of your lower selves, you integrate into a whole, complete being. The lower parts of the self sometimes seem wild, nasty, and apt to indulge in things from which there can flow bad consequences. But the lower selves have much ancient wisdom. They are full of honesty and a simple, perfect faith of the kind children have. The lower selves do not need to be kept on a short leash and beaten into obedience. Simply understanding and acknowledging the lower selves, and gently guiding them with respect, is the right way to treat them. To know both the lower and upper selves is to know yourself truly. And shapeshifting is a path that leads you to better know this.

Even with only mental shifting, great changes can occur in what we often think of as the real self, our ego and the world of our ideas. Learning that we can change our personality, intelligence, desires, and even, in rare cases, our bodies, like a change of clothes, is a deep realization. This realization shows us that all of this is, indeed, like a change of clothes. Seeing the things that stay constant shows us the real self. In this way, we come to a fuller realization of and better connection to the higher self. We know that we are divine, eternal souls with a reality beyond whatever mind or body we happen to possess at the moment. Shapeshifting is a spiritual journey, a tough one, but very rewarding. It has a purpose and reality far beyond simply "turning into an animal," or employing your shifter abilities for earthly benefits.

2

Mental Shifting

There are two ways to define mental shifting. One is to describe it as the shifting of the mind, mind-set, or mental state, partially or wholly, into that of an animal. This can happen either "lightly" or "deeply." This view of mental shifting can include everything from animalistic mood shifts to the deepest mental expression of the animal within. It does not include astral shifting, "spirit journeys," possession shifting, bilocation shifting, or physical shifting, even though all of these types generally include a simultaneous mental shift.

The second view of mental shifting divides all shifting into two categories, "mental" and "physical." The physical category includes only bilocation shifting and physical shifting (some also include possession shifting and tiny physical changes, such as eye-color changes). The mental category therefore includes any type of non-physical shift.

In this chapter, I provide information on all kinds of non-physical shifting. To avoid confusion, however, I use the term "mental shifting" only to refer to real mental shifts, not to all kinds of non-physical shifts.

When I cover the subject of astral shifting, I always call it "astral shifting," not "mental shifting."

What is mental shifting? It is the shifting of the mind or mental state to a more animalistic mental condition. Human thought patterns, habits, and ways of thinking are pushed to the background, while more animal ways of thinking come to the foreground. The weakest kind of mental shift is sometimes called an "aura shift," or a "mood shift," but the most common term used is "light mental shift." The stronger mental shifts are often called "deep mental shifts."

Everyone has an animal side hiding somewhere in the subconscious, along with an inner child and a host of other "selves." In shifters, this animal self comes to the surface more often than in normal humans. It is also more active, and cannot be banished to the subconscious for long. The animal self is not something that suddenly "possesses" the shifter during mental shifts. It is more or less present in the shifter at all times. Even when most human, the shifter has some animal instincts and feelings present. The animal self simmers on the surface of the subconscious, and rises to conscious awareness more often.

The lightest kind of mental shift occurs when an animalistic mood comes over shifters, making them feel more animal than normal, and making their senses feel sharper. They may feel a rising wildness within them, or they may want to run for the sheer joy of it. They often feel very much in tune with their physical bodies, very aware, and ready for anything. At the same time, their human thought processes are not significantly hampered. No matter how they feel inside, they still act human as far as outside observers can tell, unless they deliberately let go and act like an animal.

At a deeper level of mental shift, human thought processes are pushed more to the background. At this level, agility on two legs is often hampered. Shifters may be very clumsy trying to walk on two legs or doing anything complex with their hands. They may think less in words and more in pure awareness when in this type of shift. The world of words recedes and, if they talk to anyone, they may go slowly and pause a lot to search for words. Even though they may become clumsier at human things, they become much more agile in animal things as the shift gets deeper. They become more and more immersed in an awareness of their senses, their physical bodies, and the world around them. They may experience an urge to drop on all fours. If they give in to this urge, they find themselves surprisingly agile. At this stage, shifters may act like animals, though they can usually hold back if they are in an inappropriate environment. If they do act animal-like because of the shift, they don't act in extreme ways unless they so intend. During this level of shift, most shifters can appear fairly normal in front of others if they try really hard.

At the deepest level of shift, shifters cannot appear normal to others unless they exercise a lot of self-control or simply retire and lie down for the duration of the shift. At this level, shifters often seem to forget how to walk. If they persist in trying to walk on two legs, they simply fall until the shift is over (unless they happen to be of a two-legged species, such as a bird or kangaroo). If, however, they give in to the urge to get down on all fours, they inevitably find that they have great agility, run with surprising speed, and appear uncannily like an animal in every nuance, without even trying. It is often impossible for them to do just about anything with their hands, even something as simple as turning a doorknob. Shifters often have long spells of a kind of wordless pure awareness, though simple word-thoughts tend to drift into the consciousness now and then. Talking to shifters can often bring them out of this wordless state. If shifters look at written words, they often see only lines and shapes, without recognizing meaning. In a shift this deep, shifters may feel that human ideas about things are stupid and wrong. They may seem far away. They may act and think in very animal-like ways, such as being frightened of indoor places full of people. In extremely deep shifts, shifters may sometimes howl or growl at people or act inappropriately in front of them, without thinking much of the future consequences. Fortunately, this type of deep shift nearly always happens away from people. The mere presence of people hampers the deepest kind of mental shift.

Shifts tend to happen when the shifter has been alone and introspective for a while. They are most likely to happen at night, away from people, and when the shifter is outdoors. In most cases, shifters feel a mental shift coming on before it actually happens, and also have some idea of how deep it will go. In most cases, they can delay it until a later time, or even suppress it altogether. Some can do this simply by force of will, others must stave it off by immersing themselves purposefully in very human activities or thoughts.

How much shifters control themselves during mental shifts depends on the relationship between the animal and the human side. In truth, there are all degrees of separation or integration between these two sides. All shifters have their own particular arrangement. Shifter culture generally divides itself into two groups based on the degree of integration. Those who have the two sides fairly well integrated are called "integrated shifters." The rest are "non-integrated shifters."

There are a few rare shifters who have almost totally separate sides, like multiple personality disorder. In these cases, one side usually doesn't remember what the other did. These are often called "totemic shifters." When this happens, it is often only a temporary condition in new shifters. From the cases I've examined, I've come to the opinion that most totemic shifters are not actually people with a totally separate animal side. Instead, they are possessed during their shifts by either their animal spirit guide or by some other animal spirit. When their animal spirit guide does this, it is often to help awaken a very weak animal side. When it is another kind of animal spirit, this relationship is often of a questionable nature and not healthy for the shifter. Totemic shifters are rare.

Shifters tend to start out as non-integrated shifters, gradually becoming integrated over time. A few shifters become totally integrated very early on, without even trying. The rest of us end up working on integration for quite some time. Some shifters never become integrated, particularly those who don't try to. Integrated shifters have their animal and human sides fairly well joined; they have a direct line to their animal side. They tend to see things from both the human and animal perspectives at once. A non-integrated shifter tends to see things more from one perspective and less from both perspectives at once.

The personality that we display when out on the town with friends is very different from, perhaps even the opposite of, the personality we show at work. Not only are these two personalities different, we also feel different when assuming one or the other. Yet this is obviously not at all like the psychiatric condition known as multiple-personality disorder. Whatever we do or feel, still *we* are doing or feeling it, not someone else. We may act differently, feel differently, even desire different things and have different priorities, when in our "work mode" or our "play mode." These two personality modes may seem like night and day to some people, but they don't fight with each other. Each remembers what the other did. Indeed, you yourself may think of them, not as "personalities," but simply as the way you are at work, and the way you are at play.

This is basically what integrated shifters experience as the relationship between their animal and human personalities. To a considerable extent, integrated shifters can bring as much, or as little, "animalness" as they want into their mode of thinking, at most times. They have better access to the animal viewpoint and feelings, even when most human, and more access to the human viewpoint and feelings, even when caught in the deepest mental shift. If integrated shifters happen to be unlucky enough to have an involuntary deep mental shift in front of other people, they recognize the problem and retire as quietly as possible, often without anyone realizing that anything more than fatigue is responsible. Non-integrated shifters, caught in the same situation might, in all innocence, growl or trot on all fours, because their animal side is so removed from the human mode of thinking that they don't fully realize how many problems this will cause them later.

Non-integrated shifters remember being human, but human priorities seem unimportant. Integrated shifters have many of these same feelings, but they retain enough understanding of the human way of being, even when extremely wolfy, that they will not do anything they will really regret later. The relationship between the non-integrated shifter's wolf and human sides is like the relationship between normal waking states, and trance or dream states.

Non-integrated shifters have a tendency toward memory holes for any extremely deep mental or astral shifts, and especially for any physical shifts. When they recall the experience, they usually remember most of it, but the memory often has a dream-like quality. They feel as if they are remembering something that happened in a dream or something that happened a long time ago. This fuzzy memory of extremely deep shifts and physical shifts is lessened if the shifter comes out of the shift slowly. The memory holes are at their worst if the shifter exits the shifted state very suddenly, or falls asleep during the shift and shifts back while asleep. When a non-integrated shifter is out of touch with the animal side, the two sides may even fight, be afraid of each other, or act like separate beings in other ways.

In every non-integrated shifter, there is always some fear or resentment of one side by the other. One of the keys to integration is sharing and compromise. Your human self may be very excited when you take it to the movies or buy it a new CD. Your animal self may be very excited when you take it for a walk in the park or buy it a new ball or a rubber bone. You need to consider the needs of each self as equally valid, and try to make the compromises that will make them both happy in the long run, in much the same way that you make compromises between the needs of your workday self and the needs of your playtime self. Even integrated shifters have some conflict of interest between their two sides, but they tend to choose the best compromise automatically, even when they wish they could have it both ways, because their animal and human selves are joined. They don't play one side against the other or seriously neglect one side.

Many new shifters are somewhat reluctant to view their animal side as being fully part of them. After all, the animal likes things that disgust the human side, like rolling in the dirt. It is hard to accept that things like that can be something that you desire. It is convenient to attribute desires like this to your animal side, to forget about them and believe that they are something very far removed from anything the "real you" desires. Many desires and feelings associated with the animal side are things we have been taught since childhood are "bad," even though many of them are really good for us.

Shifters who are unwilling to accept and integrate the animal side are often unhappy, always struggling with and hating themselves. Shifters who avoid accepting their wolf aspects are more likely to have holes in their memory of being shifted. While shifted, they are also more likely to do things they will regret when back in their human mode of thinking.

The integration of the human and animal sides is often complex and difficult, but it boils down to promoting three things—self-love, self-acceptance, and honesty with the self. Animals can lie. Some birds will give the alarm signal when there is no danger, so that other birds will go away and they'll have all the food to themselves. Pets will deceive you about the fact that they made a mess indoors. Yet animals are simple, honest souls, and one thing they cannot do is lie to themselves.

People, especially civilized people, lie to themselves constantly. People lie to themselves about their real motives, beliefs, and desires; they lie to themselves about what other people think of them. Being civilized is just a constant stream of lies to yourself about the things you want to excuse, the things you don't want to admit you desire, and the things you'd rather not deal with or acknowledge. Being civilized often means suppressing your real self, and even lying to yourself, telling yourself that the mask you present to the world is the "real you." Even though civilization, indeed life itself, involves compromise and suppression, you don't have to lie to yourself about it.

When your animal side is close to the surface, ready for a shift, you start to realize all the things about which you've lied to yourself. You become closer to being one with your animal part, and start losing the ability to lie. This makes most people uncomfortable, and is one source of fear about the animal side. You may be in a relationship with someone you don't really love. You lie to yourself because you are afraid to be alone. The career you've chosen may be more what you are "supposed" to do than what you really want to do, and you may have lied to yourself about your real reasons for choosing it. You may not be living the life you really want, but lie to yourself because you are afraid of the risks or hard work associated with an alternate path. You may be lying to yourself about your religious beliefs and need to acknowledge those doubts, and perhaps mix some agnosticism into your religion. Most people lie to themselves about many things. When they start getting close to their animal side, they open up a hornet's nest of doubt and tough questions.

If you cover up these questions by lying to yourself more, that only separates you from your animal side. If you deal with these issues honestly, you become integrated more with your animal side. You don't necessarily have to make radical changes to bring your life more in line with the truth, for there are many things we cannot change. A big part of life involves compromise, disappointment, and settling for less than you would like. In order to properly integrate with the inner animal self, however, you must at least start being honest, and admit the real truth, even if you can't or won't live a life more in line with it.

DREAM SHIFTING

When the animal side is heavily persecuted by the human side, shifters often suffer from vivid dreams of wild beasts chasing them, threatening them, and eating them. The eating reflects the animal side's desire to absorb the human part and live in oneness with it. These dreams can be frightening, but dreamers often find that their wounds do not hurt, and that, once eaten, they are still alive and have become one of the animals doing the eating. In these dreams, if the dreamers voluntarily go out to the attacking wild beasts, they usually find that the beasts transform from slavering ugly brutes to very beautiful and friendly animals.

In these dreams, it is you against you, even if it seems otherwise. All you want is to be one. The animal side does not want to destroy you. It wants your acceptance. This may seem a strange way to gain acceptance, yet other parts of your subconscious often send you various frightening dreams when trying to do the same thing. Your animal self is an animal. When persecuted, it is a scared and confused animal. All it knows is that it wants to merge with your human mode of thinking, and it tries to do this in the most obvious, physical way possible—by eating it.

There are many other important dreams for shifters. In fact, dreams, because they are allied with the subconscious, are often an important way of interacting with the animal side in ways that further one's progress on the path of a shifter. Dreams can be very important for understanding the relationship between your two sides and learning to merge them. "Split consciousness" dreams, in which things are seen from the viewpoint of both selves, either simultaneously or alternately, are common in shifters.

This kind of dream is an extremely important aspect of shifting. One such dream was related to me as follows:

> *In my dream, I saw a man and a wolf. The man saw the wolf and his eyes widened in fear at having a wolf so close to him. I felt everything the man felt, and knew his thoughts throughout the dream. The wolf looked at the man, and saw and smelled his fear. I felt everything the wolf felt and knew his thoughts throughout the dream. The wolf was alarmed at having a man so close to him, and laid his ears back and bit the man. The wolf felt the pain of the bitten arm. The man knew that the wolf felt his pain. Each realized that they felt what the other felt and knew what the other thought. My view of the scene lengthened, so that I could see them from afar, and I saw that they were joined at the waist, having the same body from the waist down.*

Another dream was related to me thus:

> *Me as a wolf and me as a human were both in this dream. I saw and understood everything from both selves at once, as if I were in two bodies at the same time. I could relate the dream from either perspective, but it will make more sense if I tell it from just one. Since I'm more comfortable with my human self, I'll tell it from that perspective. I was outside with my wolf. She was being rambunctious and doggy and wanted to get into everything, including the mud, and jumped up on me. I needed to go into a store and we couldn't be separated, so I put her on a leash and took her in. She felt restricted. She knocked a few things off shelves, even though she was trying to be good. I was told to leave the store because of the trouble she caused. Outside, I was very sad. I loved my wolf, but didn't know what to do with her. Looking at her more closely, I saw she was limping a bit and I felt the pain in her paw, as I felt everything she felt. I knelt down and took her paw and looked at it. A thin, sharp rod of metal, like a huge needle, was thrust entirely through the thickest part of her paw. I knew I needed to remove it, but that it would hurt. My wolf*

knew this, too, but as an animal, she could not trust even me to cause her great pain in the interest of her future comfort. She "told" me that the only way she could let me do that, would be if I put a vulnerable part of myself under her control while I pulled out the spike, trusting her as much as she trusted me. She told me to put my tongue in her mouth while I pulled out the spike, trusting her not to bite it off. I was appalled. That was asking a lot of me. She "told" me that I was similarly asking a lot of her, from her perspective. I thought about it, and decided to do it. I placed my tongue in her mouth, feeling very vulnerable and scared, and pulled the spike out of her foot. It hurt horribly coming out, but, once out, it felt much better, and she didn't bite my tongue off. I looked more closely at her paw and saw many other spikes, even more deeply embedded. I knew I would have to remove them someday, but not that day.

SENSE SHIFTING

There are a number of types of non-physical shifts. One of these is sense shifting. Sense shifting occurs when shifters receive information from a real animal's senses. They may see what the real animal is seeing, hear what it is hearing, smell what it is smelling, or feel the wind through its fur and the earth under its paws. They may experience just one sense, several at once, or even all of the animal's senses. Sense shifting is often accompanied by telepathic contact with the animal, or by simply being aware of its thoughts, without any telepathic communication. It is also often accompanied by the sense of an "energy cord" connecting the shifter and the real animal.

In sense shifting, shifters usually receive information simultaneously from their own human and animal senses. While seeing what the animal sees, they still see out of their human eyes. While hearing what the animal hears, they still hear out of their human ears. On occasion, however, one or more of their human senses are "blanked out," while they receive information from the corresponding sense or senses in the animal. Occasionally, sense shifters even become unconscious, riding around in the animal's body, feeling everything it feels, yet not at all in control of its actions. They are merely passengers. This type of sense shift is much rarer, and borders on possession shifting. It is not possession shifting, however, because the shifter has absolutely no control over the animal's body.

When shifters see from both the animal's eyes and their own, they see, not one scene superimposed on the other, but rather two separate scenes, just as you can see one scene and imagine another in your mind without the two scenes overlapping or being superimposed on each other. The same is true when shifters feel everything the animal feels. Sense shifters do not mistake something touching the animal's leg for something touching their own human leg. Instead, they have a sense of two separate bodies—their own human body and the other distinctly animal-shaped body. Each sensation of touch belongs to one or the other. With the senses of smell and hearing, however, sensations are often mixed up with information from the shifter's human senses.

It can be very strange to see out of an animal's eyes at the same time you are seeing out of your own. It is also very educational. It gives you a small taste of what it feels like to be an animal, and hints at what physical shifting might be like someday. It teaches you thousands of little things about being a shifter. Sense shifters usually have their shifts with different species, regardless of what species of shifter they are. A wolf shifter may sense shift with cats, dogs, mice, horses, cows, snakes, and just about any other species available. Sense shifting is best done and happens most frequently with the familiar of the shifter. It is possible to do it with any animal, but the results can be unpleasant.

When I was young, I once sense shifted with a dog. This dog at once felt my presence and resented it, and went berserk. He finally jumped on my young brother and bit him badly. I felt horrible afterward. You can never tell how strange animals will react to sense shifting, and it is best to be careful. Sense shifters are usually fairly close to the animal, at least when the sense shifting starts. They usually know from which animal they are receiving sensory information. In some cases, sense shifting starts with an animal that the shifter can't see. The shifter eventually tracks it down by following sensory clues. In some cases, the animal may go well out of the visual and audio range of the shifter.

Some claim that it is possible to experience sense shifting with animals that are far away, perhaps even hundreds or thousands of miles away. Some claim to have had sense shifts of this type with jaguars, bears, and other animals that live far from the shifter. I myself am not sure whether this type of sense shifting exists or not. It is fairly rare, and, because the actual animal cannot be identified, it is impossible to gather any proof one way or another on whether this is truly sense shifting, or only a powerful vision.

I myself had a vision that might have been sense shifting with a very remote animal. It felt much like sense shifting, and was very vivid. I could see, feel, smell, and hear everything the wolf did, in incredible detail. I had the vision in the afternoon, but the setting of the vision was at night, as if the wolf were on the other side of the globe. In my location, it was fall; in the vision, it was winter, with ice forming over puddles and snow everywhere. It was quite cold, so the vision must have been set far to the north as well.

Possession shifting is similar to sense shifting. In it, you become unconscious and enter an animal's body during astral travel. In possession shifting, you are more or less in control of the body. In most cases, since the animal itself is still in its body, the two of you are in there together. In some cases, the animal's soul is either temporarily ejected, or still present but "asleep" or pushed to the background. It is best to practice possession shifting only with a familiar.

ASTRAL SHIFTING

Another type of non-physical shift is astral shifting. Astral shifting is the shapeshifting of the astral body. Usually, astral shifting refers to the shapeshifting of the astral body during trance or astral travel, but the astral body can also shapeshift while the person is awake and active. This active type of astral shifting is often indistinguishable in its effects from a light mental shift.

Astral shifts, as I've defined them, involve leaving the body via astral travel. Many astral shifts are very like the traditional "shamanic journey to the spirit world," except that the journeyer assumes animal form when there. In this type of astral shift, shifters go into very deep trance and find themselves in a strange wilderness, sometimes populated with mythical plants and creatures as well as with more ordinary ones, as in many normal shamanic journeys to the spirit world. They may have an experience much like dream shifting, or they may have a more "visionary" type of experience, such as direct meetings with animal spirit guides. Often, a lesson must be learned or a problem surmounted while they are there. They may also gather special kinds of wisdom. One use of this type of astral shift is to enter certain areas of the "spirit world" that are off-limits to humans. Shifters can enter these areas only by totally shedding their human nature for a time and leaving it behind them.

Another type of astral shift occurs when shifters travel in the more normal areas of the astral plane that correspond to areas in this world, instead of its "spirit world" areas. This resembles most normal astral travel, except that shifters have their mental states shifted to the animal side and feel "enveloped" in an astral animal body.

In a third type of astral shift, shifters enter a trance state.[1] In this type, shifters remain in their bodies, but in a trance, not aware and active as in mental shifting. This type is occasionally mistaken for physical shifting by those who are inexperienced and who were unobserved during the shift. Shifters often retain only fragmentary memories of the experience.

In this type of astral shifting, shifters go very deeply into trance and begin feeling extremely intense sensations of heat in their extremities, accompanied by realistic sensations of change in part or all of their bodies. They begin to feel that they have the body of an animal, but they also are often dimly aware of the room that they are in. They often have very vivid flashes of running as an animal, sometimes accompanied by small, weak motions of their arms and legs. They may have disjointed impressions of a jungle or wilderness through which they are traveling, as in the shamanic-journey type of astral shift.

---

[1] Quite a number of very interesting astral shifting experiences, including this third type, as well as methods for invoking them in those who are not shifters (it is possible for non-shifters to experience astral shifting, because the astral body shapeshifts so easily) are related in *Where the Spirits Ride the Wind* by Felicitas D. Goodman (Bloomington and Indianapolis: Indiana University Press, 1990), pp. 128–140. *Deerdancer* by Michele Jamal (New York: Arkana, 1995) also has some exercises.

Astral shifting is spontaneous in some shifters. They may feel tired, go off somewhere and lie down, and suddenly find themselves in an astral shift. Most astral shifts are induced, however, once shifters learn how to trigger them. In induced astral shifts, shifters usually go deep into a meditation state until they enter at least a light trance. Many normal humans can experience astral shifts, even though they aren't shifters, if they try hard and follow the right instructions. Astral shifts are not one of the phenomena that define one as being a shifter. The astral body shapeshifts so easily that one does not have to be a shifter in order to experience an astral shift.

One of the defining characteristics of a shifter is that they have two etheric bodies instead of one. Normal humans have just one etheric body, a human etheric body that, if visible (as to psychics or under special circumstances), looks much like a carbon copy of their human body. Shifters have this human etheric body, but they also have an animal etheric body. This second etheric body is less "solid" and not as strong as the human etheric body. It is most "solid" and defined in its extremities, in the paws, tail, and head area, and more nebulous in its middle areas. Normally, the animal etheric body is carried around stretched over the human frame, with the extremities fairly well lined up with the corresponding parts on the human body, and the rest stretched somewhat out of its true shape.

Many people wonder how someone can have two etheric bodies. It's quite simple. As I stated in chapter one, etheric matter has a property that physical matter doesn't have: it can occupy the same three-dimensional space as other etheric matter. A shifter's animal and human etheric bodies overlap and are somewhat intertwined. Shifters are not the only case of someone carrying two etheric bodies within them, occupying the same space. Certain mediums also have this ability. During séances, partially materialized etheric arms and legs sometimes thrust out from various parts of their bodies. This phenomenon is well-known and is referred to as "pseudopods" in spiritualist literature.[2]

---

[2] Pseudopods are among the most common paranormal events reported at séances of physical mediums. There is a detailed record of a very well-documented séance by one of the most famous physical mediums in *Natural and Supernatural*, by Brian Inglis (Dorset, England: Prism Press, 1992), p. 389.

Having a second etheric body in the form of an animal is held, in shifter society, to be one of the main things that defines shifters. This second etheric body may be felt and may manifest in a number of ways. Sometimes it manifests in out-of-body travel—not astral travel, which only involves the astral body, but etheric travel, which involves the etheric body. When shifters engage in etheric travel, they may be etheric traveling with either their human or their animal etheric body. Etheric traveling with the animal etheric body is called "etheric shifting." As in regular etheric travel, sometimes the etheric body becomes "closer" to this plane, and partially "materializes" as a ghostly form. This form is usually transparent, and usually cannot directly affect physical objects. Occasionally, however, it is close enough to the physical to do such things as knock over objects, leave footprints, or shed a few hairs and leave them behind. Eyewitnesses say that this form often has glowing eyes.

In a few cases, it may look solid instead of transparent, but may retain non-physical qualities, such as being able to pass through walls or suddenly disappear. When the etheric body partially materializes and becomes visible, it is often called "apparition shifting," because an apparition or "phantom" seems to have been formed. I have come across many cases of eyewitness sightings of apparition shifting, including cases where the apparition formed by the shifter was glimpsed by several people, who all agreed with each other and with the shifter on the particulars of the occurrence. Etheric shifting and its rarer variation, apparition shifting, are both very difficult to accomplish. Most cases occur spontaneously. Shifters may feel tired and lie down, or go into trance during meditation, and suddenly be thrown into an etheric shift without quite knowing how or why it happened. Very few shifters claim to be able to engage in etheric shifting at will.

PARANORMAL ASPECTS OF MENTAL SHIFTING

There are some paranormal aspects to some mental shifts, and sometimes these aspects are experienced without any mental shift. These include more-than-human strength, speed, agility, or senses, as well as the rare supernatural occurrences that border on physical shifts, such as eye-color changes and the growing of tiny patches of fur. Those who experience supernatural aspects to their mental shifts are often called "berserkers."

We get the word "berserker" from the Scandinavian warriors. The name comes from the bear-sark, or bear-shirt, that these warriors wore. Although you will probably find contrary claims in some modern books on werewolf folklore, Norse folklore makes it very clear that berserkers were not shapeshifters, but rather mental shifters with paranormal powers. Berserkers could draw on the animal for strength, speed, and senses beyond the human, but they did not physically change in any way.

In ancient Scandinavia, these abilities were honed and used specifically for war. Modern berserkers usually don't train their abilities for fighting. Berserkers are simply mental shifters who exhibit paranormal effects or abilities frequently in their mental shifts. Many mental shifters have had occasional experiences with berserker powers, but few experience these powers regularly, and even fewer can invoke them at will. There are a number of shifters who go into medium-to-deep mental shifts whenever they are seriously threatened. These are sometimes called "the true berserkers," indicating those who use mental shifts for self-defense or fighting skills. In these shifters, either the animal side is very protective, or it has been "trained" to manifest when they need to fight.

It is commonplace in shifter packs that when a berserker gets backed into an alley in the bad part of town, he or she can usually get out unscathed, even when facing armed opponents. In most cases I've encountered, shifters never even had to fight. They just shifted mentally, causing an "aura" of pure animalistic energy to suddenly surround them. This, along with the look in their eyes and their uncontrollable growling, scared away their enemies. In those situations where they had to fight, they fought ferociously, by instinct, and often displayed supernatural strength or speed. The Scandinavian berserkers are famous for fighting with complete and utter ferocity, like angry bears. There was no technique to their fighting, so it was very hard to use countermoves against them. They fought by pure instinct. It was said that they terrified all enemies, vanquished some of the best warriors, and bit through iron shields.

There has been a great interest in cultivating berserker powers for martial arts and street fighting. Some of my shifter friends have pointed out that some societies involved with advanced martial arts or street fighting use exactly the same techniques that we shifters use to "awaken" a new shifter. These fighters, however, then bend the inner animal toward aggression, defense, and anger. That, of course, is the use to which the Scandinavian berserkers were put. I do not believe that it is good to link the inner animal to fighting and anger in this way. Many of those who purposefully develop their berserker powers and bend the inner animal toward fighting, find that the way to integration and physical shifting is blocked.

One of the most common berserker powers is the ability to run faster or jump higher than a normal human can. In one case, I personally observed a berserker bounding along, jumping about six feet in the air with every step. When I say six feet, I mean that the bottoms of her feet were at about that height at the peak of each bound. And she was not even a very athletic person!

Even though the paranormal effects of the berserker sometimes occur without any mental shift at all, they are usually connected to mental shifts. They are especially likely to occur during very deep mental shifts and with high shifting energy. One common effect of deep mental shifting with very high shifting energy is that, when you "return to human," you find that the spit in your mouth has that dry, disgusting texture and taste it often has when you first wake up in the morning. This is the hallmark of having reached a relatively deep trance state; though, in the case of most mental shifts, it is an open-eyed and active trance state, not like what people usually associate with "being in a trance." This spit is often called "wolf spit" by shifters. Berserkers are particularly likely to experience "wolf spit," especially during mental shifts in which they display the more paranormal berserker powers.

Heightened senses are also fairly common to berserkers. In werewolf movies or novels, the werewolf often runs around with full-time superhuman senses while in human form. This is not accurate. Heightened senses usually come and go. Moreover, they range from just a little better than normal to superhuman, or anywhere in between. There are few shifters who have heightened senses all the time, especially if those senses are anywhere near the "superhuman" category. In some cases, the heightened senses are just a heightened awareness of the senses that you usually have. In other cases, the senses themselves are definitely sharper. In a few cases, the heightened senses are so sharp as to be downright paranormal.

One of the more common types of heightened senses is heightened hearing. At a low level, this is simply hearing better than normal. In the strongest manifestations, which often happen during mental shifts with high shifting energy, the whole way of hearing changes. Every detail is sharper. In fact, so many quiet sounds are distinctly heard that the sounds all crowd in on your awareness and are somewhat distracting and confusing. Everything sounds much the same, and yet different. The shifter may also hear ultrasonic or subsonic noises.

When heightened smell occurs, it is often independent of any shift. In fact, some shifters have a full-time heightened sense of smell (more so than with any other sense). With heightened smell, one is distinctly aware of smell most of the time. Everything smells much richer, more detailed and varied, but not necessarily stronger. One often starts really noticing the distinct smells of people, and even gaining the ability to distinguish them by scent.

Heightened sight is one of the least common types of heightened sense. It usually occurs only in deep mental shifts, in shifters with high levels of shifting energy. It is often accompanied by eye-color changes. "Heightened sight" is actually a misnomer, for some aspects of the sight become worse, especially color vision. Wolves and most other mammals are colorblind. This does not mean that they do not see color at all. Like colorblind humans, they can distinguish color somewhat. Everything does not look like a black-and-white TV. It means that they see red and green as basically the same color, and divide the color spectrum into a handful of colors, instead of the hundreds or thousands of tints that humans can distinguish. Dogs, in color tests, see blue and yellow best, and wolves probably do too. Cats are less colorblind than canines. Most animals can also see very slightly into the ultraviolet and infrared range.

Most shifters agree with this view—from mental shifters who experience heightened sight to those who claim physical transformation. They say that every detail sharpens and stands out, especially in the dark. The reason that wolves and many other animals are colorblind is that it allows them to see better in the dark. What their vision lacks in color, it makes up for in being able to gather light, and distinguish fine shades of light and dark. Being extremely sensitive to the tiniest shading of light and dark translates into incredibly sharp and detailed vision. Where we detect hundreds of shades of color, an animal detects just a few. Where the animal detects hundreds of shades of light and dark, we detect just a few.

The first thing shifters usually notice is that the color seems to wash out of things, so that shades of black, white, gray, and lots of brown make up most of the color spectrum. Many things are tinted with blue or yellow, and a few things have a strange, inexplicable iridescent "glow" in colors the shifters can't identify. Many shifters describe them as brilliant neon-like colors that they have never seen before. Everything comes into extremely sharp focus, especially things in deep shadow, and things seem almost to be leaping out at them, the details are so clear. Anything that moves, in particular, seems to "leap out" from the background and become even sharper.

Sometimes, the eye color will temporarily change. I have seen this myself, even though it's only happened to me a few times. I've also heard a number of first-hand reports of shifters who have seen this phenomena in another shifter's mental shift, so it is not just the imagination of those that experience it. Science also admits that this kind of sudden eye-color change exists, because too many psychiatrists have seen multiple personalities suddenly change eye color with a personality switch. When this type of eye-color change happens over a matter of minutes, it is simply a gradual change of tint. When it happens in a matter of seconds, a rim of the new color appears in a circular ring on the outer rim of the iris and spreads inward. If the shifter has blue eyes that are changing to yellow, it often happens in two stages. First, a rim of green appears on the outer part of the iris and spreads inward so the iris becomes green. Next, a rim of yellow appears and spreads inward to color the eyes yellow. Eye-color changes almost always reverse themselves when the mental shift ends, or even before it ends.

Sometimes shifters may grow a very tiny patch of fur. This is fairly rare, yet I've heard enough reports of it, and seen enough evidence, that I believe it exists. I once saw it happen to a fellow shifter. I didn't actually see the fur growing, but it wasn't there before the mental shift and it was afterward. It was definitely real fur, growing right out of his skin. He had it for quite some time afterward, too. These patches of fur usually appear on the belly, in about the region of the second chakra, and sometimes they appear on the chest or throat. They are seldom much bigger than a quarter. It seems that they appear during a very deep mental shift. Sometimes the fur immediately slides back into the skin or "evaporates" into ectoplasmic "fog," and sometimes it persists indefinitely.

When these spots are examined, they don't seem much like a hairy patch. They are much more like fur, with the hairs unlike normal body hairs, growing very thick and close together. The color is usually white or pale yellowish, this being the usual color of a wolf's underbelly fur. Fortunately, these patches are very easy to get rid of. If you shave them off once, they will grow back much thinner. If you shave them off twice, usually only a few lone hairs will grow back.

There are sometimes other strange side effects associated with mental shifts, especially in those shifters who have high levels of shifting energy, or who regularly experience berserker powers. One of these is that sometimes the skin changes to a distinct grayish hue, or sometimes a whitish color. In some cases, this goes so far as to fade to a pure white, like paper. This is a characteristic that is reported in shapeshifting legends from around the world.

In *Dance of the Dolphin*, by Candace Slater, a collection of modern shapeshifting folklore from Brazil, witnesses of shapeshifting dolphins frequently reported that their skin was white as snow right before turning into a dolphin, and immediately after returning to human form.[3] When

---

[3] Candace Slater, *Dance of the Dolphin* (Chicago: University of Chicago Press, 1994), p. 208.

they had not just transformed, however, the *botu,* or weredolphins, were said to be nearly indistinguishable from normal humans, except that they sometimes had a small hairless indentation on the top of their head, a vestigial blow-hole. For this reason, they often wore hats.[4]

In some cases of mental shifting, especially those connected with skin that turns whitish or grayish, the skin may actually jump, crawl, and twitch in the weirdest way. It may feel as if many tiny hairs were squirming underneath the surface. This often looks as if the skin were being pushed from underneath by something, not as if the skin were simply twitching. Often, when this happens, shifters will have a feeling all over their body of a great "tension" and "pressure," as if they were going to burst if they did not shapeshift. These symptoms can be alarming, but they are completely harmless.

I have come across a few cases where the phenomenon of *elongation* is experienced in conjunction with mental shifts in which the skin turns grayish or whitish. Elongation is a phenomenon that has been reported in folklore all over the world. It has also been an object of study for some of the more modern paranormal investigators, and is probably best known as a phenomenon associated with spiritualist mediums. Elongation occurs when the body becomes somewhat out-of-phase with normal physical matter, and becomes partially like etheric matter. Matter in this state is often called "ectoplasm." The body stretches and elongates—the torso stretching from three feet to six feet long, or an arm stretching out far longer than its normal length, for example. This is generally an involuntary state, and is often quite brief, with the stretched part going back to its normal length and size fairly soon after elongation.

One side effect, often associated with grayish or whitish skin in mental shifts, but much more common than elongation, is the phenomenon of the skin oozing a grayish or pale-white "fog" that clings to the skin and crawls over its surface. The accounts of how this looks and behaves are exactly the same as the accounts of ectoplasm in its fog-like form. From this, I've concluded that this substance must be ectoplasm.

---

[4] Slater, *Dance of the Dolphin*, p. 92.

One of the most common berserker-type side effects is a keen awareness of (and partial manifestation of) the etheric animal body. The feeling of having animal "phantom limbs," such as a tail, paws, muzzle, or wolf ears, is an experience that many shifters have had, even if only once or twice. It may happen in conjunction with a mental shift, or outside of any mental shift altogether. A person with an amputated limb can often still feel the missing limb. What they are really feeling is the remaining "etheric limb," a part of the etheric body that corresponds to the amputated part. In the absence of any sensations from the physical part, they are able to notice the sensations from the etheric part. In much the same way, a shifter may distinctly feel, sometimes in incredible realism and detail, a phantom tail, muzzle, ears, paws, or even larger pieces of an extremity. The most common phantom limb felt is the tail, for the same reason that amputees can best feel the etheric where they don't have a limb. Humans have no tails. In order to fully feel an etheric paw, you need to somehow bypass the sensations and signals coming from your real hand. There is no such problem with a tail, because you have no real tail to "override" in order to feel the sensations that are coming from the etheric tail.

Phantom limbs are not truly there, in the sense of the real world. They pass right through any clothing that is worn over that part of the body. In those rare times that they won't, it is very uncomfortable to sit on an invisible scrunched-up tail. Phantom limbs are not visible, except sometimes dimly to psychics, and sometimes animals can see or sense them. When I am very healthy, I can grow phantom wolf ears at will. When I was younger, one of my amusements was to sit next to cats that liked me, and then suddenly grow phantom wolf ears. No matter how still I sat both before and after the change, the cats always knew and would suddenly run away looking terrified.

In most cases, this manifestation of phantom limbs is, as far as physical reality is concerned, mostly in the mind of the shifter, a shift in psychic perception more than anything else. In some cases, however, especially in conjunction with deeper mental shifts in shifters with high levels of shifting energy, the etheric body can manifest as "phantom limbs" to a greater extent than normal, an extent that is more than a mere shift in perception.

Many shifters who are supernaturally strong or swift during mental shifts credit their strength to the muscles of their etheric animal body. Many of those who can run on all fours swiftly credit phantom wolf legs with keeping them properly balanced and providing muscle power. I have also heard reports of shifters leaving wolf-paw prints even though their hands and feet looked fully human, prints presumably made by invisible, yet partly solid, etheric wolf paws.

Another "phantom limb" phenomenon that is frequently reported is phantom fur. Only twice in my life, when concentrating very strongly, was I able to call up phantom fur at will. Some shifters, especially those in cold climates, have learned to do this. Phantom fur is more "solid" and closer to being physical than other phantom extremities. This is useful, because it can sometimes keep the shifter warm—not just with a false warmth, but with skin warm to the touch to other people, in some rare cases even when the shifter has been out in winter weather for hours, stark naked! In some cases, when someone runs a hand just above the skin of a shifter manifesting phantom fur, he or she can faintly feel the fur.

Quite a number of shifters believe in the traditional powers of the berserker, or at least they believe in some of those powers. Many shifters have actually experienced some of these phenomena, even if only once or twice briefly, and even if they didn't quite realize what was happening to them at the time. Yet there are a fair number of shifters who simply refuse to consider the existence of physical shifting. Physical shifting is much harder to believe in than berserker powers. It is even harder to simply keep an open mind about it.

There are many people who believe in various aspects of the paranormal. But among New Agers, flakes, the superstitious, and others interested in the supernatural, "werewolves" are believed in very little. Even the most superstitious seldom believe in werewolves. So it is no wonder that even shifters, who are pretty close to being "werewolves" themselves, don't necessarily believe in actual physical transformation.

It is certainly true that some of the legends that purport to be shapeshifting legends show the hallmarks of legends about berserkers in costume. There are even fairly modern accounts of wolf societies of mental shifters and those who practice wolf medicine that lend weight to these theories. From the era of the Wild West come many stories of the Native Americans of the great plains who wore wolf skin while imitating wolf mannerisms to an uncanny degree for the purpose of cultivating "wolf medicine," or sneaking up on buffalo, or scouting and traveling through enemy territory in disguise. Modern shifters practice the art of skinwalking using homemade costumes. Some shifters never use costuming in this way, but some swear by it as one of the most potent ways to connect to the inner animal. I suspect that many ancient skinwalkers were not deliberately trying to create "werewolf legends" either, but were just trying to grow and learn as shifters.

The legends that sound like berserkers in costume are much more common in legends from the earlier eras, from pagan or immediately post-pagan times. They are virtually absent from the legends of later centuries. I believe this is because these legends reflect a time when wolf societies, similar to those that frontiersmen encountered in the Americas, were still alive and flourishing in Europe. Later on, however, the church's influence and suppression of all things associated with pagan practices caused most of these societies to fragment. Therefore, the later legends mostly involved true physical shifters. Since the European population was increasingly well-educated and less superstitious, the sightings of people in costume, regardless of their berserker powers, were less likely to make it into legend.

I think that those who refuse to believe in physical shifting, and try to explain the phenomenon with technical explanations of how this and that shifting phenomenon could be combined to mimic physical shifting, are simply afraid to believe in the possibility of physical shifting. Some shifters, when they have it proven to them that berserker phenomena exist, despair of ever finding physical shifting. When they find something can imitate physical shifting in some ways, yet not be physical shifting, they say to themselves, "Well, this must explain the legends," and stop hoping to find anything more.

However, berserker phenomena show that there is something real and paranormal associated with werewolf legends. Berserkers and what they are able to do are lesser manifestations of the same phenomena that lead to true physical shifting in its more developed form. The same wolf etheric body that lends a wolf's abilities to a berserker, can, at a more physical level of manifestation, actually become material enough to be a physical thing, via either bilocation shifting or physical shifting. And true physical shifting is only taking berserker phenomena a little farther, to its logical conclusion. If one can exist, why not the other?

CHAPTER 3

Familiars and Spirit Guides

Historically, the term "familiar" has been used in three ways. One describes an animal spirit, usually a guide, who is strongly associated with a person, another describes a real animal who assists a person in magical or spiritual matters, and a third describes a totem or power animal.

A totem or power animal is not a real animal, and it is not an animal spirit. One of my totem animals is a raccoon, but there is no real raccoon or spirit raccoon associated with me. This species merely reflects my personality and has an archetypal influence and symbolic meaning for me. A totem animal represents an abstract quality. For example, the bald eagle is the national bird, but there is no particular bird, real or spirit, that people point out as "the" national bird.

To avoid confusion, I use three separate terms to denote the three ways in which "familiar" has traditionally been used—totem animals, animal spirits, and animal spirit guides. An animal spirit guide is a guide for a person (a guide in New Age terminology is a "guardian angel"). There are also "animal spirits" that are just "stray" animal spirits. I will use the term "familiar" to refer only to real physical animals.

Familiars provide a point of contact with the animal world. They are teachers of animal ways. They are also parent figures to shifters. Shifters are born human, to human parents. The animal side of a shifter is largely an orphan, with no animal parents or teachers, no knowledge of animal ways except by instinct. The familiar acts as teacher, a valuable point of contact with the world of real animals. Shifters form bonds with their familiars, thereby strengthening their own animal self.

Animal spirit guides have a similar purpose. They teach shifters what it means to be an animal, in ways that only another animal could teach. But animal spirit guides also have a greater purpose. They function exactly like regular spirit guides, except that they also embody the nature and qualities of a particular species, and must remain true to this nature. The only way their nature is truly different from that of a real animal is that they always have human or more-than-human levels of intelligence, as normal spirit guides do.

It is generally believed that most shifters have one or more animal spirit guides. Not all shifters are aware of these, just as most people are generally unaware of their ordinary spirit guides. Even psychics don't necessarily know their own individual spirit guides, though most psychics have a vague sense of their collective presence. Some shifters claim that they have no animal spirit guides, and that they are psychic enough to sense the presence of any if they did have them. These claims of having no animal spirit guides are more common among more advanced shifters. Simple mental shifters are most often aware of their animal spirit guides. Shifters who are very new to the art or who are struggling and learning about shifting are also much more likely to be aware of the presence of animal spirit guides.

I am of the opinion that many of those who manifest the "higher powers" are right in their belief that they don't have animal spirit guides, even though this runs counter to standard shifter beliefs. I believe that animal spirit guides appear in the first place because the shifter needs teaching and guidance in the ways of animals. Those who have achieved the "higher powers," or who have otherwise reached certain goals, do not need animal spirit guides any more, so the guides withdraw. Those that are most likely to be aware of the presence of animal spirit guides are the novice shifters.

Those shifters who have animal spirit guides usually have only one. The species of that spirit guide corresponds to the species into which the shifter shifts. Sometimes shifters have two or more animal spirit guides of the same species. Few shifters shift into two different species, but those who do generally have an animal spirit guide for each of those species. For instance, a wolf-bear shifter would have both a wolf spirit and a bear spirit guide. Occasionally, shifters may have an extra spirit guide of a different species from the one into which they normally shift. I've known quite a number of wolf shifters who had an extra cat or fox spirit guide.

It is particularly common among mental shifters, especially for those who are artificial shifters, to start out as fox shifters and later turn to some other species. Fox spirit guides very often provide an introduction to shifting. Those who go through this often get a new spirit guide of the new species when the changeover occurs, but keep the old fox spirit guide for a while. Shifters don't often get a new animal spirit guide. It usually happens only when the shifter is young or new to the art, and has a species changeover, such as changing from a fox shifter to a wolf shifter. It also occasionally happens at major life events, such as when a close loved one dies. In this case, the old spirit guide is generally replaced by one of the same species, but some shifters may experience a species changeover and acquire a new animal spirit guide.

Some novice shifters do not bond with the fox or any other species. They mentally shift, and show all the other typical signs of being a shifter, but are not bonded to any particular species. In this case, they often go through a dozen or so species in short order, along with the accompanying spirit guides, before they bond truly with one species. This is always a temporary phenomenon. When this hectic time is over, the shifter generally has only one animal spirit guide, and does no more species switching.

Those who do have animal spirit guides often find them very useful. Shifters tend to become aware of their animal spirit guides gradually, most often in dreams. Sometimes I am aware of the presence of my wolf spirit guide while I am awake, and generally sense the message she is trying to give me. These episodes are vague, however, and mostly useless. I often meet with my wolf spirit guide in dreams, and here she is very vivid and real, and often communicates things very clearly and precisely. Some shifters have visions of their animal spirit guide during meditations. Some rare shifters actually see their animal spirit guide, ghost-like, as it follows them around all day. I've also come across a few cases of psychics who could see an animal spirit guide following a shifter around.

It is common for shifters to have a very dramatic meeting with their animal spirit guide shortly before they have their first mental shift. In most cases, this occurs as an extremely vivid and dramatic dream—the kind of dream that seems extremely real, causes the person to wake up covered with sweat, and sticks vividly in the memory for days afterward. Many of these dreams are birth/death/rebirth experiences. Shifters may experience being torn to shreds and eaten by animals, only to find that they have become one of the animals. Some dreams may involve the flesh simply falling off the body, bit by bit, for no apparent reason, and animal parts growing in the place of what has been lost. Sometimes they are as simple as meeting a very wise animal, and suddenly realizing that you are of the same species. Some of these dreams are puzzles, and recur until the shifter-to-be finally meets the spirit guide in the right way.

In a few rare cases, the animal spirit guide meets the shifter-to-be in an even more dramatic way. In one case, a woman's first mental shift was presaged by a truly paranormal meeting. She woke up at night, feeling as if she were in some strange sort of trance state, and feeling a strong call from "others." She followed this call to a certain place outside, where she saw many spirit wolves. They somehow "told" her that she was one of their pack. She played with them, wrestling and chasing, as a child would play with dogs, and feeling as if she were in a strange trance the whole time. The wolves left many tiny bites on her in the course of playing, just as a dog will sometimes play-bite too hard and scratch the skin. In the morning, even though she half thought it was all a dream, there was evidence that she had been outside during the night, and amazingly, she did still have the many tiny bites. Animal spirit guides do more than just give shifters messages in dreams and visions. There are mental shifters that say that their animal spirit guides trigger mental shifts, and guide them through mental shifts.

A shifter's familiar is a real animal, one that serves in a very special way and may interact with the shifter's animal spirit guide(s). The familiar may be a "channel," allowing shifters to see, hear, and feel what the animal senses, or even to occupy its body temporarily. Some shifters also have a telepathic bond with their familiar, and can read its thoughts. The familiar can be a channel for the animal spirit guide, allowing it to act through the familiar to communicate with the shifter. Having a familiar can be very beneficial, especially for mental shifters who are still trying to develop their skills. The familiar is an animal, and thus can teach shifters a lot more about being an animal than they could figure out instinctively. Moreover, the animal spirit guide communicates more easily through a familiar than through subtle signals and rare visions.

Creating a bond with a familiar is not difficult. In fact, many shifters make their pets into familiars without even trying. Some shifters have only one familiar, but many have two or more. The familiar does not have to be the same species as the shifter. Housecats are common substitutes for tiger shifters and for every other kind of cat shifter. Dogs are common familiars for wolf shifters. Familiars don't even have to be close to the right species, even though closer relationships work better. As silly as it may sound, a wolf shifter may have hamsters, ducks, or any sort of animal as familiars.

Curiously, a familiar of the "wrong" species will, with time, come to resemble the species for which it is a substitute, both in personality and body. A man I knew had two Labrador retrievers who acted as his familiars, and as channels for a bear spirit guide. These dogs, while still looking like dogs, walked like bears, and somehow physically resembled bears. This resemblance was not imagined. Strangers who saw the man walking his dogs would often comment on it.

There are certain properties that are unique to familiars that allow you to distinguish them from normal pets. There must be love between shifters and their familiar. The bond is unusually strong. Shifters couldn't think of harming their familiars, and they typically feel a very warm fondness for them, a feeling somewhat similar to that of being in love. Shifters tend to think of their familiars, not as mere animals, but as beloved friends, twins, sisters, or brothers. When separated from them, they miss them and think of them often. Shifters typically never forget to feed, water, and walk their familiars.

Familiars often seem to understand things beyond what most animals of the species should understand, especially those things the shifter is trying to communicate. Familiars become particularly devoted to their shifters, and it is clear to everyone that they like them more than anyone else in the family. Some familiars are affectionate with others, and other familiars pretty much ignore everyone else. Shifters remain particularly in tune with what their familiars are doing, feeling, and thinking, and familiars remain similarly in tune with their shifters. Sometimes familiar and shifter communicate telepathically.

Some superstitious folk believe that werewolves are possessed, sometimes by an animal spirit, but more often by a demonic entity. In nearly all cases, this is not true. In some cases, shifters are indeed possessed by their animal spirit guides when they shift. This occurs mostly in young shifters, where the spirit guides do this to help them "learn the ropes." Later, they outgrow it. It is also often true that shifters are partially possessed by their animal spirit guides during bilocation shifting. In neither of these instances is the possession total. The animal spirit guide is a benevolent entity, that never ejects the shifter's soul from the body during possession. Both the shifter and animal spirit guide are in there together. The animal spirit guide may greatly influence the shifter's mind during these episodes, but only by way of wolflike feelings and such, not by domination and suppression of the shifter's free will.

A familiar and an animal spirit guide perform an important function in a shifter's life. A shifter is not a real animal. Neither is a shifter completely human. Shifters live largely in human society, spend most or all of their life in a human body, and are taught and raised by human parents. Shifters need real animals to nurture and teach them their animal side. This is where familiars and spirit guides are important. The familiar is a real animal, and the animal spirit guide is a real animal in spirit form who is also wise, intelligent, guiding, protective, and parentlike.

Familiars and animal spirit guides, especially working together, can teach you a lot about your animal side. They can also heal a broken heart. If you grew up as a shifter without having a familiar and without being aware of your animal spirit guide, you probably felt alone, neglected, orphaned, and out of place, even if your parents were very loving. If your animal side grew up wild and angry at the world, you may find that you become hateful and destructive whenever you bring your animal side to the surface, and you may be afraid of it. The love and protective care given by familiars and animal spirit guides can make all the difference, and can calm your inner animal self. If your animal side is angry, destructive, and feels unloved, it is time to cure that problem by obtaining a good familiar or trying to get in touch with your animal spirit guide. It is very important for shifters to be knowledgeable and responsible about their craft. The truths you need to know are buried in your own instincts. When you were a child, you always knew what was right and unfair by instinct. Your animal spirit guide can help develop those same instincts for your animal side.

Familiars can also help. It is very helpful to be able to observe and learn from a real animal. Relating your human and wolf sides emotionally and having visions of your animal spirit guide cannot teach you everything. Choosing and training a familiar can be very important. You should not simply choose the cutest kitten or puppy. You shouldn't even use health as a criterion. It is not smart to buy the runt of the litter, but if this happens to be the animal meant for you, it is the best choice. You need to pick out the animal that calls to your soul, the animal that has a special understanding in its eyes. If in doubt, watch carefully, because your animal will choose you. If all the other puppies are more interested in food and mother, but one seeks you out and gives you a special look, that may be the one. Please do not base your choice on a fear that if you don't choose an animal, it will be killed. The world is full of animals that will be happier in the afterlife than with the wrong owner, and your future familiar may also be in need of rescue—more, actually, because it needs you in a spiritual way.

There are many possible future familiars out there for you. You may want to delay getting a familiar until you find an animal that has both the "rightness" about it and other desirable characteristics. One important thing to consider is fur color. When working with a familiar, the fur color of the animal will attract certain energies. Avoid animals with black fur. Black is not an "evil" color. Black soil is the richest soil, and the magical symbolism of black goes back to the beginning, the origins, and the creative processes. I have had a couple of wonderful familiars who were black. However, black does tend to attract unsavory spirits and bad energy. If you are a young, inexperienced shifter, or are a person prone to morbid thoughts, depression, and envy, you should avoid having a black familiar, unless there are many positive indications. If the black animal has even one small white spot, it balances the energy and reduces the potential danger.

Another way to balance the energy is to make sure you have another familiar of a different color. Black familiars can be extremely powerful. Black cats, in particular, seem to be very strongly connected to the other worlds. Black dogs have a much stronger tendency to be evil than any other black animals. There is a lot of folklore about demonic black dogs, much more so than black cats. Red, orange, or ginger-colored animals have a very strong connection to the fire element. These animals are particularly suitable familiars for fox shifters, and for people who are trying to build up their inner fire.

White animals have a strong connection to the divine and to wisdom. If you need divine help or wisdom, a white animal is a good choice. White is connected to purity and innocence. One of the best familiars I ever had was a beautiful white dog. For a wolf shifter, a dog is a very suitable familiar, especially a medium-to-large breed that is intelligent and has pointed ears. Breeds that are particularly suitable are collies, German shepherds, chow chows, akitas, huskies, samoyeds, and various mongrels that have the right features.

Wolf hybrids are not suitable familiars at all, and neither are full wolves usually suitable. I know wolf shifters who have tried both. Wolf hybrids are obscene, artificial animals. Both wolf and dog, they have a schizoid, weird, sneaky nature and split selves. If you adopt one as your familiar, you will inherit their neuroses and your nature will become more split and chaotic under the influence of their split selves. Many wolf shifters say that there is nothing worse than a wolf hybrid.

Wolves and wolf hybrids are intelligent animals with an intense need to roam far and wide. Both tend to become extremely aggressive (or withdrawn), neurotic, and unhappy in captivity. It is very important that familiars not be abused. They must be loving and trusting, not resentful, and they must want to be with you. Conditions that may be more than adequate for a dog may be abusive and neglectful for a wolf or wolf hybrid. For this reason, among others, pet wolves can seldom be familiars. Sometimes wild wolves can.

Wolf shifters who live in the extreme northern United States, Canada, or Alaska often report that they have a wild wolf "adopt" them and become their familiar. The wolf will probably never allow itself to be touched, but it will appear and show itself at close quarters fairly often. Sometimes wild foxes or other wild animals will also become familiars.

Some breeds of dogs have associations with other species. Beagles have connections with raccoon energies, as they are bred to hunt mostly raccoons, and, like all hunters, they partake of some of the nature of their prey. In a similar way, terriers, bred to hunt rats, partake of the nature of rats. They even resemble rats and act a bit like them, which is why some call them "rat dogs." Other terriers partake of the nature of badgers, because they hunt by digging in the same manner as badgers. In the same way, Irish wolfhounds partake of some of the nature of wolves. Just look at the expression in their yellow eyes, and you can see the wolf nature clearly. Some breeds of cat have special qualities. Siamese cats have a dainty, feminine, Oriental energy, and a strong sexuality. Both Maine coon cats and Japanese Bobtail cats have energies that connect to the primeval wildcat. Abyssinian cats have an energy that connects to ancient Egypt and to species of cats that live in a dry or hot climate.

The eye color of a familiar and the eye color of your animal spirit guide is important. Blue eyes share some of the qualities of white fur, and are genetically linked to white fur. Blue is also the color of many young animal's eyes, before they change to the adult color. Blue eyes are innocence and youth. Blue is often genetically linked to blindness in animals, especially in horses. Blue may signify being too innocent, naive, or "blind." Green eyes are often the eyes of the "witchy" individual. Green eyes often signify connections to the other worlds, the world of wild nature elementals, fairies, and devas. Green eyes may signify psychic abilities.

Brown eyes are earthy. Brown-eyed animals may be practical and trustworthy, with their feet on the ground. They may also find it less easy to rise to the higher realms. Yellow eyes are very special. Most wolves have yellow eyes, and so do most owls. In nature, yellow eyes are often associated with species that need to see very well, especially in the dark. Yellow eyes are a bit of the yellow Sun or yellowish Moon to carry with you. Yellow eyes are a blending of nighttime energies with those of the day. They often symbolize mystic knowledge or ancient wisdom. People often find yellow eyes both frightening and haunting.

Orange eyes are mostly found in species that are not nocturnal. They are a fire symbol; foxes have orange eyes and orange fur. Gray eyes are said to carry potential for a clear view of the future, and are often connected with unusual paranormal abilities.

There are two other eye colors that I should mention: red and purple. They are extremely rare. Some reptiles and pigeons have red eyes, and I believe purple eyes are found sometimes in hummingbirds. I've heard a few shifters say their spirit guides have purple eyes. These shifters were unbalanced and not quite sane. Red eyes are a universal symbol of evil. Sometimes, when your animal side is upset and feeling abused, you may see it, or yourself, in a vision as having red eyes. This is a potent signal of danger. It means you should wake up and start paying attention before things get worse.

It is best to choose young familiars, for it is harder to train an adult animal. When dealing with your familiar, you need to act as if you were dealing with a friend. You may be used to treating animals as playthings or servants, or you may be a softy who likes to spoil them rotten. Neither approach is correct. You must treat familiars with considerable love and respect, and with an appreciation for their personality and individuality.

Your familiar must be treated as a peer. Trying to force your will on a familiar is always bad. One of the reasons that the familiar needs to be open and trusting toward you is that these qualities are absolutely essential for both sense shifting and possession shifting.

The bond of trust between shifter and familiar is important because the familiar may also sense-shift or, rarely, possession-shift, into you. When this happens, it feels somewhat uncomfortable and invasive to have your familiar in your body with you, and you may be very exhausted afterward. This is what it feels like to the familiar when you sense or possession shift into it. Your familiar is not just a teacher and a door into the world of animals. It learns things about being human from you. Many familiars show much more human intelligence and understanding than any other animal of their species. They become a bit human, even as you become a bit more integrated with your animal side. They are also in tune with your thoughts, and sometimes almost "borrow" your intelligence in some ways. It is my belief that familiars are animals destined to be born as humans in their next life, and that they become familiars in order to learn about being human.

The bond between shifter and familiar can cause trouble when the familiar dies. In myths, the lives of shifters are caught up with their familiars. When the familiar dies, the shifter dies too. This is not literally true in real life, at least not in modern times. If a shifter has only one familiar for many years, its death may be a physical shock, even beyond the grief. The shifter may be weak, disorientated, and even occasionally suicidal for some time afterward. The way to avoid this is to have more than one familiar at a time. The shock of the death of any familiar is much less, even if the grief is the same, if there is another familiar still living.

Many people ask, "Why are so many legends about predatory species of shapeshifters?" There are prey-animal species of shifters, both in modern times and in legend. These are not nearly as common, however, as the predatory species. In legend, we find deer, horses, boar, and rabbits as some of the most common prey-animal shifters, but these are far outnumbered by the more common wolves, cats, and bears. In modern times, we find this as well. I've known of a few prey-animal species in modern shifters: a few rabbit shifters, a couple of moose shifters, and one kangaroo shifter. But the herbivores are definitely outnumbered by the predators.

Different people have had different ideas about why this was so. To many primitive societies, the reason was quite clear. People who became shapeshifters on purpose tended to become predators, because it is much easier to be a part-time animal as a predator than as prey. You could move around more easily, as there is a lower species density, and you are not constantly trespassing on someone else's territory or running into them. You are also not likely to be made into a snack by some predator! A were-animal is always a highly inexperienced animal, not having the benefit of being raised by animal parent(s), taught animal things, or even spending all that many hours in the physical form of an animal. A were-animal may take years of regular shifting to accumulate the life experience that a real animal acquires in a few weeks.

An inexperienced predator only has the problem of not being able to catch prey—not a big problem, since the were-animal presumably eats in human form and spends little time in animal form. This is probably a contributing factor to the legend that were-animals are hated and feared primarily because they kill livestock. A very inexperienced predator would be unlikely to be able to kill anything other than livestock. But an inexperienced herbivore is in grave danger, for predators do not just pick off the weak and old, they also prey heavily on the unaware. And you can't get much more inexperienced than an adult prey animal who has only spent a few hours in the physical form of an animal.

Those who become shifters on purpose, and who have some control over what species they choose, therefore tend to choose predatory species. This also has some relevance for hereditary shifters. In hereditary shifters, where being a shifter runs in the family, the family often tends toward one species. It does not mean that all shifters in that family are going to be that species, but they will tend toward that species. If many lines of hereditary herbivore shifters died out in the past because of predation, that would explain why few are around now.

In my personal opinion, there are other possible reasons why predators far outnumber herbivores. I believe that the prevalence of predatory shifters is due more to reasons of the spirit and nature of human beings rather than to predation. Many shifters have the strongest bond with animals of a predatory nature. The two most common types of shifters are canines and felines. The most common pets are dogs and cats. Herbivorous primates, such as the ape and gorilla, are highly developed, but shifters don't use them to manifest. The average shifter, if forced to join animal society, would probably be happier in a wolf pack, lion pride, or fox family than in a deer herd, rabbit warren, or chicken coop. Being socially similar makes dogs and cats more satisfying pets and comrades. In my experience, people who become shifters are much more likely to "connect" with a predatory species, and "become" that species.

Predators and herbivores tend to be inhabited by different types of souls. In the cycle of reincarnation, I think that souls grow to be herbivores, and later "graduate" to the level of predators, and even later go to the human level. I think that predators are inhabited by higher souls than herbivores; the two tend to be on two different levels entirely. This has to do with the spiritual meaning of the role of predator and prey (something worth studying for any shifter). While there is generally a gulf between a human soul and that of a herbivore, there is a certain kinship between a human soul and that of a predator, such as an eagle or leopard.

In medieval times Europeans had different ideas about why werebeasts were predators—at least the "official" view, propounded by the church, was quite different. As time went on, the church's viewpoint dominated the richer, more varied viewpoint found in folklore. In the church's view, most or all werewolves and other werebeasts were evil sorcerers who had made a pact with the devil. The church's doctrine stated that these evil sorcerer-werebeasts tended to choose predatory animals such as wolves and bears because they had an unholy desire to tear and rend flesh and commit acts of violence. These predatory animals seemed better suited to these tasks.

WOLVES

The wolf, more than any other animal, has come to symbolize the wilderness, for wolves re-establish themselves much more quickly than bears or large cats, unless persecuted by the technology and fervor of modern times. Early Europeans saw wolves return whenever wilderness returned. In modern times, the wolf is seen as a symbol of the wilderness, for wherever the wolf is, that is true wilderness.

In Europe, when war and famine ravaged the land, and farmland and pastures gave way to wilderness, the wolf returned just as fast as the wilderness.[1] Thus the wolf became a symbol of famine, war, and death as well. Wolves were seen as wild beings, lurking, always waiting for a chance to revel in the bad times of humanity. They were often viewed as a symbol, sometimes even a cause, of conditions that were evil and horrible for the human beings living through them. If the wolf was profiting, humans must be suffering.

Wolves are a major "power" animal. Much of their magic has to do with power. Like all power animals of this type, they are generally viewed as either very good or very evil by any particular culture. This is because power, while being neither good nor evil in itself, can be used for either good or evil. In some cultures, wolf medicine was used mostly for good, and got a very good reputation, as in most Native American cultures. In other cultures, the power contained in wolf medicine was used primarily for evil, and so that culture became convinced that the "essence" of wolf is evil. Ravens, often associated with wolves, are another power animal that is generally regarded as either very good or very evil.

Most Native American cultures saw wolves as very good animals, symbolizing the very best that a human could attain. Wolves were good warriors and hunters. They were smart and strong, and acted in wise ways. Wolves could make it on their own, as lone wolves, or as part of a well-organized pack. This particular characteristic of wolves symbolized the best traits to which human beings could aspire. To most Native American societies, the best human beings were strong and wise and could make it on their own,

---

[1] "Whereas in 1300 wolves had been largely confined to the Far North, Russia, and mountainous regions," Douglas claims, "they made a distinct comeback in the succeeding centuries . . . in the 1420s, wolves were allegedly seen roaming through the suburbs of Paris." Adam Douglas, *The Beast Within* (London: Chapmans, 1992), p. 92.

but could also do well in a group, and contribute to others, helping to teach and raise up the next generation. Wolves were the only animals of the American continents that really did this. Native Americans saw, in wolf society, something admirable, something similar to the way human society was run, yet something only the best of human societies even approached.

Most Native American societies admired the way wolves dealt with food. The wolf, more than most other large predators, tends to "waste" food. Wolves learned to cache their kills. When they had eaten the majority of a carcass, they often hid the rest by scraping dirt or snow over it, while they went off to do more hunting. Most bears and large cats will stay with a carcass until it is finished, but wolves often try to accumulate carcasses during times of plenty, just as we keep extra food in the refrigerator. This habit of caching is not the same as "wasting" food, as the early Europeans often interpreted this behavior, attributing it to bloodlust and gluttony. The wolves return to their caches in times of poor hunting. One inevitable side effect of caching, however, is that other animals help themselves to the wolves' food.

Most Native American societies saw this as proof that the wolf was truly a kind soul, a good, benevolent creature. They saw that the wolf not only provided for itself and its immediate group, as the good warrior did, but also provided for those less fortunate out of their surplus, as every truly kind soul did. Indeed, even though the wolf doesn't really intend to supplement the diets of a host of other creatures, it doesn't really object to this pilfering either. Biologists are often baffled by the fact that wolves pass up chances to kill the creatures that pilfer their caches. In fact, surpluses from wolf caches have a very important function in the environment. Especially in the arctic regions, many small predators would have difficulty getting through the hardest times in the winter (especially young experiencing their first winter on their own) if not for wolf kills. This characteristic of wolves made many Native American societies view them as unusually sacred animals that gave to others, as well as providing for themselves and their own group.

Wolf magic has often been put to use in certain types of endeavors. Wolf magic has to do with the concepts of competence, in a group setting or alone, organized group maneuvers, and hunting. Wolf medicine has often been cultivated by hunters, especially those working in a group. As Rudyard Kipling writes in *The Jungle Book*, "The strength of the Pack is the Wolf, and the strength of the Wolf is the Pack."[2] This is a very eloquent statement of the essence of what wolf magic is about. Wolf magic is about the interplay of strength alone, and strength with others. Even in situations where one is alone, wolf magic still invokes qualities that are related to the kinds of things involved in the strength of a group

Because these qualities of strength, competence, hunting, and group endeavors are involved in wolf magic, it has often been used for war. Wolf magic has often, unfortunately, been invoked by those who wished to practice warfare more successfully. The Indians of the North American plains used wolf pelts for many different purposes—for medicine and magic, for hunting, and for war. The Pawnee used wolf magic for war and scouting more than any other plains tribe.[3] They wore wolf pelts while scouting in enemy territory or trying to steal horses, and they imitated the wolf in the way they moved to try to invoke wolf medicine. In the sign language used on the plains in the old West, the sign for "Pawnee" was exactly the same as the sign for "wolf." However, none of the Native Americans used wolf war magic in the excessive way it was used in Europe, and especially in Scandinavia.

Europeans found wolf magic useful for purposes of war. The wolf was often seen as a symbol of death, destruction, and war. Wolf gods were often war gods as well. The qualities of intelligence, group maneuvers, ranking, and hunting found in the wolf are qualities that human beings found useful when engaged in war. Sadly, this has made a very bad reputation for the wolf in Europe. Wolves were often painted on war shields. The barbarian hordes that brought the downfall of the Roman empire often howled like wolves during warfare, and imitated other mannerisms of the wolf.

The Scandinavians made particular use of wolf magic for war, and, though they considered war to be a positive thing, their wolf myths are

---

[2] Rudyard Kipling, *All the Mowgli Stories* (New York: Doubleday, 1954), p. 91.
[3] Barry Lopez, *Of Wolves and Men* (New York: Scribners, 1978), p. 111.

more frightening that those of any other people. Their mythic wolves were often depicted as giants, as in the myths of giantesses who rode gigantic wolves, with bridles made of live snakes. Like Fenris, Nordic wolves of myth were often portrayed as all-powerful, unstoppable forces of destruction and war. Given the opportunity, they drank rivers of blood, ate the Sun itself, destroyed all they could. Even the Scandinavian gods were deeply frightened of mythic wolves, and could just barely and temporarily restrain some of them from their destructive habits. According to Norse myth, eventually Fenris would escape and destroy all the gods.

Sadly for the reputation of wolf magic, the Nazis, who were notoriously superstitious and involved with evil mysticism, also cultivated wolf war magic. They took their inspiration especially from Scandinavian mysticism, and misused sacred Scandinavian runes, the Indian swastika and the double-S rune. They also called themselves werewolves and engaged in the most despicable mass destruction the world has seen for some time.

Because of its associations with war magic, and especially the way this was abused in Europe, the wolf received a very bad reputation. People cultivating wolf magic today should realize, however, that these horrors of the past have nothing to do with wolf magic itself, only with humans and the uses to which they have sometimes put wolf magic. Those tapping into wolf magic today, unless they are deliberately tapping into particularly horrid mythic powers, such as that of Fenris, need not fear awakening any powers of war and destruction.

The Europeans, though they paid much less attention to it than to the destructive myths, also recognized the good and sacred qualities of the wolf that Native Americans so admired. European culture took many of its views from Greco-Roman and Celtic culture. Greco-Roman culture had mixed views of wolves. Originally, the wolf was a very sacred animal, perhaps the most sacred of all. Rome was supposed to have been founded by Romulus and Remus, sacred twins suckled by a she-wolf. The major festival, Lupercalia, was held in honor of the she-wolf, as well as for other reasons. Wolves were strongly associated with both light and prostitutes. Since prostitutes were often held to be sacred in Greco-Roman culture, this is not as negative as it might seem at first.

Many minor deities had wolfish aspects. The two most important gods, Zeus and Apollo, were originally wolf gods, and are still worshipped in that aspect by some of the backcountry folk, such as the Arcadians. Even city people acknowledged that Zeus and Apollo had strong connections to wolves, though they became increasingly uncomfortable with this, and, in later times, the myths changed so that Zeus and Apollo bore wolfish names because of their zeal to destroy wolves, who were harming the flocks.

The city people were distinctly uncomfortable with the fact that the Arcadians still worshipped Zeus and Apollo as wolf gods, and connected these ceremonies with decadence and disgusting things, such as human sacrifice and cannibalism. Greco-Roman culture was also the source for what is probably the most famous werewolf of early myth: King Lycaon, from whom we get the term "lycanthropy." It was often said in Rome that Lycaon was the very first werewolf, but this is untrue, for we have records of earlier werewolf myths.

Lycaon was revered by the Arcadians, and their sacred rituals were designed to imitate the events of the myth in which Lycaon became a werewolf. The myth of Lycaon shows evidence of being very old. In the myths of Arcadian origin, Lycaon is the "good guy." In later legend, however, Lycaon is the incarnation of evil, irrevocably mixed up with human sacrifice and cannibalism, and justly punished by the gods by the "horrible fate" of becoming a werewolf . . . something that the Arcadians actively sought, and didn't think was such a horrible fate.

Though Greco-Roman culture has a fair amount of benevolent werewolf and wolf folklore, and even shows evidence of originally perceiving the wolf and werewolf in a wholly sacred light, it is distinctly uneasy about both. Especially in the later times, there seems to have been a distinct smear campaign against the wolf and werewolf, probably because of the dependence on sheep herding, sheep being particularly vulnerable to wolves.

European culture took a lot of inspiration from Greco-Roman culture, and inherited many mixed views of distinct discomfort with the wolf and werewolf. European culture, however, also took its mythic and symbolic views from other sources, and one of these sources is Celtic culture, which dominated pre-Christian Europe. The Celts happened to be a people for whom neither the wolf nor the other common werebeast species (bears, cats, and foxes) were particularly sacred or important. If the wolf had been an important sacred animal for the Celts, we probably would have a more positive view of wolves and werewolves in Western culture. The major sacred animals of the Celts were, in fact, animals that were seldom sacred for any other culture.

The Celts did not view the wolf as evil, they simply didn't pay much attention to it. Most cultures have been obsessed with the wolf; to consider it unimportant was rare. The Celtic view of werewolves is almost entirely benevolent. They were often seen as noble souls, and, not infrequently, as heroes. At worst, they were comic figures or subversive, but seldom actually evil. Views inherited from the Celts persisted in Europe in some places, mixed with the new Christian views. The good qualities of the wolf that are so admired in some cultures relate to the female wolf—particularly the mother wolf.

The evil wolf is almost always symbolized by the male of the species. The good, sacred wolf is the mother wolf. When appeal is made to wolf magic in a positive way, it is often the mother wolf that is invoked. She is seen as very maternal. In myth, she suckles humans. Those Europeans who wished to become benevolent, not evil, werewolves appealed to feminine wolf spirits. Young Roman men who wished to become werewolves celebrated a sacred marriage with Lupa (a wolf goddess and minor deity) during their celebration of the festival of Lupercalia.

FOXES

The fox is an animal whose magic and power is particularly important to shifters. Wolves, cats, and bears have little "shapeshifting" magic associated with the magical "essence" of the species. Foxes, however, are different. The fox is a shifty animal, with a shifty nature. There are other species with a strong "shapeshifting essence" or connection with shapeshifting magic, notably the butterfly, swan, and frog, but none of these are common shifter species.

Some shifters are definitely identified with a particular species from birth, or from an early age, long before their first mental shift. Most shifters don't really "solidify" as a particular species until later, however. Most start out being strongly connected to the animal magic of one of the little folk of field and wood, such as the badger, otter, squirrel, mouse, rat, raccoon, rabbit, skunk, or weasel. (Incidentally, most furries are strongly connected to the magic of a particular species of one of the little ones of field and wood.) After that phase, they go through a brief fox phase (there are few permanent fox shifters), then solidify as their final species, usually a wolf, bear, or cat. The fox is thus a very special animal to shifters. It represents a gateway to shifting, and is often called "the gateway animal."

The fox occupies this special position for a number of reasons. It is the only one of the most common shifter species that has strong connections to the magic of shapeshifting. The fox is both one of the little ones of field and forest, and one of the major shifter species, so it serves as a convenient "bridge" for moving from one kind of animal magic to another. It also has another characteristic that makes it a "gateway" to shifting. The fox, although technically related to the canines, has a mix of canine and feline characteristics, behavior, lifestyle, and "magical essence." Foxes look like canines, but have slit eyes and retractable claws, like a cat. They are a blend of canine and feline. Since the vast majority of shifters end up as either canines or felines, the fox is perfect to serve as an introduction to shifter-hood, allowing the shifter to experience both canine and feline energies before "solidifying" as one or the other.

The energy of the fox is feminine. Male fox spirit guides are rare. Although the fox is a feminine influence, there is a fairly equal mix of male and female fox shifters. Male fox shifters tend to be quite feminine in some ways. The fox is not necessarily a good spirit guide, since it tends to be capricious, two-faced, teasing, and of a shifty nature that one can never quite trust. The energies of the fox are quite strongly connected to those capricious energies of the side-planes that relate to the fairy or deva kingdom, that are inhabited by the mythical beings we call "fairies" and "elves." Fox shifters and any other type of fox person would do well to study the magical and spiritual characteristics of the fairy and deva kingdom, for many of these characteristics also apply to the fox.

The essence of the fox is connected to the magic of "invisibility." Fox people, whether fox shifters or just people with "fox medicine," tend to go unnoticed easily, even when they don't wish to invoke this power of "invisibility." Quite a number of fox people I've known could walk up to people unnoticed, say "Hi," and scare them out of their wits. The fox is an extremely sexual influence, with a kind of playful, kinky sexuality, rather than the raw sexual power that animals such as the horse bring with them. It is especially connected with flirting and sexual teasing. Especially when the fox first enters your life, you may be in great danger of finding yourself juggling several inappropriate lovers at once, without quite knowing how you managed to get into this situation.

This is especially true for young men, who handle excess sexuality much less responsibly than either women or older men. Do not worry, however, for the fox brings an energy that is perfectly compatible with monogamy—it is a monogamous species, but will create excess sexual energy and tension that has to be dealt with, especially before you've gotten used to it.

Fox people also have a quality that can be powerful if used wisely, but it tends to get them in trouble. They are very lucky and tend to believe in this luck too much and too often try to push the boundaries of what they can get away with. The fox is strongly connected to the element of fire. The elements of fire and water are both related to the energies of shapeshifting. Some shifters think that fire is even more strongly related than water. As none of the other common shifter species have a really strong connection to these elements, this is another reason to view the fox as a gateway to shifting.

CATS

Felines are probably the second most common "species" of shifter. In some areas that have no wolves, werecats are the most common in the legends. Cat shifters are feminine, coy, silent, proud, and full of ancient mysteries and secrets. Most wolf shifters are not thought of as particularly "canine" people, probably because "canine" nature is fairly close to human. Wolf characteristics don't really stand out as being that different from human characteristics. But cat shifters are much different in this regard. They are almost always known as "feline." This is because feline characteristics are quite distinct from human characteristics, and nearly everyone has seen domestic cats engaging in behavior patterns that they recognize as feline. Of course, very few have any inkling of just how catlike these people really are!

Cat shifters tend to withdraw from everyone and "crawl off into a corner to lick their wounds," especially when their pride is hurt. This often causes hurt feelings in friends who try to comfort them, and who don't understand why they aren't reacting in the typical human way. Real cats tend to be very promiscuous and form few bonds in their sexual relationships. This has an effect on cat shifters. It often causes them to be very sexual people, though it does not usually make them promiscuous. Cat shifters still form typical human bonds with a significant other, but their relationships with lovers tend to be more of a "buddy" relationship than what you would typically expect. Cat shifters may be very attached to their lovers, and enamoured of the sexual relationship, but they are not quite in love with the lover in exactly the way other people are.

Cat shifters are not completely solitary. They cherish relationships and need them, but don't have the gregarious group nature that humans and wolves both have. One advantage to this is that cat shifters have the ability to walk quickly and easily away from bad relationships, as soon as they go bad. It is said in shifter culture that, if strange things are going on in your pack and suddenly all the cats start leaving, the pack is probably becoming a bad thing, either degenerating into a cult or souring in some other way. Cats are free of unnecessary ties and simply leave when it's time. When cat shifters are in a bad relationship, they are invariably the abusers, not the abused. This has given them an undeserved bad reputation.

Cats are not connected to evil more than any other species, but if the cat's energy sours and becomes evil, it becomes extremely evil. Cats are naturally selfish beings, full of pride and prone to regard themselves as gods. Anyone with these characteristics, who is also evil, is going to be extremely evil. Cats are also predators that enjoy torturing their prey. They are often tempted to "torture" for no reason at all, seeing anyone around them caught in a bad situation or having a bad day as "easy prey." If cat shifters give in to this temptation often, they get a bad reputation as someone who "kicks people when they are down" for the fun of it. These feline tendencies are responsible for the bad reputation that cats have had in various cultures. For example, in the Middle Ages, when cats were strongly associated with black magic, thousands were burned.

The vast majority of cat shifters are either tiger shifters, puma shifters, or leopard shifters. The tiger, puma, and leopard each have qualities unique to their species, but, for the most part, these are mainstream cats. Their energies are pretty much the same as general cat characteristics. There are a number of other felines that have very specific energies—for example, the lynx. Everywhere lynx are found, folk wisdom claims that they are a hybrid of wolves and cats. This is, of course, not true. But, in a metaphysical sense, it is. The lynx combines the spiritual essence of the wolf and the cat.

Almost all felines have distinct, defined markings, such as stripes or spots with clearly marked boundaries. Most canines have markings that are less well-defined, markings that are shaded, with various colors blended together and fading one into the other, with no pattern of stripes or spots showing through.[4] We see this kind of canine coloration especially in wolves and coyotes. In the lynx, we see a coat coloration of shaded layers of gray and brown, closer to the canine than to the feline. The lynx is also an animal with practically no tail. The long tail is one of the distinct characteristics of felines. The lynx is also approximately the same size as the wolf, and has another pseudo-canine characteristic: occasionally, one male and one female will form a permanent, monogamous bond, with the male helping to raise the young. This is unlike the usual pattern in felines. In some species, polygamy occurs, and sometimes, as with lions, the male helps with the young. But actual pair bonding in felines is almost unheard of. On the other hand, pair bonding is pretty much the rule in canines,

---

[4] In fact, the interested student can learn much about the mystical nature of canines and felines by studying the symbolic significance of clearly defined patterns versus mottled, shaded, undefined patterns.

with the exception of the domestic dog. It is also interesting that the gods and goddesses associated with the lynx, such as Freya, are associated with wolves. Lynx shifters are often cat people with an exceptionally strong wolf influence, or wolf people with an exceptionally strong cat influence.

Lion shifters are another type of feline with distinctly different energies. Most lion shifters are male—one seldom runs across lioness shifters. Lion shifters tend to be "kingly" and divine. They are good leaders, and are often highly respected people. One of the best, most intelligently run packs I have ever seen was led by two lion shifters who did an amazing job of keeping a group of shifters with diverse species, interests, religions, and beliefs from the constant bickering that characterizes too many packs. The downside of lions is that they tend to be proud and superior, and often have difficulty seeing things from the underdog's point of view.

The snow leopard is another cat species that diverges from mainstream cat energies. The snow leopard is a big cat that lives in the Himalayan Mountains. It is endangered, and is known as one of the world's most beautiful cats. There are many strange legends associated with the snow leopard, and the shifter would do well to study these in detail. The snow leopard is an emblem of invisibility. It is superbly camouflaged. Its feet often leave no tracks in the snow, for they are heavily furred, and it drags its tail behind it to wipe out its tracks. Snow leopard people tend to have a strong connection to the magic of invisibility, though this tends to manifest in somewhat different ways than in fox people. The snow leopard is often thought of as a spirit cat or ghost cat because it is white and ghostlike. It is also reputed to be a vampiric animal, draining its prey of blood and then leaving it. Snow leopard people seldom practice actual vampirism, but often have traits associated with the vampire—beauty, seductiveness, and sensuousness that hides a dark side.

The snow leopard is often associated with the guardian to the spirit world or the world of the dead, and with the life/death/life cycle. This is unusual: canines often play this role in myth, but felines seldom do. The snow leopard is held by many to be a divine animal—not divine in the earthly, kingly way of lions, but divine in a more ethereal, refined, spiritual way. It is often associated with the higher qualities in Buddhism. In fact, some Buddhist saints are said to have the ability to transform into snow leopards.

BEARS

Bear shifters are common. The bear is a decidedly male influence, though this influence manifests in a very different way than the female influence of the fox. While there is a fairly even mix of male and female fox shifters, almost all bear shifters are male. I've known of very few female bear shifters. Despite this, however, most bear spirit guides are female. I think this happens because the spirit guide has to remain utterly true to the nature and essence of the animal the guide is representing. Just about any male bear would be uninterested in guiding and protecting another, but the mother bear is a fearsome and wonderful guide and protector. The spirit guide remains true to the spirit of bear by being a mother bear. Bear shifters are truly fortunate in having such a powerful and wondrous guide.

Bear shifters tend to be powerful people, but they are calm and laid-back most of the time. They tend to be very friendly. They do have some serious flaws, however. It is difficult for them to become angry, but when they do, they become incredibly angry and are not easily placated. Whether angry or not, they have a tendency simply to sweep others and their wishes aside, without noticing they are doing so, just as a large, powerful bear will sweep smaller creatures aside with no effort. Bears are short-sighted creatures with small eyes, so bear shifters tend to be "shortsighted" in a symbolic way. They tend to be stubborn and form opinions quickly, often before all the information is in. They then cling to these opinions regardless of the evidence.

The bear has been spiritually important to many peoples. It is sacred to most Native American peoples, being one of the most important animals in their metaphysics. It is also sacred to the Scandinavians of pre-Christian Europe. From the evidence left behind by cave paintings, it is believed that prehistoric peoples had extensive bear cults, and that bears were sacred to them. Those who are bear shifters, or who simply have bear medicine, would do well to study the extensive magical lore of the bear.

RELATIONSHIPS BETWEEN SHIFTER SPECIES

The wolf, the fox, the cat, and the bear are the four most common shifter species. Each has its special place within the framework of the magic of shapeshifting. Moreover, there is a certain type of symbolic relationship between these four animals (see figure 2). The bear, in symbolic terms, is "on top." It is the most sacred of these animals and occupies the position of the divine essence, the mother, giver, and protector. The cat, in symbolic terms, is to the left and below the bear. It belongs to the magic of yin, of left-handedness, of feminine essence, of intuition instead of reason. It is also solitary, belonging to the inner world of the self. The wolf is to the right of and below the bear. It belongs to the magic of yang, of right-handedness, of a more masculine essence, of reason and the outer world. It is magically connected to the group, to organization, to planning. It is not solitary and separated, like the cat, but is able to be either solitary or gregarious. The fox is the gateway animal. It has its place in balance, half canine and half feline.

In accordance with this arrangement, each animal has a certain relationship to the others, for the purposes of the magic of shapeshifting. The bear is sacred, and so bear shifters have an unusual amount of access to "divine energies" through their bear spirit guide. The wolf is able to "call on" the bear for help. That is, wolf shifters are often able, in times of need, to attract into their lives some of the divine essence of the bear. In nature, wolves sometimes hunt bears in the spring, when they are weak from hibernation. It is said that wolves relish bear meat more than any other, and that traps baited with bear meat are the most successful in capturing wolves. This is symbolic of the way that wolves can sometimes draw on the essence of bear for "nourishment," in magical terms.

The cat is generally not able to call on the bear, or on any other animal, for help. Cats are fairly independent and self-contained. Wolves (canines) and cats (felines) tend to be opposed to each other, just as our own domestic dogs and cats are usually at odds. Foxes are often able to call on either wolves or cats for help in times of need. In fact, it is not at all uncommon for fox shifters to manage to attract a full-time wolf or cat spirit guide into their lives, in addition to their own fox spirit guide.

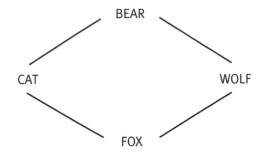

ELEMENT	LEFT-HAND YIN QUALITIES	MOTHER ANIMAL DIVINE QUALITIES	RIGHT-HAND YANG QUALITIES
Air	Owl	Eagle	Raven
Fire	Cat	Bear	Wolf
Water	Dolphin	Seal	Shark
Earth	Snake	Turtle	Crocodile

Figure 2. Relationships between werespecies. The four species most common in shifting have certain relationships to each other, and especially to the three most common birds in shifting: owl, eagle, and raven. They also have special links to the most common reptiles and water animals found in shifting, according to elemental correspondences. Fox is not in the regular chart, for she has a unique place in shifting as the "gateway" animal.

The fifth most common type of shifter is the bird. It is hard to tell which bird species is most common among shifters, but the top three, which far outnumber all the rest, are owl, raven, and eagle. In the category of eagle, I include all hawks and falcons, which, in a magical sense, are nothing more than smaller and less powerful eagles. The owl, raven, and eagle all have a particular relationship one to the other that is very like the relationship between the cat, wolf, and bear. Ravens are linked with wolves, and occupy much the same place among the birds that the wolf occupies among the mammals. The raven is the right-handed bird, linked with reason and organization. In much the same way that the wolf can call on the bear for help, raven shifters can often call on eagle energies and characteristics in times of need. The eagle occupies much the same place among the birds that the bear occupies among mammals, for the purposes of the magic of shapeshifting. (In more general magical terms, the eagle is more connected to the lion than to any other mammal.) The eagle, like the bear, is a very sacred animal, with a close connection to divine essence.

The owl occupies much the same place among the birds that the cat occupies among mammals. The owl is the left-handed, yin, feminine bird. This is true beyond the context of the magic of shapeshifting. Cats and owls have long had a close association in folk wisdom. Owls have been called "cats with wings." Like the cat, the owl is solitary, self-reliant, and self-contained. Just as canines and felines tend to be bitterly opposed, so are owls and ravens. Real owls and real ravens get along poorly, with ravens often "mobbing" owls during the day and owls often preying on ravens at night. The owl is also thought of as "opposed" to the eagle, for the eagle is the symbolic ruler of the day, while the owl is the symbolic ruler of the night. In shifting culture, there is no bird that corresponds to the place of the fox among the mammals. The fox is completely unique in its relationship to the magic of shapeshifting.

These magical relationships between wolf, fox, cat, bear, eagle, owl, and raven are quite self-evident if you've spent enough time watching shifters of these species. If you spend enough time around shifters and listen to them talk about their experiences, you can actually see these relationships in action. I do feel obliged, however, to expand this structure into a larger one, gleaned from my own personal experience.

One night in a dream, while I was in the process of writing this book, my wolf spirit guide came to me and started talking about the relationships between the four most common mammals and the three most common birds. She told me that this easily observed part of the structure was, in fact, only a part of the overall structure.

She pointed out to me that Western esotericists have always assigned certain animals to the elements of earth, air, fire, and water. Fire corresponds to mammals, air to birds, earth to reptiles, and water to fish and water mammals. She said that, while I had accounted for the fire and air animals, I needed to include the common shapeshifting species for each of the other two elements, earth and water, in order to complete the structure. (For an encapsulated view of these relationships, see figure 2, page 75.)

Of the earth animals, reptiles (turtles, snakes, and crocodiles) are the most common shifting species. I get this mostly from the legends of physical shapeshifters, for there are very few modern reptile shifters. Turtles occupy the "top" position among the reptiles for the purposes of the magic of shapeshifting. They have always been associated with the divine and sacred. In Asia, turtles represent a symbolic bridge between heaven and earth—the underside of the shell is square (a symbol of earth) and the topside is round (symbol of heaven). All of the legends of shapeshifting wereturtles that I've ever come across involve very large sea turtles. These legends are found in seacoast societies all over the world, but especially in Asia. Wereturtles are usually female. Curiously, many of these legends relate that those who can physically transform themselves into turtles also acquire the sea turtle's very long life-expectancy (real sea turtles can live hundreds of years) and resist aging. There are many legends of people who turned into sea turtles, spent a few years in the ocean, then return home to find that a hundred years have passed. Yet they are still young.

Among the reptiles, the crocodile occupies the right-hand position, associated with yang, reason, and order. Werecrocodile legends are quite common wherever crocodiles are found. There are even supposed to be modern werecrocodile legends still popping up in Africa. The snake occupies the left-hand position, associated with yin, intuition, and mystery. Most weresnake legends involve large constrictors, not poisonous snakes.

The three most common shifting species of water animals are the shark, seal, and dolphin. The seal occupies the "top" or "divine" position among the water animals. Wereseal, or selkie, legends are common wherever seals are found, particularly in Scotland. The species represented in wereseal legends were almost invariably "real seal" species, not any of the species of sea lion. Seals differ significantly from sea lions in that most seal species are better adapted to water, and worse adapted to land (an advantage for any seal physical shifter—after all, you've already got a good land form!). In most species of seal, the male and female are of comparable size, instead of the monstrous males and tiny females found among most sea lion species. Seals also tend to be less gregarious and tend to pair bond, or even sometimes mate for life, while sea lions rule over massive harems. From studying the legends, I believe that the species of seal most often involved in selkie legends were the gray seal and the monk seal, both of which have largely disappeared from their former range.

The left-hand water animal is the dolphin. Shapeshifting dolphin legends are found pretty much everywhere that dolphins are found. Particularly common are the legends that involve people turning into various species of freshwater river dolphin, such as the pink-skinned *botu* of the Amazon River.[5] The right-handed water animal is the shark. Sharks are opposed to dolphins just as strongly as canines are opposed to felines. Wereshark legends are common along the west coast of Africa and in Hawaii.

My wolf spirit guide pointed out to me that there are certain types of connections between the elements as well. For instance, when a wolf or raven shifter goes bad, they take on the worst qualities of the two lower right-hand animals—shark (water) and crocodile (earth). They take on ravenous destruction. The same thing happens when cat or owl shifter goes bad: they begin to take on the worst qualities of the two lower left-hand animals—the excessive sexuality of the dolphin and the cold fearsomeness of the snake. Even the divine animals are not immune to this. When an eagle or bear goes bad, the shifter tends to take on the worst qualities of turtle and seal: the slowness and inhibitions of the turtle, and the overly emotional, subconscious connectivity of the seal. This may manifest as an inability to get along well on "land." ("Land" symbolizes the outer world, "ocean" the subconscious, and "source" the inner world.)

My wolf spirit guide said that there are other significant connections and magical implications that can be derived from this structure, but I was unable to comprehend them. She also said that shifters, of whatever species, can gain insight and wisdom about shifting by doing "pathworking" exercises on this structure. Pathworking is a kind of shamanic, visionary spiritual practice whereby the magic worker literally "explores" the

---

[5] In fact, there is an entire book devoted mostly to legends of weredolphins of the Amazon River. See *Dance of the Dolphin,* by Candace Slater (Chicago: University of Chicago Press, 1994).

magical correspondences and connections of a particular magical structure, in the realm of dreams and visions. The best known example of this is the practice of pathworking on the qabbalistic "tree of life." I haven't done any pathworking on the structure of shifting animals, because I've never been trained in pathworking and don't know quite how to do it. Hopefully, other shifters will take up this task and discover more about the basic mechanics of the magic of shapeshifting.

OTHER CANINE SPECIES

While cat shifters are spread through many feline species, most canines are wolf shifters. Other canine shifters have, however, characteristics distinct from wolves. Coyote shifters are not uncommon. In magical terms, the coyote is unlike the wolf, even though many people tend to think of it as a little brother to the wolf. The coyote has a magical essence that is almost exactly the same as that of the jackal. Indeed, it lives a life more like that of a jackal than a wolf. The coyote has often been called "the American jackal."[6] Most Native Americans consider it to be an unlucky and unreliable totem animal, although not necessarily evil. The coyote is the "wise fool," often childish, often foolish, but also possessed of a deep, primitive wisdom. Coyote people tend to go through life looking like bumbling fools one moment, then in the next, they are suddenly two steps ahead of everyone else. Coyote people can go far in life, but only if they keep an incredibly tight rein on their foolishness. This is particularly difficult for them, because they have great difficulty perceiving their own follies, and tend to be unable to differentiate their greatest mistakes from their greatest accomplishments.

Coyotes are also liars. This is simply part of their nature. Coyote people may not intend to lie, may not even realize they are lying, because they are caught in their own illusions. Nonetheless, they spread misinformation around them constantly. I've learned never to believe anything that a coyote person tells me, unless I'm able to check it out myself and see that it's

---

[6] Jackal shifters are not uncommon, though they are very similar, in metaphysical terms anyway, to coyotes. The Old World jackal has the same metaphysical and magical qualities as the coyote.

true. They even change their own beliefs on the facts of this or that story, so that they may tell the same story a different way every few months. Coyote people have great potential, great power, and great wisdom, but most of the time, it is wasted.

Friends of coyote shifters commonly say that they are both their greatest friends and worst enemies. They love them deeply, but also want to strangle them half the time. In my friendship with a coyote shifter, I have found much the same thing. This individual was truly a great personality, and often spouted uncommon wisdom, yet constantly managed somehow to get me involved, without my consent, in the most hair-brained schemes. After being "taken for a ride" too many times, I finally terminated the friendship, though there are times when I wish I hadn't, for I still miss this truly wonderful individual. This coyote shifter left quite a trail of upset ex-friends behind, and most of these past and present friends report having a difficult, love/hate relationship with this individual.

Just as many people equate coyotes and wolves, so do many equate wolves and dogs. Wolves and dogs are quite different, especially in terms of their magical essences. Most societies, although not our modern society, have considered wolves and dogs to be opposites, fundamentally opposed. Most also considered one to be good and sacred, and the other to be the incarnation of evil. Most Native American societies consider the wolf a very good, sacred animal, and the dog lowly, cringing, and dishonorable. Some Native American societies even believe that the dog has no soul. In Medieval Europe, it was just the opposite. Dogs were the archetype of loyalty and faithfulness, dependent on human approval, willing to lay down their lives for their masters. The wolf was the opposite: wild, in full rebellion against God's original plan for animals, and even daring to steal from man and decimate his flocks of sheep.

The wolf, partly because it was the only large predator (and thus, a significant threat to livestock) that was able to re-establish itself quickly, became a symbol of all the wild animals who dared to rebel against God and man by following their own "selfish" interests instead of "properly" serving man. They became a thorn in man's side by stealing. Bears and large cats could be quite troublesome to livestock as well, but there weren't that many of them (so that their predations were felt less keenly) and a slower reproductive rate, so it was easy to permanently eliminate them from certain areas.

In reality, none of these societies grasped the whole truth about the nature of wolves and dogs. The essence of both wolf and dog is neither evil nor good. They embody both positive and negative traits. Dogs can be cringing, unhealthy dependents with no honor or self-direction, or they can express the qualities of loyalty and faithfulness in much healthier ways. Dog shifters are certainly quite nice people to have as friends, not just because some of them tend to be submissive, but because they are very companionable and honest. They genuinely enjoy others and are usually quite aboveboard, so you never have to wonder where your place is in the friendship or whether or not they really like you. Many dog shifters are assertive, contrary to their "submissive" image, but they tend to be assertive in a way that is very pleasant to others. Sometimes you don't even notice their assertiveness. Dog shifters are often quite protective of those they care about, and they have an unusually strong ability to protect themselves. In mythology, dogs are associated with the gateway to the world of the dead or the spirit world. They are also associated with qualities of motherhood.

Dog shifters often identify with breeds such as collies, German shepherds, Dalmatians, or Labrador retrievers. Sometimes they consider themselves to be one of the species of truly wild dogs, such as the wild dog (or "painted wolf") of Africa, the dingo of Australia, the rare "raccoon dog" of Europe, the pariah of India, or the dhole of Asia.

In legend, the werehyena was usually female, and most hyena shifters I've known have been female. The hyena is a very female species, though its femininity is different from that of foxes. The fox is feminine, shifty, and flirty, while the hyena brings forth more of the raw, primal power of woman. It is said that the energy of the hyena hearkens back to a mythical time when women were the leaders and men were less important. Hyenas have an assertive femininity that is not always pretty in the way it shows itself. Hyenas possess the power of the crone, the grandmother, the wise old woman, whereas foxes possess the power of the maiden or girl. Hyena shifters tend to be women with a strong sense of their own power, who know where they are going and don't mind if they have to step on people to get there. Even if they are doing exactly what everyone else is doing, they tend somehow to sound more coarse. They often "rock the boat" to get what they want, and are not always popular.

Hyenas are one of the ancient groups of mammalian predators that have existed longer than "modern" mammals. They've been with this world, like the canines, felines, bears, and weasel family, through many ages, and were once a major family of carnivores, with many species and wide-reaching distributions. Hyenas, though they look vaguely canine and live in packs, are much more closely related to cats.

Their decline is not entirely due to human beings. Hyenas are an ancient type of mammal, with a build and structure that predates modern mammal groups. Hyenas and their kin were forced out by the rise of more modern types of animals, such as wolves, who were more efficient. They hearken back to an earlier stage in the world's evolution, in some ways a more crude stage, but also a more primal stage, a more earthy stage—full of certain types of ancient knowledge. Those with hyena medicine, whether shifters or not, can tap into these valuable resources, which are beyond the reach of most people. Hyena people may, therefore, seem more crude, primitive, and even backward.

There is a small but significant number of shifters who claim that their species is not a real species. They claim to shift into something that has never existed as a species in this world—dragons, for example. This phenomenon has piqued my interest, and I've spent time tracking down cases and trying to figure them out. Many shifters don't take this group seriously.

Being an open-minded person, however (after all I believe in werewolves), I decided I should at least investigate something thoroughly before I decide to dismiss it. For starters, there is a precedent in legend for this phenomenon. There are a number of legends about people who shapeshifted into dragons[7]—in fact shapeshifting is one of the mystical

---

[7] In fact, transformation is a common feature of dragon legends, for example, Margaret, the transformed dragon of the Castle of Bamburgh, and the daughter of Ypocras, both from Northumberland in Britain. See Paul Newman, *The Hill of the Dragon* (Bath, England: Kingsmead Press, 1979), pp. 123–127.

qualities that many cultures have assigned to dragons. There are also quite a number of legends about people who periodically turned into some unnatural animal. One of these was the *callicantzari* of Europe, who changed into an incredible variety of monstrous forms, none of them natural and some that mixed various animal and human parts in grotesque and strange ways. The more commonly reported callicantzari forms were two-legged or four-legged shaggy forms with pig snouts and gigantic claws on the hind and front feet, and a naked, ropy, long tail like a rat. Interestingly, the mythical centaur is one of the creatures that the ancients considered to be a type of callicantzari. In the Americas, we have much the same sort of creature in the windigo.

Another instance that hearkens back to legend is that a fair number of cat shifters permanently remain "undifferentiated felines." That is, they have a very strong connection to feline energies, and are absolutely sure they are cat shifters, but regularly "see" their form as several different species, or even as a combination of the characteristics of several different feline species. They have "solidified" as feline, but not as any particular species of cat. I've never known an "undifferentiated canine," but it is quite common for people to be "solidified" as an eagle shifter or rat shifter, but not know exactly which one of the many species of eagle or rat that they are.

This recalls ancient legends in which a fair number of werecats are described as feline, but combine the characteristics of more than one species. This raises an interesting question. It is certainly possible for a mental shifter to be "solidified" as an undifferentiated feline, but is it possible for a physical shifter to manifest as a feline combining the characteristics of more than one species, effectively becoming a "species" that has never existed?

Some sorcerers who practiced shapeshifting were said to be able to choose their form, even from animals that didn't exist. In Scandinavia, where, in ancient times, shapeshifting was common and well-known, one of these strange forms that frequently appears in the legends sounds exactly like a pterodactyl. It was described as a huge, leathery bird with wings like a bat's, that was about the size of a person. Scientists estimate that the largest species of pterodactyl weighed no more than 200 pounds, so this definitely puts pterodactyls in the correct weight range for an animal that can be physically shifted into with ease. Some shifters who have looked at these "werepterodactyl" legends think there may be a small number of pterodactyl physical shifters around, accounting for the occasional well-documented pterodactyl sightings that occur every so often.

These legends raise the question of whether an animal need exist in the flesh in this world for it to be available as a species for either mental or physical shifters. To answer this question, a number of things must be considered. For one thing, I'm sure that a person can be a mental or physical shifter of an extinct species. After all, look at wolves and tigers. Both animals are on the verge of extinction, tigers more so than wolves. They have been eliminated from the vast majority of their original range. I have never actually known a tiger shifter who lived near real tigers, or who ever saw them outside of zoos. Moreover, most wolf shifters live in areas where wolves have been extinct for a hundred years or more. Yet wolves and tigers are both major shifting species, and I believe that, even if they do become extinct, we will still have an abundance of wolf shifters and tiger shifters.

It certainly weakens the accessibility for an animal to be nearly extinct or extinct, but it doesn't necessarily make them totally inaccessible. After all, what do shifters access when they access the "energy" of a species? They are not accessing the real animals out there, for the most part. Instead, they are accessing a kind of collective subconscious of that species, a coherent, highly structured form that exists on etheric, astral, or other planes of non-physical existence.

Esoteric doctrine states that every species has a "collective subconscious" and essential structure on the higher planes. This construction is most often called the "morphogenetic field" of a species. The morphogenetic field of a species does weaken if a species disappears from the physical realm. Yet portions of it will always exist on certain planes, available for those able to tap into it, for the purposes of working with the "medicine" of the species, and perhaps even for those who are to become shifters of this species.

Many of those who claim to be shifters of mythological species, such as dragon shifters, have pointed out that the "essence" of the dragon is perfectly available on the higher planes. Indeed, many work with the "medicine" of the dragon in much the same way that one works with a real animal. It does not matter that real dragons have never existed. Their other-plane essence is particularly strong—so strong that every culture in the world has the dragon as a major mythological beast. These shifters say that, if it is so easy to access the energies of dragon for other paranormal purposes, why is it so hard to accept that someone could be a mental dragon shifter?

Some shifters have pointed out evidence in the legends of people accessing the morphogenetic fields of extinct species. For an example, when a physical shifter changes into a species much smaller than human, it tends to shift into a large version of that species. A physical rat shifter, for example, will generally turn into a rat the size of a small dog, not the size of either a human being or a real rat. Some have pointed out that, in the relatively recent past, such as during the last Ice Age, our ancestors lived alongside giant versions of many of our modern species, giant species that are now extinct. A few of these larger versions of our more familiar species have survived: for an example, there is a species of otter that can grow to six feet.[8] Might physical shifters of legend that turn into large versions of small animals have been accessing the "energy" of the larger, extinct species? After all, you can't just take a normal rat, and make it the size of a small dog. Many internal changes, such as bone structure, muscle distribution, and lung capacity, must occur or the dog-sized rat won't be able to walk or function very well. A larger species of rat that had evolved that way, however, would already have solved these problems.

There is another clue to the accessibility of an extinct species that is found in some bear shifters. There are a number of bear shifters who have distinctly "seen," for their entire life, their bear form as having a long tail. A number of extinct species of bear had tails. Today's bears have very

---

[8] The giant otter, *Pteronura brasiliensis*.

short, almost invisible, tails, but we know our ancestors lived alongside bears with tails during the Ice Age, because they painted cave art of them. Might these "tailed" bear shifters be accessing the morphogenetic field of an extinct species of bear?

To what extent might some shifters be able to access the essence of animals that do not physically exist in this world? Do some shifters access the energies of extinct species, species whose morphogenetic field still lingers? These are some very interesting questions to consider, and perhaps shifters of the future will be better able to investigate these questions and clear up the mysteries.

CHAPTER 4

Bilocation Shifting

I n many shapeshifter legends, transformation is described like this: the werewolf becomes unconscious, and a wolf body materializes "out of thin air." This wolf is really the werewolf in wolf form, and it wanders about doing whatever it feels like doing. Later, it returns and dematerializes, or is reabsorbed by the human body. The werewolf's human body then regains consciousness. This is bilocation shifting, so called because it resembles another phenomenon, bilocation, in all but one detail. In normal bilocation, the body that materializes is a carbon copy of the human's own body. In bilocation shifting, the body that materializes is an animal body. Examples of bilocation shifting are common in folklore from all over the world. In fact, it often seems that bilocation shifting is far more common than physical shapeshifting.

One classic case of bilocation shifting happened in 1879 to a miller named Bigot, at Serisols. One morning Bigot's wife got up early to do the laundry, and left her husband asleep in bed. She saw an animal in the corner of the yard that looked like a dog. She threw something at it and hit it in the eye. The animal immediately disappeared, as if it were a ghost. At exactly the same moment, Bigot woke up screaming in his bed, and yelled that he had been blinded. From that day on, he was blind in one eye. His own children swore this story was true.[1] In this case of bilocation shifting, the animal form was seen dematerializing, so it was not a case of the mere possession of an existing animal body. Another bilocation shifting case involved an old woman named Sally Walton who lived in Lancashire at Cloughfoot Bridge.

> A farmer, who dwelt near, awaking one night saw a large black cat sitting at his feet and watching him intently. Laying hold of a knife that was close at hand, the farmer hurled it at the cat, striking one of its fore-legs. The animal vanished, leaving no trace anywhere. The very morning after it was noticed that old Sally had her corresponding arm wrapped in a kerchief.[2]

One of the hallmarks of bilocation shifting is that the body, in its animal and human aspects, somehow exists in two different places at one time, as if the laws of three-dimensional reality had been superseded by some other type of reality. Bilocation shifting, like physical shifting, always has the characteristic of repercussion: wounds received by the animal body are also received, at the exact same place, by the human body. People who are merely possessing a real animal's body do not receive its injuries, and might not even suffer any harm if the animal dies while they are occupying it! However, modern investigators of folklore often assume that people believe that shapeshifting happens in one of two ways—physical transformation of the human body, or possession of a real animal's body. Tribal beliefs about the spirit-body being able to materialize, either in normal human form or in the form of an animal, as in the case of the beliefs of the Banyang,[3] are often too subtle for most of those investigators to comprehend fully. Furthermore, when investigators probe native peoples, ask-

---

[1] Montague Summers, *The Werewolf* (Secaucus, NJ: Citadel Press, 1973), p. 238.
[2] Montague Summers, *The Werewolf*, p. 199.
[3] Adam Douglas, *The Beast Within* (London: Chapmans, 1992), p. 21.

ing them whether they believe the transformation is accomplished either by physical means or by possession, they are often frustrated by their inability to get a straight answer.[4]

One reason for this is that people's beliefs are often different from the choices that are offered by the investigators. These beliefs are subtle, based very much on non-Western thinking, and difficult to understand. Another reason is that, in order for people observing shifting phenomena to know whether it is bilocation shifting or physical shifting, they either must observe a materialization or dematerialization of the animal body, or a physical transformation, or they must find where the unconscious human body is concealed while the bilocation animal body is out prowling. Injury-transference, or if the person is missing while the animal prowls, or the person knowing what the animal did in ways that are hard to explain, are all traits that exist in both bilocation shifting and physical shifting. In folklore, it is far more common for people simply to accumulate vast amounts of circumstantial evidence that someone is a shapeshifter. It is rare that they actually witness a physical transformation or a materialization of the bilocation animal body. It is somewhat common to uncover bilocation shifting by finding the unconscious human body while the animal body is out prowling. There are cases, however, in which the evidence does not show whether it was bilocation or physical shifting.

The Scandinavians have a fair amount of shapeshifting folklore that shows that even simple peasants understood far more about the mechanisms of shifting, and about the difference between bilocation and physical shifting, than did the peasants of central Europe. The Scandinavians have many words that refer to shapeshifters, as well as words that distinguish various types of shapeshifters and various mechanisms for shapeshifting. In Scandinavia *Ham-farir* signifies "the *'faring'* or *travelling* in the assumed shape of an animal, fowl or deer, fish or serpent, with magical speed over land and sea, the wizard's own body meantime lying

---

4 "As Endicott noted, the anthropologist in Malaya could not even discover whether an alleged werewolf, or weretiger, was supposed to be a man who physically turned into a wolf or a tiger, or an animal that a man's spirit periodically possessed." From Brian Inglis, *Natural and Supernatural* (Dorset, England: Prism Press, 1992), pp. 35–36.

lifeless and motionless."[5] *Ham-farir* thus appears to refer to bilocation shifting. "Among the Finns and Lapps it is not uncommon for a magician to fall into a cataleptic condition, and during the period his soul is believed to travel very frequently in bodily form, having assumed that of any animal. . ."[6] The Finns and Lapps obviously knew of out-of-body types of shifting.

Gaspar Peucer also relates beliefs in bilocation shifting: "Those who are changed suddenly fall to the ground . . . and there they lie without life or motion. Their actual bodies do not move from the spot where they have fallen, nor do their limbs turn to the hairy limbs of a wolf, but the soul or spirit . . . quits the inert body and enters the *spectrum* or φασμα of a wolf, and when they have glutted their foul lupine lusts and cravings . . . the soul re-enters the former human body . . ."[7] The Rev. Sabine Baring-Gould also speaks, more explicitly, of beliefs in bilocation shifting: "the human body was deserted, and the soul entered the second form, leaving the first body in a cataleptic state, to all appearance dead. The second *hamr* was either borrowed or created for the purpose"[8] (*hamr* is a Norse word for "shape," specifically referring to the animal shape of a shapeshifter). Here again, we have a reference to the form being created, not simply taken over from an existing real animal.

Montague Summers calls attention to beliefs in the actual creation of an animal spirit-body: "When it is asked how is this metamorphosis then effected, Thyraeus sums up various opinions . . . some . . . consider that the form of an animal is superimposed in some way upon the human form. Others again believe that persons are cast in a deep slumber or trance . . . and that then the astral body is clothed with an animal form."[9] Among various esoteric authorities of the modern age, the idea of actual physical transformation of the human body is often ridiculed, but ideas about bilocation shifting and other types of out-of-body shifting are taken much more seri-

[5] Montague Summers, *The Werewolf*, pp. 9–10.
[6] Sabine Baring-Gould, *The Book of Were-Wolves* (London: Senate, 1995), p. 165.
[7] Montague Summers, *The Werewolf*, p. 78.
[8] Sabine Baring-Gould, *The Book of Were-Wolves*, p. 16.
[9] Montague Summers, *The Werewolf*, p. 92.

ously. Lycanthropy is often explained as a kind of shapeshifting of the spirit body, which can then appear to others while the human body sleeps.

When approaching shapeshifting from the point of view of the paranormal, it is far easier to explain the existence of bilocation shifting than physical shifting. Out-of-body travel, etheric manifestations, and materialization of the human double are all widely believed in, and form a big part of the foundation of paranormal and New Age beliefs. To believe in bilocation shifting, one need only believe that the spirit-body can shapeshift and materialize in this form.

Eliphas Lévi (a respected authority) believes that lycanthropy exists, and is of the opinion that werewolfism is due to the "sidereal body" (an older term for either the astral or etheric body), which is affected into animal shape by a person's habitual thoughts, and can wander about at night as a fairly solid phantom animal, while the werewolf lies asleep.[10] C. W. Leadbeater, another noted authority, also believes that werewolves exist, and that they are formed by the materialization of one of the subtle bodies,[11] though his view of werewolves would have them particularly evil in nature. Westerners of the 19th and early 20th centuries felt that animals such as the wolf were particularly evil, and therefore any person becoming one must simply be manifesting their inward evil in their outward form.

According to Adolphe d'Assier, in *Posthumous Humanity*, the astral or etheric body is more fluid than the physical body, and, for this reason, may take on animal form. He warns that, when one is dealing with an animal phantom, one should not immediately assume it to be the ghost of an animal, for in some cases it is a "lycanthropic manifestation of the human phantom."[12]

---

[10] "This author gives it as his opinion that werewolfry is due to the 'sidereal body,' which is the mediator between the soul and the material organism,' . . . in the case of a man whose instinct is savage . . . his phantom will wander abroad in lupine form, whilst he sleeps . . . dreaming he is a veritable wolf. The body . . . will receive the blows and cuts dealt at the fantastical shape," Montague Summers, *The Werewolf,* p. 102.

[11] "His view is that certain astral entities are able to materialize the 'astral body' of a perfectly brutal and cruel man who has gained some knowledge of magic, and these fiends drive on this 'astral body', which they mould into 'the form of some wild animal, usually the wolf,' to blood and maraud." Montague Summers, *The Werewolf,* p. 102.

[12] Frank Hamel, *Human Animals* (New York: University Books, 1969), p. 265.

Ghosts and Hauntings

To fully understand bilocation shifting, it is first necessary to understand regular, human bilocation. Normal bilocation itself can best be understood as a logical extension of other paranormal phenomena. It is easiest to start with the phenomena associated with ghosts and hauntings. Ghost and "hauntings" phenomena are probably the most common, and most widely believed in, paranormal phenomena. It is debatable how many "ghost" phenomena are actually caused by spirits of the deceased, or by some kind of left-over astral "imprints" they left behind, or by some other kind of spirit entity that is not deceased. Yet even the most skeptical of the believers in the paranormal believe that the "raw phenomena" of hauntings exist, even if they don't agree on exactly what causes them, or on whether the living really linger behind as the beings we know as "ghosts."

Haunted houses are extremely common, and just about everyone knows someone who has seen a ghost or experienced some kind of haunting phenomena. The phenomena associated with hauntings are some of the best-documented supernatural phenomena, and also some of the most common. I believe that anyone who seriously and reasonably investigates haunting phenomena comes to believe in them, if they are not hardened skeptics. I don't really have the time or space to go over a detailed proof of the phenomena of haunting, but much has been done in this field before, and hauntings have more available proof than any other paranormal phenomena. Interested readers would do well to undertake their own inquiry into this field.

In most haunted houses, people may see a half-transparent ghost from time to time or feel a presence. In others, the phenomena may be much more physical in nature. The ghosts may make objective, recordable noises, move objects, leave footprints behind, or materialize blood, slime, or powder. In some of the most physical hauntings, the ghosts may even seem to become, briefly, semi-solid and able to affect physical things. In rare cases, they may seem as solid and physical as you and I. It is in this rarer kind of "full materialization" of the ghostly body that I'm principally interested here.

This kind of materialization is more common than many people think. In it, the ghost seems to become fully physical, at least in most ways, although it can dissolve and disappear at any time. This body feels real and solid to the touch. It also looks very real and solid, and there are even some well-documented cases where it had an actual pulse or was able to eat! People who encounter the ghost may have no idea that they are talking to a ghost, until it suddenly disappears or they learn that that person is dead, and has appeared to others. Interested people should research ghost phenomena. There are thousands of examples of this type of thing, and many books of recent American ghost sightings from firsthand accounts. You don't have to find some dusty tome of third-hand accounts gathered in the Middle Ages, as is the case with werewolf folklore. You might even seek out the nearest haunted house and stay there until you see some ghost phenomena for yourself. "Haunting" phenomena are very real, and quite common.

Among students of the paranormal, it is well-known that matter does not exist only on the material plane. Astral and etheric matter also exist. Every living body has an astral body and an etheric body. Ghosts may have an etheric body that sometimes, temporarily, seems to become fully material. It is a little-known fact that the living can be "ghosts" too. Since everyone has an astral and an etheric body, all that is required is out-of-body travel. The "haunting" phenomena produced by the living during out-of-body travel can be anything from a "presence" felt or dimly seen by others, to partial "ghostly" materializations, or objects moved or sounds made by the etheric body. In fact, there is not much difference between the phenomena that are produced by out-of-body travelers glimpsed by others, and the phenomena produced by ghosts. Ghosts are simply made of the stuff left over when the physical body dies, stuff that we all have while we are still alive. It should not be surprising, then, that the living can sometimes appear as "ghosts," exhibiting the same characteristics and phenomena, when engaging in out-of-body travel.

It is this capacity of the living to "materialize," to a greater or lesser extent, during out-of-body travel that sheds light on how bilocation can be possible. Since all living beings have etheric bodies, just as ghosts do, it is possible for the living to leave their bodies and produce a physical form, a carbon copy of their human body that can appear ghostly or as a solid materialized form. After all, a ghost is simply those parts of the person that are left behind after death, and we all have those parts while we are still alive. By leaving the body, and then "fully" materializing the ghostly etheric form, we can achieve "bilocation."

In true bilocation, the materialization of the etheric body is even more extensive than the phantoms produced by out-of-body travel. It becomes, seemingly at least, as solid as a real physical body. There are differences between it and a true physical body, but these differences are slight. A bilocation body can affect physical objects just like a true body. It can eat and digest, it seems just like a real body if seen or touched; it leaves footprints. But a bilocation body is not quite physical, though it is very close to it. It is inherently unstable. Strong light shining directly on it can cause it to dematerialize, and can even injure it with burns. If injured, by light or otherwise, it may dematerialize, and the injury will simultaneously show up on the unconscious real physical body.

How does bilocation occur? First, the person becomes unconscious. A deep trance state or other state of unconsciousness is required. Bilocation can occur during ordinary sleep, but it usually occurs during some strange trance state. After the real body becomes unconscious, the bilocation body materializes. It may materialize within sight of the unconscious physical body, in which case witnesses can see it slowing materializing, like a foggy ghost fading into view and then becoming more and more solid, sometimes with foglike ectoplasm exiting the unconscious body and augmenting the bilocation body. More often, it materializes some distance from the real body—in some cases, even miles away.

After the bilocation body has materialized, the unconscious real body often becomes pale and stiff as a board. The breathing slows, and it loses actual weight and becomes quite light. In fact, these symptoms are also found in cases of partial materialization of the etheric body,[13] as well as

---

[13] See *Psychic Self-Defense*, by Dion Fortune, for one example of these symptoms in conjunction with partial materialization (York Beach, ME: Samuel Weiser, 1992), p. 50.

the full materialization that we call "bilocation." In most cases, bilocation is not an event that is under control of the person doing it. Most well-documented cases in the records of psychical research are described as spontaneous. There are also some well-documented cases of people who have had partial control over the phenomenon, but these are more rare. Moreover, the person couldn't reproduce the phenomenon on demand, and could rarely control the location where the bilocation body materialized. There are also some cases, particularly older cases in the folklore, where people have had fairly exact control over their bilocation ability. According to Carlos Castaneda, the sorcerers Don Juan and Don Genaro both claimed to be able to engage in bilocation at will (although it took both of them a very long time to learn how to do it in the first place), and he saw some evidence of this ability.

Many Christian saints, as well as the holy men and women of many different religions, have been credited with the ability to bilocate. Not all of these reports are necessarily true, but a number of them are quite well-documented. Regarding Alfonso Liguori: "Liguori's most celebrated miracle took place in 1774 when, preparing to celebrate mass, he went into a trance and on coming out of it two hours later, said he had been at Pope Clement XIV's death-bed in Rome. This caused some amusement to those present. 'We were all tempted to burst out laughing,' Sister Agatha Viscardi was to recall. But then those who were in attendance at the bedside of the dying Pope Clement described how they had not only seen, but talked to Alfonso; he had led them in prayers for the dying."[14]

PHYSICAL MEDIUMS

Bilocation shifting, as well as regular bilocation, involves many of the same mechanisms that are involved in physical mediumship. In order to fully understand bilocation shifting, it is helpful to go over examples of similar accounts from physical mediums. Physical mediums are those mediums who produce distinctly physical phenomena during their

---

[14] Brian Inglis, *Natural and Supernatural*, p. 136.

séances, notably materializations of spirits, pseudopods, apports, ectoplasmic forms, and precipitation of ectoplasm.

A medium is a person who holds séances, often in the spiritualist tradition. Most mediums communicate with the spirits and produce nothing more spectacular than occasional levitations of small objects, spirit voices, or dim partial materializations. Some mediums, however, called physical mediums, regularly produce physical and semi-physical phenomena. Their abilities lie in an area that causes a lot of temporary changes in the phase of matter and subtle matter: etheric matter becomes ectoplasmic as it slowly comes closer to the physical, and physical matter temporarily dissolves into the etheric realm.

This is what we are most interested in here. A physical medium has powers over the state of matter, in a supernatural way. Yet these powers can be fairly random in nature. It takes a pretty powerful physical medium to be able to effect a specific paranormal outcome with a specific physical object just when they want to do this. Most mediums operate only in trance. Normally, the powers are allowed to "play around," manifesting strange things, but not necessarily in accordance with the medium's conscious will.

One of the phenomena of physical mediumship is called "apports" in spiritualist literature. This occurs when an entire object, usually a very small one, is "phased out" into the etheric plane, so that it "disappears" from this realm. The object can then be sent through walls, retrieved, put into a locked safe, or "linked" with a solid ring in a way that it couldn't, under the laws of ordinary reality, without breaking the ring. While the object is "phased out" into the etheric, its normal physical boundaries don't exist, so it can simply pass right through other objects. However, the object always re-establishes itself. Physical matter, made temporarily etheric, has a strong tendency to return to the physical state, and etheric matter, made temporarily physical, has a strong tendency to return to the etheric state. It is extremely difficult to do this to anything other than a very small object, which is why apports are usually very small.

Mediums can also take etheric matter and bring it partially or "fully" into the physical state. I use quotes, because I do not believe that, except in the most extraordinary circumstances, etheric matter can ever become truly physical. "Full" materializations of etheric matter look exactly like true physical things. They feel real and have most of the properties of true physical objects. There are always subtle, yet important, differences, however, from true physical matter. Etheric matter can become partially or "fully" physical in a number of ways. Most of the time, the materializations are partial and the matter appears as ectoplasm. "Ectoplasm" is a term used in spiritualist circles to refer to etheric matter that has become partially physical. It can be fully visible to everyone, psychic and non-psychic alike, although it has not yet become "fully" materialized. It is in an undifferentiated state that the ancients called "first matter."

Ectoplasm can appear in a number of forms. One of the most common forms is a precipitation of slime or powder that forms in the air. There is never any evidence of the slime or powder when the séance is over, however, for ectoplasm always returns to the etheric. It also commonly appears as a white, or occasionally grayish, fog that forms in the air. On rare occasions it materializes as a paste-like substance, resembling white clay or cake batter that condenses from the ectoplasmic fog. This paste-like form of ectoplasm often writhes and crawls like a living thing, and may spontaneously sculpt itself into various forms. Spirits who are present sometimes inhabit it and cause it to form itself into crude faces, hands, or occasionally even complete people,[15] though they often can't maintain any of these shapes for long and the stuff collapses. The paste-like form of ectoplasm often "evaporates" into the ectoplasmic fog, then fades away. In rare instances, it solidifies even more and seems to become fully physical for a short time, but this is rare.

One of the more rare and dramatic manifestations associated with the physical medium is the materialization of the spirit guide. This also involves conversion of matter from the etheric to the physical and vice versa, but in a much more controlled and guided fashion, for there is

---

[15] One of the more famous examples of a materialized complete human form, involving the famous medium Florence Cook, is related in Brian Inglis, *Natural and Supernatural*, p. 267.

already a "template" present for the stuff that is being materialized. The spirit guide serves as this template. This phenomenon has a direct bearing on the phenomena of bilocation shifting. It is, indeed, just like bilocation shifting except that, in all cases of physical mediums materializing spirit guides that I've run across, the spirit guide being materialized resembled a human being, not an animal.

This phenomenon of materializing spirit guides is very significant, in that it forms an essential link between regular bilocation and bilocation shifting. In regular bilocation, the body that is materialized is a carbon copy of the human's own body. In the materialization of a physical medium's spirit guide, however, the body formed is human, but definitely a different body than the medium's normal human form.[16] The "template" for the materialized spirit-guide body is borrowed from the spirit guide instead of from the physical body of the medium. In bilocation shifting, the materialized body formed is an animal body, the template for the materialized body being borrowed from either the animal spirit guide of the shifter, or from the general essence or morphogenetic field of the species. The materialization of the spirit guide of the physical medium shows that bilocation can indeed happen with a body that is not just a carbon copy of the human's own physical body. So, if you believe in bilocation and the materialization of spirit guides, as many people do, it is not a big leap of faith to believe in the type of werewolves that exist as bilocation shifters. If one can exist, why not the other?

When bilocation shifters start to shift, all sorts of weird feelings run through their bodies and they may suddenly be soaked with sweat. They may want to lie down, which is best so they don't fall over and hurt themselves when they pass out. They quickly become unconscious. Any friends watching report that their bodies become very pale, very cold, and often as stiff as a board. In addition, they often become unusually light and are easily lifted, as if they weigh only a fraction of their normal weight. These symptoms are also found in regular bilocation.

---

[16] Brian Inglis, *Natural and Supernatural*, pp. 297–298, shows an example of this sort of thing.

Materialization and Dematerialization

The next stage in bilocation shifting is the materialization of the animal body. It can appear anywhere from right beside the unconscious human body to within about a mile of it. The bilocation shifters that I have talked with say they have no control over where the animal body materializes. If the animal body appears next to the human body, any friends watching can see it slowly solidifying, like a ghost, first foggy, then more and more solid. Whitish fog ectoplasm may actually be seen exiting the human body, especially from the mouth, and augmenting and solidifying the wolf body. When the wolf body materializes far away, its materialization presumably happens in much the same way, but there are seldom any witnesses.

Once the wolf body has formed, it contains the shifter's consciousness and personality. The bilocation shifter has truly turned into a wolf. This wolf is completely solid and real in nearly every way. It leaves footprints, it breathes, it gets hungry and eats, it eliminates waste. If touched, it feels solid and real. Yet it is an inherently unstable body. For instance, if it is wounded it will bleed. If the injury is serious, it will almost certainly dematerialize immediately and involuntarily. It is sensitive to light—bright light can force a dematerialization. Turning a bright flashlight on the wolf body suddenly will almost certainly dematerialize it, and often leave the human body with burned skin in a corresponding place. If the wolf has not dematerialized by dawn, dawn will usually force this. The stability of the animal body and its sensitivity to light will vary from shifter to shifter. In legend, some bilocation shifters could go abroad as wolves by day, but they still tend to do it on cloudy days.

When bilocation shifters experience a forced dematerialization, it leaves them exhausted and weak. Moreover, any injury they receive in wolf form will immediately appear on their human bodies, to the surprise of any friends watching. When they become human again, they usually have a pretty good memory of what they did as wolves. In modern cases I've come across, bilocation shifters typically have a clearer memory of what they did as a wolf than physical shifters do. When they become human again, their wolf bodies dematerialize and their human bodies simply wake up, feeling much better than when they passed out. Indeed, they feel much as they do when waking up normally. In folklore, bilocation shifters were often the most common type of werebeast, often more common than the type that transforms the physical body. In modern times, they seem to be much more rare than true physical shifters. I believe that there is a reason for this. In other centuries, regular bilocation was more common. There is evidence that it was taught, by methods now lost to us, and that it was an ability enjoyed by many witches. Folklore also indicates that bilocation shifting was easier for a normal person to learn than physical shifting. If bilocation shifting is not much beyond ordinary bilocation, then perhaps, in the time of the legends, it was not much trouble for a witch who already knew regular bilocation to learn bilocation shifting.

Assuming the Animal Form

Physical shifters can and do have different masses in their human and animal forms. That is, they can turn into animals that weigh either less or more than their human forms. This does not violate the law of the conservation of mass any more than the materialization of spirit forms does. Mass is not created or destroyed, it is simply drawn out of, or put into, storage in the etheric realm.

Physically shifting into an animal form that weighs more is much easier. Shifters have little problem turning into large animals, like horses or bears, even though those animals may have many times their human mass. Physical shifters who shift to small species, such as foxes or rats, will often turn into larger versions of these animals—not as large as their human form, but still much larger than these animals normally get. Werefoxes may be the size of collie dogs, and there are legends of wererats the size of terriers. There are instances of normal-sized werefoxes, but, outside of bilocation shifting, none of normal-sized wererats, at least in the folklore I know.

There seems, nonetheless, to be a limit beyond which a physical shifter cannot shrink. The only way to turn into a very small animal seems to be through bilocation shifting. In many of these instances, especially those involving very small animals, the animal body forms inside the bilocation shifter's mouth and crawls out. Since this very tiny bilocation animal body forms from solidified etheric matter, ectoplasm, it forms most easily inside the mouth. There are many physical mediums who can only materialize ectoplasm in their mouths,[17] while others can materialize it most easily there. The reason for this is simple. The mouth is an open space, not occupied by any physical matter. Yet it is very solidly inside the body, within the inner layers of the aura and deep inside the etheric body, where the etheric body is most dense and can most easily solidify.

In many primitive societies, it was believed that the soul exited through the mouth when people dreamt or engaged in out-of-body travel. It was also believed that hostile spirits trying to possess the body entered it through the mouth. This was the basis for the practice of exorcism by the forced swallowing of mice. The hostile spirit was believed to latch onto the mouse in the mouth, or at least to be confused by the presence of another astral and etheric body (that of the mouse). This made it easier to eject.

When the bilocation shifter's body is tiny and materializes in the mouth, it simply crawls out. These very small forms are often small weasels or, most commonly, shrews. Sometimes they are small birds, bats, or even small fish. They are rarely mice, perhaps because a mouse is so vulnerable and likely to get eaten. As tiny as it is, a shrew seems vulnerable, but even things a hundred times its size think twice about bothering a shrew. Shrews are fierce predators that perform feats comparable to a man killing an elephant barehanded. I am not sure just where the dividing line is for how small a physical shifter can be. There are reports in legend of physical shifters turning into normal-sized rabbits. I think that I'm correct, however, in saying that only a bilocation shifter can turn into something mouse-sized.

---

[17] Some interesting, well-documented cases of a physical medium who was particularly famous for materializing ectoplasm in her mouth are related in Brian Inglis, *Natural and Supernatural*, pp. 434–435.

Some shifters claim that they can separate from the animal etheric body, remaining connected to it with only a cord of "energy." They claim to be able to let it temporarily loose to walk beside them, four-footed, rather than keeping it roughly stretched over their human bodies. Some say that this is the first step to learning to project a ghostly body, and, eventually, a real, solid, bilocation animal body.

It's useful to get trustworthy friends to watch your unconscious human body while you are running about as an animal. For one thing, any disturbing of the body can have bad consequences. For another, some wandering spirit may occasionally try to possess your empty body. The mere presence of watchful friends will keep most such spirits away. In some cases, the breathing may become dangerously slow, or the body may chill too much, and it is best to have friends nearby who can get help if this becomes health-threatening. After all, all out-of-body travel is potentially deadly, and especially out-of-body etheric travel, which can dangerously slow down the vital signs.

Bilocation shifters, like all other shifters, have animal etheric bodies as well as human bodies. In some shifters, this second etheric body is rather undeveloped and malleable, while in other shifters, the animal etheric body is more "solid" and developed. This second etheric body tends to be fairly well-developed in the extremities, and is roughly stretched over the human body most of the time. In physical shifters, the second etheric body is also roughly stretched over the human one while they are in human form, but it tends to become much more developed. Physical shifters, more than any other kind of shifter, tend to have very strong, "solid," and well-developed animal etheric bodies. Bilocation shifters, unlike physical shifters, don't necessarily have etheric bodies that are very well developed. In fact, their animal etheric bodies are often less developed than those of the average mental shifter. Many bilocation shifters say that they "borrow" some of their animal shape from their animal spirit guide. In fact, many report that they jointly inhabit the bilocation body with their animal spirit guide, sharing control. Some bilocation shifters can materialize this body either as a copy of their regular human body or as their wolf body. This is yet another instance in which bilocation shifting resembles regular bilocation.

The Myth of the Silver Bullet

One persistent modern misconception is that werewolves can only be killed by a silver bullet. This particular myth has been promoted in werewolf movies, probably because it made the werewolf scarier and a better monster for horror fans. A monster that is too easy to kill never makes a strong impression. Many werewolf novels have elaborated on this concept in a "science fiction" kind of way. The reasoning is that, if werewolves are shapeshifters, they are immune to bullets because they can simply shapeshift the wounded flesh back to its unwounded state. After all, if a creature can change its whole body in a few minutes or less, what is so difficult about sealing up a bullet wound? Silver, on the other hand, is somehow disruptive to the werewolf's body chemistry. Many of these novels claim that werewolves are allergic to silver and can't touch it.

This line of reasoning is false, for, even in physical shifters, the shapeshifter doesn't transform in a purely physical way. Instead, the physical matter of the human body becomes partially etheric in nature, in which state it can flow from one template to another. Sealing up a wound is something entirely different, and something that shapeshifting will not do. The templates are subtly linked. If one template is wounded, the other is as well. Shuffling the physical matter to the other template cannot heal a wound. Unfortunately, when people start believing in werewolves, they often take the novels and movies too seriously. The silver-bullet myth is found in the old legends. It is found there only rarely, however, and only under special circumstances. The truth is tied up with bilocation shifting, and bears little resemblance to how things are portrayed in the movies. Shifters have no trouble handling or being around silver. In fact, silver has an affinity with shifters. Silver is a metal of the Moon. Many shifters wear silver jewelry and love silver. The legends agree with this. If a werewolf or other shifter were truly allergic to silver, they wouldn't be able to touch silver coins. When most of the werewolf legends were born, silver coins were quite common. If werewolves had trouble touching silver coins, the legends certainly would have reported it. In fact, the "silver bullets" were usually not bullets, but silver coins scooped from pockets and stuffed into old-fashioned guns that could shoot just about anything.

In most legends, werewolves could be injured as easily as normal wolves. When the shapeshifter was wounded in animal form, it retained the same wound in human form. This happens in both bilocation shifting and physical shifting, and is called "repercussion." Repercussion plays a big part in many legends as the main proof that someone is really a shapeshifter. The legends tell us they were often killed by being stabbed or shot in animal form. They were caught in traps and had their hands or feet mutilated. In most legends, silver was unnecessary if you wanted to injure or kill a shapeshifter.

There is some truth to these silver-bullet legends, but it only applies in special cases. Silver bullets were supposed to kill, not just werewolves, but also vampires and all sorts of ghosts and apparitions. Silver bullets can injure *partially materialized etheric forms* that normal bullets, for some reason, cannot touch. Partially materialized etheric forms can also be injured with knives but, for some reason, bullets can't seem to touch them—as if something moving extremely fast, like a bullet, is somehow "out of phase" with the reality of the materialized etheric form. Partially materialized, and even "fully" materialized forms, such as those that occur in bilocation shifting, do not have all the characteristics of true physical reality. Although they can be almost indistinguishable from fully physical objects, they are still somewhat "out of phase" with normal physical matter.

It seems to be true that normal bullets pass through materialized bilocation bodies and other etheric forms without even touching them. So it is bilocation shifters—not physical shifters—who are immune to normal bullets. Moreover, it is only the materialized animal form that is immune, not the physical human body. I haven't found any legends of physical shifters being immune to normal bullets. Most of the silver-bullet legends center around small animals—wererabbits and werehousecats—and not werewolves. And most small werebeasts of legend were probably bilocation shifters.

Why are silver bullets different from lead bullets? Here we have to think about the etheric, and about the characteristics of various substances. Various nonliving objects have corresponding "copies" of themselves in etheric matter on the etheric plane. These etheric copies or "ghosts" may be nothing more than faint smatterings of stray etheric matter clinging in the shape of the object, or they may be fairly well-developed objects on the etheric plane. Larger objects, organic objects, objects that have been the object of many human thoughts (such as those handled frequently, or those with lots of emotional associations) and objects made of certain special materials tend to have more "solid" etheric counterparts. This phenomenon is responsible for such things as ghost trains. Nonliving objects can sometimes have etheric counterparts that are just as persistent as human ghosts.

Silver is one of the few metals that is assigned spiritual qualities. Silver has a "soul" of sorts. This means that silver objects have a strong etheric counterpart, not any kind of self-aware "soul." This etheric counterpart of silver can injure etheric forms, while merely physical bullets pass right through. A gold bullet (gold is another "spiritual" metal) would probably work just as well as a silver bullet, but I doubt anyone has tried it. People have tried bullets made of elderwood,[18] and these are supposed to work just as well as silver.

This theory of silver bullets fits in with the phenomena described in folklore, and with well-known paranormal principles. The theory that any shapeshifter can just seal up wounds is false. Shapeshifter wounds don't just seal themselves. That is entirely an invention of modern fiction.

---

[18] Frank Hamel, *Human Animals*, p. 10.

Physical Shifting

When most people think of shapeshifting, they think of physical shifting. In truth, physical shifting is the most dramatic manifestation of shapeshifting. There are many people who are truly shapeshifters, deep down in the very fiber of their being, who have never experienced a physical transformation. Physical shifting is one of the rarest types of shift. There are many who doubt its existence, and there are many who feel that it used to exist, but does no more. There are also many who believe in physical shifting. I am one of them. I used to be doubtful about physical shifting, thinking that maybe it existed only in the Middle Ages, but not anymore.

My mind was changed by a number of things. As I studied shapeshifting folklore and accounts of modern physical shifters, I began to notice similarities with many other types of paranormal phenomena. As far as I know, no paranormal investigator has ever gotten a shapeshifter inside their labs to study. But there are years and years of well-documented research by paranormal investigators into things like ectoplasmic materializations, and much evidence for it, and many believers in it. If physical shifting shows evidence of being just a rare and specialized application of ectoplasmic materialization, then it is not so hard to believe in. If one exists, why not the other?

I was impressed by the sincerity of many modern physical shifters and some of the evidence they could produce. When people have physically shifted quite a number of times, those who live with them are likely to witness a transformation sooner or later. The families of physical shifters are those most likely to claim that they have seen such transformations. Those families are also most likely to speak up if they feel it was just a strong vision or hallucination. They would be unlikely to support a family member in a mistake or delusion. Besides family members, those who have experienced many physical shifts often have other witnesses. Witness testimony, especially when several witnesses agree on details, is fairly substantial evidence. Not every physical shifter has this kind of evidence, but some do.

Another piece of credible evidence is that physical shifters get few benefits from disclosing this information, and are often hounded and harassed. Other shifters may hound them and pretend to be their friends, hoping they will reveal some hypothetical secret of physically shifting, or that the ability will somehow rub off on them. They may accuse them of lying, and constantly demand proof. Many shifters are afraid to believe in physical shifting, because they fear being disillusioned if they discover that it doesn't exist. These shifters want to promote the doctrine that shifting is only mental and spiritual in nature, so that they don't have to face the frightening possibility of the existence of higher powers.

Those who like to set themselves up as gurus and advisors see physical shifters as potential sources of power and credibility. They like to pull physical shifters into their little cliques, and then try to get them to support their particular view of what shifting means and how it should be done. They like to attract prestige and more followers by associating their little group with a real shapeshifter, the "ultimate" possible power of shifting. Gurus who try to do this are of less-than-proper moral character, and are often abusing their friendship with the physical shifter. Many physical shifters thus try to hide their ability from other shifters. They see how badly others are mistreated or abused, and they would rather not go through the same thing. Most only tell their close friends..

When a physical shifter is "outed" accidentally, or when they are inexperienced and don't realize the consequences of talking openly until it's too late, they often end up leaving the pack, going into hiding, and refusing to associate with any shifters. Occasionally, some information can be squeezed out of them, but they are mostly not interested in being known as physical shifters, because they have experienced the consequences.

I've known five physical shifters fairly well. I've briefly talked with a number of others. Some people who are not physical shifters themselves have passed information to me from physical shifters that they know or used to know, and some information comes from physical shifters who passed information and stories from physical shifters that I don't know. I've also used information from legends of physical shifters to fill in some of the holes, to substantiate some of the more rare phenomena, and to help support the same information I've gotten from modern physical shifters.

The information from physical shifters who've never met each other matches to a large degree. This information also matches the legends. I've come to understand the legends a lot better by talking to actual physical shifters, and I've come to better understand some of the experiences of actual physical shifters by studying the vast volume of shapeshifting folklore and legends. I've concentrated on the most substantial information, those facts on which most physical shifters agree. In the discussion below, I've indicated my own opinions and speculations, and that information that is not as well supported as the rest.

The number of physical shifters cited below might lead you to believe that they are more common than they really are. In truth, physical shifters are fairly rare. I've had contact with many more than most shifters do because I've spent years seeking them out, and treating them with dignity and respect when I find them, so that they do not simply feel abused and want to get away from me. I also believe I was a physical shifter in a former life, and I've used this information to "sniff out" physical shifters better than most shifters can.

I estimate that there is one physical shifter for every twenty to fifty mental shifters. In my broad definition of "physical shifter," I include those who used to physically shift years ago, but who have lost the ability, and all who claim to be physical shifters and have some evidence to support their claim. If you narrow down that definition to include only those who are physical shifters right now, and who also have very good evidence, "physical shifters" would be much more rare than one in twenty or even one in fifty.

The idea found in popular media that physical shifters transform with every full Moon is far from the truth. Physical shifts are more likely to occur on or near the full Moon, but just about every physical shifter goes through many full Moons each year without transforming. Transformations are also fairly likely to occur on or near a new Moon, and they sometimes happen entirely removed from either Moon, or even in the daytime. From what I've seen, the average physical shifter transforms two or three times a year. They also go through phases, lasting from a few months to about a year, when they transform very regularly, and they sometimes have periods when they go for a few years without any transformations.

There are a few who transform approximately every other full Moon. I even knew one of these for a short time. There are also supposed to be a few who physically shift very regularly, about once a week. I haven't talked with any of them, but I've heard rumors of them and have talked to one physical shifter who said he knew one. Legend also relates that some physical shifters transformed frequently, even as often as every night. I do not think this was very common, even in the days of legend.

TRIGGERING A PHYSICAL SHIFT

In many werewolf novels, physical shifters change more than once in the same day, or each day for several days in a row. This is far from reality. Every novel and movie I've come across greatly exaggerates how frequently werewolves change, how easily the change happens, and, in cases where the werewolf gains some power over the changes, the ease of triggering shifts at will. Physical shifts occasionally happen entirely by accident, or even when the physical shifter tries to resist the change, but this is rare. The first few physical shifts may even happen by accident. The physical shifters don't really intend to attempt a physical shift, but simply follow their instincts, feelings, and desires. They are led to the right way before they quite know that the path they are traversing leads to physical shifting. In fact, some physical shifters who have now lost that ability claim that the first few physical shifts, the ones that happened at least partially by accident, were the easiest, and that things got more difficult with time, as they learned enough about the warning signs of a physical shift that it was less likely they would have one by accident.

Most physical shifts are induced, to a greater or lesser extent, once the physical shifter learns the conditions and techniques that tend to trigger them. Even so, "at will" physical shifting is rare. Physical shifters need to wait until shifting energy is at the right level, get in the right state of mind, and make sure all the conditions are conducive to the shift.[1] It generally takes a few hours of this to induce a physical shift, and there is no guarantee that a physical shift will even happen. Even those who are pretty good at this and who can create the right conditions fail about half the time.

The mental state of a physical shifter in animal form varies. It can be anywhere from a very deep mental shift (wholly animal but with the memory of being human) to an average-level mental shift (human insights and thought processes sometimes drifting to the surface or being available when needed). The modern myth of a "ravening beast" mentality is entirely false. Unless werewolves are very evil people to begin with, or have harbored intense hatred against someone for a long time, they will not be dangerous. Werewolves do not see humans as prey, and they do not lust after human flesh. They are not the killers that they are made out to be in movies. They may try to jump on friends and fawn on them like a friendly dog, however, scaring those friends rather badly. In many legends, a

---

[1] The techniques for causing physical shifts are discussed in detail in chapter 7.

scared friend kills a werewolf who behaves in just this manner, and the even is labeled a werewolf attack. Many "evil werewolf" legends got their start in just this sort of innocent, and tragic, event.

How mentally wolflike a shifter is during a physical shift varies from shifter to shifter, and even from one shift to the next in the same shifter. Over a long period of time, the mental state tends to retain more and more of the human mentality. That is, those who have been physical shifters for a long time tend to be able to call forth more human mentality when needed. I have never heard of physical shifters who had an entirely human mental state while in animal form.

In physical shifters who are in animal form, there is always a fair degree of animal instincts, desires, and thought processes. These tend to overwhelm the human mentality and push it to the background. Remember, the physical shifter actually has an animal brain while physically shifted, and this affects the thought processes. Most physical shifters are very much just "dumb animals" when shifted. In fact, thinking in too human a way, whether by accident or on purpose, tends to trigger the shift back to human. This is actually the explanation for a piece of shapeshifting folklore. It is common shapeshifting folklore that to call a werewolf by its name will cause it to change back to human form[2] (or, in some legends, change back and also be cured, though I really doubt that). Most physical shifters cannot understand words when in animal form. Their hearing is entirely different, and, since they actually have an animal's brain, the part of their brain that processes language is gone or vastly changed (in other words, shapeshifting is not a good way to eavesdrop on people!). A person's name, however, lies at a deeper subconscious level than language. It is the one sound we always start at, or hear across a noisy room. The very sound has been etched into our subconscious. Calling a

---

[2] As in this Danish tale: "There was a man in Hjörring named Niels Løt, a merchant and inn-keeper; his wife's name was Karen. Old Skytte-Kraen in Astrup had accused her of being a witch and Niels challenged him to prove it. They took the matter to court. A large black dog followed Niels to court. Skytte-Kraen was asked to prove Karen was a witch and he turned to the dog and said: 'Stand up, Karen, and answer that.' There she stood naked in the courtroom. The husband took off his overcoat and threw it over her." Barbara Allen Woods, *The Devil in Dog Form* (Berkeley and Los Angeles: University of California Press, 1959), pp. 93–94.

physical shifter by name often brings an involuntary return to the human mental state, causing a shift back.

Most physical shifters have fairly good control over the change back to human form. It is much easier to trigger than the change to animal form. Simply thinking in too human a way can trigger a change back, and this sometimes happens accidentally. Even though physical shifters have a much greater control over the change when in animal form, however, this doesn't necessarily mean they will change back when and where their human side desires. The wolf side may think that it's perfectly okay to change back to human a few miles from home and the nearest clothing, though it usually has more sense than that. If they plan to change back to human form in front of a loved one whom they want to let in on the secret, they, as a wolf, will likely feel that it is far more interesting to roam around the woods instead. In fact, any plans they make as humans before shifting are likely to seem stupid or unimportant once they are in animal form.

This is endlessly frustrating to those who wish to use their physical shifting to further their human purposes. For this reason, those who want to have these powers just to do "neat" things with them would be better off not pursuing the path of physical shifting. Physical shifting is for people mature enough to be able to accept it, deal with it well, and enjoy it for what it is. It is for those who want simply to experience the quiet beauty of being truly wolf (or whatever other species), without needing anything more.

INTEGRATED AND NON-INTEGRATED SHIFTS

Physical shifting occurs when the human body actually changes into an animal body. Hands turn into paws, the face elongates into a snout, and the human body becomes indistinguishable from a real animal. All physical shifts happen in the same basic way, but the characteristic details and symptoms vary according to whether the shifter is integrated or non-integrated.

There are three major things involved with physical shifting. One is very high levels of shifting energy (and the strong animal etheric body associated with it), another is the ability to move into a state of mind in which you can completely "let go," another is the state of integration of the shifter. Those with manifestations of the paranormal during mental shifts (berserkers) always have very high shifting energy. Very high shifting energy alone, however, is not enough to trigger a physical shift. All physical shifters must also have the ability to "let go." (For more information on "letting go," see chapter 7.)

The third major thing involved in physical shifting is the state of integration of the shifter. If the shifter is integrated, the physical shift happens slowly and smoothly, finishing in a matter of minutes. This does not require inordinately high levels of shifting energy; a level slightly less than that needed for berserker powers will usually suffice. It is also possible, but not common, for the shift to be stopped in the middle, or reversed before the full animal form is reached. This slow type of physical shifting is most often called "classical physical shifting" (or "classical shifting" for short) because it resembles the classic, slower type of shift seen in werewolf movies—except for the fact that the shifter achieves full wolf form instead of remaining in the "wolfman" form seen in the movies.

If the shifter is non-integrated, but manages to physically shift anyway, the shift requires enormous amounts of shifting energy. The shift happens very suddenly, the shifter is pushed "over the edge" forcibly by the incredible amounts of shifting energy fueling the shift. It usually takes only a few seconds to complete itself. For this reason, I have chosen to call this "instantaneous shifting." Both types of physical shift involve the same basic phenomena and mechanisms. Instantaneous shifting simply has more extreme symptoms and side-effects because of the very large amounts of shifting energy involved. The symptoms of classical shifting are all similar to those of instantaneous physical shifts. They are simply slower, more stable, and less volatile in nature. In instantaneous shifts, the human and animal sides are separated, and the physical shift switches suddenly and violently between them. In classical shifts, the two sides are joined, they are part of the same continuum. The classical shift is also a continuum, slowly changing in a stable, continuous, connected way.

The instantaneous shift is more like a dam bursting, while a classical shift is like a river gradually descending into a valley. Instantaneous shifting is more like shape switching, and classical shifting is more like shape changing. However, both are still basically the same phenomenon, only differing in the degree of the symptoms. Many classical shifters have experienced the instantaneous type of physical shift once or twice. Some instantaneous physical shifters have experienced a classical physical shift, though usually a faster than normal one. If a shifter learns physical shifting first, and then later becomes integrated, they will at first be an instantaneous physical shifter, then their shifts will slow down and become more classical as they become integrated. Physical shifts whose symptoms fall between the instantaneous and classical type do happen, but these are rare.

INSTANTANEOUS SHIFTS

To a much greater extent than any other type, instantaneous shifters build up great amounts of shifting energy and expend much of it in their shifts. Instantaneous shifters are very affected by the phase of the Moon and every paranormal current, much more than the slow type of physical shifter. They usually build up shifting energy for a month or longer. When within several days or a week of their shift, the level of shifting energy is so high that they experience what is commonly called "the fever." The fever is a condition of very high tension that is caused by holding very large amounts of shifting energy within. It occurs in nonphysical shifters as well. The symptoms of the fever are typically a great restlessness and yearning, cramps (especially in the area of the second chakra), an intense sensation of tingling, itching, twitching, or engorgement of the skin, and headaches. The fever can be mild or extreme. Instantaneous shifters, within a few days of a possible transformation, usually have very strong symptoms of the fever.

In instantaneous shifters, within a few hours of the physical shift, the symptoms of uncomfortably high shifting energy become noticeably worse. Within a few minutes of the physical shift, the instantaneous shifter feels an incredibly urgent need to run off and hide somewhere where their animal personality feels "safe" (generally away from people). They often also experience a gut-wrenching nausea or pounding headache at this time, and most commonly feel that they are going to vomit. The physical shift itself is painless, and they are instantly relieved of any symptoms of the fever as soon as it occurs.

When the time of the physical shift itself comes, one of two things happen. Either they do physically shift, or the shift aborts at the last second. If the shift aborts, they experience an immediate sharp reduction of shifting energy as it deflates. They feel immediate relief from the fever. They may be thrown immediately into a short-lived mental shift, or simply be left in a normal condition.

If the instantaneous shifter does physically shift, it happens very suddenly. Often the skin turns whitish or grayish just before any physical shift or close call. Usually, grayish ectoplasmic "smoke" oozes from the skin and covers much of the body, and the shifter suddenly falls onto all fours. The physical change from fully human to fully animal takes only a few seconds, and looks much like a blur, especially since the foglike ectoplasm clinging to the skin obscures the form. This sudden shift is often accompanied by a great rush of wind moving around the shifter, sometimes with a sharp sound like a thunderclap. Occasionally, the instantaneous shifter glows extremely brightly for an instant during the shift.

At the moment of the instantaneous shift, the shifter's mind is thrown into extreme confusion. When the confusion sorts itself out, the mind has changed and become very wolflike. The shifter no longer thinks in words, only in emotions and sensations. Instantaneous shifters tend to have much more of an animal mentality; their instincts overwhelm them more. They also have more trouble remembering their shifts clearly. The animal, however, remembers being human much better than the human remembers being an animal, whenever there is any memory barrier. While both bilocation shifters and classical physical shifters usually have excellent memories of what they did as animals, the instantaneous shifters usually have poor memories of what they did as animals, although they usually remember the shift itself and its immediate aftermath vividly. Part of this memory problem arises from the fact that the instantaneous shifter is not integrated, so memories do not get accepted as well by the human side. I think, however, that it is partly also due to the instability and volatility of the actual shift, the way it strains the mind, almost literally taking it apart and putting it back together suddenly and with great confusion. Mental shifts that happen extremely suddenly are often accompanied by similar fuzzy memories and memory holes of the time spent shifted.

When instantaneous shifters are physically shifted into their animal form, their shifting energy is continually being burnt away. When the energy runs out, in several hours generally, they change back to human form suddenly, in much the same way that they transformed into animals. In most cases, they get tired and go to sleep when their shifting energy starts getting low, and they simply wake up human, having experienced the return shift while asleep. If they can avoid going to sleep, the memory of their shift is dramatically improved. They remember their time as animals much better, because their memories are not mixed up with their dreams and the sleep state.

CLASSICAL SHIFTS

Those who manage to fully integrate their animal and human sides, and who become physical shifters, become classical shifters. Classical shifters take from two to ten minutes to change from fully human to fully animal. The length of time varies, even in different shifts experienced by the same shifter. Classical shifting is much easier to trigger than instantaneous shifting, but is harder to complete. Many of those who experience classical shifts have frustrating experiences with it, because, once started, there is no guarantee that it will finish. If the shifter loses the right state of mind in the middle of the shift, the shift stops there and immediately brings the shifter back to the human form.

All physical shifting tends to deplete shifting energy, and another physical shift cannot occur until that energy is built up again. Normally, for a classical shifter, this takes at least a day and often a month. But classical shifters don't "burn" shifting energy in the intense way that instantaneous shifters do. After a physical shift, the amount of shifting energy will still be fairly high. In instantaneous shifters, when the shifting energy has run down, they are forced to return to human form. They rely on shifting energy, and a constant supply of it, simply to maintain themselves in animal form. In a classical shifter, there is no need to continually use up lots of shifting energy to maintain animal form. It seems as if classical shifters don't need shifting energy to stay animals any more than they need it to stay human, although that may be an exaggeration. I've never heard a reliable report of a classical physical shifter remaining in animal form for more than a few days at a time, although legends do report that some werewolves could remain in wolf form for a few months, or even for years.

THE PROCESS OF PHYSICAL SHIFTING

The actual physical change of a classical shift is similar to instantaneous shifting, but much slower. In the classical shift, the first changes are the same as with almost-physical shifts: eye color, skin changes, or smoke-like ectoplasm.

The first truly physical change to occur is the growing of fur. The fur appears first in small patches that spread outward over the entire body. These patches of fur often appear first on the belly, in the general area of the second chakra. The hair on the head and other body hair thickens and changes texture to become fur, then spreads out from these areas as well. At this point in the change, the werewolf somewhat resembles a fur-covered human. Though we have few detailed descriptions from legend of what a werebeast's physical transformation is actually supposed to look like, what we do have agrees quite closely with the information I've gotten from modern physical shifters. From many different cultures and places, those physical shifters who changed slowly first got a peculiar skin color and then grew fur,[3] before other changes became very noticeable.

Only after fur has covered most of the body do other changes become noticeable. The face elongates into a snout, the hands change to paws, the feet lengthen, with the heels becoming a wolf's hocks and the front developing into paws. Then a tail grows, leg and arm proportions change, the

---

[3] As in the case of one werehyena in Abyssinia, who changed in front of some girls who had been teasing him about the rumors that he was a werebeast. He first had a change in skin color, then began to grow hyena fur, and slowly kept changing until he was fully a hyena. Frank Hamel, *Human Animals* (New York: University Books, 1969), p. 80.

torso lengthens, the hips narrow into the slender pelvis of a wolf, and the shoulders narrow and disappear into the torso. The result is a creature that is a wolf in every way. Instantaneous physical shifts look much the same, but happen much more rapidly.

The way in which the physical change progresses is very significant and has much to do with the wolf etheric body. During physical shifting, the changes of shape and proportion are happening to all parts of the body at once, but they are happening at different speeds in different parts of the body. The change happens the fastest in the extremities: hands, feet, ears, nose, and tail. The hands and feet are very pawlike and have almost completed their change, and the head is very wolflike, at a point when the rest of the body still resembles a furry human. The change completes itself first in the extremities, with the torso changing slowest of all and being the last part to complete its change. The change occurs in this way because of the shape and nature of the etheric wolf body. Like the human etheric body, the etheric wolf body is somewhat fluid and flexible. Normally, the etheric animal body of a shifter is most "dense" and easily felt in the extremities, sometimes in the form of phantom tail, ears, muzzle, and paws. These extremities line up fairly well with their human counterparts, with the rest of the wolf etheric body "stretching" roughly over the human frame.

The extremities of the physical body change first and fastest, because the more solid extremities of the "phantom animal body" (the only parts that are fully their right shape and also lined up with the corresponding human parts to begin with) fasten onto the extremities of the human body and change it into their own shape. As the completed change spreads out from those extremities, more and more of the nearby etheric wolf body can stop being stretched over the human frame and assume its true shape, lining up correctly with the corresponding human part. Subsequent parts can then change.

During a physical shift, what really happens is that the solid matter of the physical body becomes partially etheric in nature—less physical and more like ectoplasm. This phenomenon of the actual body becoming less physical and somewhat closer to ectoplasm in nature is found in some physical mediums, saints, and magic workers. As the physical body becomes somewhat ectoplasmic, the skin may turn pale, or even white as snow. In some cases, it becomes grayish. When the physical body becomes partially ectoplasmic, it is no longer completely subject to the rules of physical matter. During a physical shift, the physical matter of the human body disassociates itself from the etheric human body, and "flows" into the ready template of the animal etheric body. The animal etheric body is the blueprint and container, without which physical shifting could not occur.

The mechanisms involved in physical shifting are exactly the same as those involved in some other commonly accepted paranormal phenomena. In order to explain these mechanisms, I'll have to go back to some of the phenomena associated with physical mediums. The etheric plane, the physical plane, both the animal and human etheric bodies, and the physical human body are all involved in physical shifting. How can the physical matter of the human body simply flow into a new shape and assume the shape of an animal body? First, the physical human body becomes closer to the etheric in its state of matter. At this point, the physical matter of the human body has become something other than simply physical. It has moved closer to the etheric plane and become partially like etheric matter. It has become ectoplasmic. It is matter in a state somewhere between the purely physical and purely etheric. It is still fairly close to being physical, and has most of the properties and characteristics of physical matter, but it is not quite physical at this point, not quite of this world. At this point, the no-longer-quite-physical matter of the human body is induced to flow out of its usual "container," the etheric body, and into the ready "container," or "template," of the animal etheric body. Here it solidifies back to the fully physical state in the form of an animal body.

This whole process sounds hard to believe—strange, unusual, and unlikely. Yet it is very similar to commonly accepted phenomena that are sometimes connected with physical mediums. If physical shifting is simply a more rare and dramatic example of a phenomenon, then it is much easier to accept. For example, the often-reported side effect of grayish, whitish, or even snow-white skin sometimes connected with smoke-like ectoplasm crawling over the skin, is a state that has often been reported in accounts of physical mediums. These symptoms are believed to signify a body that is becoming closer to the etheric in nature, becoming partially ectoplasmic and less purely physical.

Another phenomenon connected with physical mediums, and reminiscent of physical shifting, is called "elongation" in spiritualist literature and in accounts of paranormal investigators. Elongation occurs when the medium's body becomes partially ectoplasmic in nature, and then part of it stretches out far longer or wider than it ever could by any normal means, then goes back to its natural shape and size. I have come across reports of elongation occurring in modern shifters, but not in physical shifters. Elongation is like physical shifting that tries to happen, but has nowhere to go. Since there is no etheric "template" to flow into, the ectoplasm simply stretches and changes shape and then returns to its normal shape. Obviously, some mental shifters have some of the keys to physical shifting, but no "template" for their body to use, so they simply experience a little elongation and then go back to their original form. Physical shifting is simply the phenomenon of elongation, but with a ready template—a strong and "solid" animal etheric body.

Ancient legends from around the world agree that most people who are hereditary physical shifters usually experience their first physical shift between the ages of 16 and 20. In modern America, however, this is not true. It is much harder for a person living in a modern culture to physically shift, and so, if it happens at all, it usually happens later in life. The usual age for a modern shifter's first physical shift seems to be between 25 and 40. What is it like to experience a physical shift? They say it is as if your senses "explode" around you. A wolf's senses are so much more sensitive than a human's that it is almost like being thrown into some kind of drug trip. One of the functions of assuming a wolf mind when physically shifted is to be able to handle this barrage of stimulation.

This sensory barrage is one of the reasons that physical shifters often roll on the ground and roam around sensing everything. Those who have physically shifted many times get used to this overwhelming sensory barrage, and it begins to feel normal. They get used to their new senses, and from then on they feel horribly blind and deaf and numb, in comparison, when in human form. Just as a badly nearsighted child feels normal even though he or she can't see, when the child gets glasses, the child suddenly feels as if he or she is living in some sort of wonderland. Then the child begins to see this as normal, and feels blind without glasses.

I, myself, even with great effort, haven't turned up very many cases of modern physical shifters. Of those that I've known, most have been werewolves. There was one werefox that had a pretty good case, and a werebear that I never knew much about and only talked with once. But I do believe that physical shifters of species other than wolves are out there somewhere. I also have heard unsubstantiated rumors of the existence of other modern physical shifter werecats, werefoxes, and werebears.

OTHER TYPES OF PHYSICAL SHIFTS

There are cases of odd types of physical shifting found in legend. One of these tells of two-form physical shifters; that is, shifters who periodically physically transform into two different species of animal. The most common pairing found in legend is the bear/wolf physical shifter particularly common in Norse legends. There are many shifters who have two mental animal sides, and a few who have three. In most of these cases, one of the animal sides is dominant; all are not equal. In my opinion, if the shifter became a physical shifter, only the dominant side would manifest physically. However, I don't have any evidence to support this. I've never known a two-form mental shifter who developed into a physical shifter. I've heard rumors of modern two-form physical shifters, and even spoken with people who claimed to be two-form physical shifters, though they weren't able to produce enough evidence to convince me that they were even physical shifters, let alone the two-form kind.

In some cases, however, two animal sides may have manifested physically, because legend reports a number of instances of two-form physical shifters. Here we are talking about a rare phenomenon within what is already a rare phenomenon. I also suspect that being a two-form physical shifter might require some magical technique that has been lost to us. I believe that, as in regular physical shifting, a "template" is needed for two-form physical shifting. In this case, it would require the presence of two animal etheric bodies that would be very hard to obtain and maintain. This is probably why so few two-form physical shifters exist, even in legend.

Another odd phenomenon of physical shifting is called "breaking out." I have never heard of a modern case of this, but it is common in legend. This occurs when a physical shifter running around in animal form gets hurt. In many legends, werebeasts attack sheep and the shepherd hits them hard with a staff or a spear. At this moment of pain, a piece of the shifter's human body pushes up through the surface of the wolf body like a ghost's hand through a wall, "floats" around on the surface of the wolf body, perhaps moving entirely to the other side of it, and then submerges. The aspect of this floating human part is often ghostly. In some legends, it is part of a human face that enables observers to recognize who the werewolf is. This is evidence for the fact that the etheric body is closely connected with physical shifting. When shifters are in wolf form, they still carry their wolf etheric body and their human etheric body around with them. Their wolf etheric body is perfectly matched to their wolf body; it is the template for that form. At this time, their human etheric body is somewhat diffuse, and stretched roughly over the physical wolf body. Breaking out occurs when part of the etheric human body comes loose under stress and gathers enough substance to be visible. Breaking out does not, as far as I know, ever happen in reverse. That is, wolf body parts do not materialize and float about the human body.

Another phenomenon reported in legends involves the whole body changing into animal form except for perhaps a few toes, or an ear, with the unchanged part remaining completely human.[4] When this happens, it is accidental. I suspect that the reason the part of the body didn't change is either that it had a weak corresponding wolf etheric body part, or the

---

[4] As in the case of Jeanne Perrin, who when "going through a wood with Clauda Gaillard, Clauda, grumbling that she had received so few alms, darted into the bushes and there came out a huge wolf. Jeanne Perrin, crossing herself and letting fall the alms she had collected, ran away in terror, for she swore that this wolf had toes on its hind feet like a human being. There is a strong presumption that this wolf was no other than Clauda Gaillard, for she afterwards told Jeanne that the wolf which attacked her would not have done her any harm." Montague Summers, *The Werewolf* (Secaucus, NJ: Citadel Press, 1973), p. 123.

corresponding wolf etheric body part didn't quite fasten on the physical body during the change. The unchanged part is usually small. When this phenomenon happens in legends, it causes observers to realize that the animal they are seeing is really a shapeshifter.

Shapeshifters in legend sometimes fall to the ground and roll around vigorously, simultaneously transforming to animal form. Superstitious peasants relate that this rolling on the ground was some sort of magic action or ritual that causes the physical shift. Modern psychologists have used this to try to link beliefs in shapeshifting to epileptic fits, even though medieval peasants knew all about epilepsy and weren't likely to mistake it for physical shifting. From talking with physical shifters, I know that these shapeshifters were not causing their transformation, as peasants thought. Nor were they involuntarily thrown into some kind of fit during their transformation. When a physical shift occurs, it is most likely to proceed if one remains quite still during the entire transformation. Movements, especially sudden movements, tend to dislodge the etheric matter that is clinging to the body and causing the transformation.[5] Brushing against, or rolling against, a solid surface dislodges it even more. For those trying to prevent a physical shift, rolling around on the ground represents a last-ditch, desperate attempt to halt the process. The werewolves of legend who were rolling around on the ground while transforming were trying desperately to stop the shift from happening, but were unsuccessful.

One of the most universally reported characteristics of physical shapeshifters is that they have very white teeth. This has been true even in situations like that of Pierre and George Gandillon (a famous werewolf case in 1584 in Naizan, France).[6] These two had been forced to live apart from other humans for a long time. They were starving peasants who were

---

[5] This is yet another reason why it is very rare in legend for a werewolf to be seen roaming around in a half-transformed state. The partially transformed state is unstable and not likely to tolerate the werewolf's movements. In all my listening to people who claimed to have seen evidence for shapeshifting, I have only come across two instances where the werebeast was supposed to be roaming around half-transformed, instead of in full animal form. In one, a group of teenagers (now adults) was chased by a werewolf in this state; in another, a man saw his friend turn into a creature like a furry person with a dog's head. Neither story had enough evidence to convince me it was really true, although, like many of these stories with little evidence, they might be true.

[6] Montague Summers, *The Werewolf*, p. 229.

sickly and filthy, with scraggly hair and thick, yellow, broken nails. Yet both of them, in this state, had bright white teeth. This is all the more unusual because dental care was uncommon at the time. Jean Garnier, another famous werewolf tried in 1603, was also described as having very white teeth.[7] Jean was a malnourished vagrant. Unlike most werewolves of legend, he was in such a state of physical health that he horrified even the people of that time. He's the last person in the world you'd expect to have very white teeth—yet he did.

All the physical shifters I've known have had fairly white teeth. I believe the white teeth of the legends is mentioned because white teeth really stood out as abnormal, for most adults had stained teeth. Today, white teeth hardly stand out because most people have them. I believe that unusually white teeth are caused by the process of regular physical shifting. The teeth get reformed without the stains. This does not correct crookedness, nor does it remove cavities that already exist. Indeed, there are a number of legends about werebeasts who were killed in animal form and retained the fillings of their human counterparts.[8] The tooth reformed around the filling. There are also legends of earrings and nose rings remaining in the ears of animals who were really shapeshifters in animal form,[9] as well as legends of wereboars with rings embedded in the front hoof of the boar form.[10]

Many people think that it is unlikely that female werebeasts could possibly experience physical transformations during pregnancy. Even

---

[7] Elliot O'Donnell, *Werewolves* (Hertfordshire, England: Oracle Publishing, 1996), p. 126.

[8] Walter Skeat claims, "The belief is very strongly held, and on one occasion, when I asked some Malays at Jugra how it could be proved that the man really became a tiger, they told me the case of a man some of whose teeth were plated with gold, and who had been accidently killed in the tiger stage, when the same gold plating was discovered in the tiger's mouth." See *Malay Magic* (London: Frank Cass & Co. Ltd., 1900), p. 161.

[9] Frank Hamel tells us that "Coffin brought himself to believe in these native stories, and quoted in evidence of their truth that he had often seen a certain kind of earring in the ears of hyaenas [sic] shot, trapped and speared by himself or his friends, identical with those which were commonly worn by the native servants." See *Human Animals*, p. 79.

[10] "The belief, though not quite so general at present as it used to be, cannot be considered extinct yet," says Summers. According to it, Turks, who have led a particularly wicked life . . . turn into wild boars, and the ring worn by the man on his finger is retained on one of the boar's forefeet." See *The Werewolf*, p. 149.

though many modern shifters think that this is likely the truth, I disagree. There are legends of shifters who experienced physical shifting during pregnancy. One of the most telling factors, however, is what the legends don't say. I have been unable to find any folklore that says that pregnant werebeasts can't change. If it were true that they couldn't change, there would be at least some folklore about it. Folklore and folk wisdom is full of all sorts of ways to "cure" werewolves or inhibit their shifting. Folklore also relates that medieval people were particularly concerned with preventing wives and daughters from physical shifting. Male werewolves had certain manly rights. But women had few rights. Men greatly feared their wives' ability to physically shift, and enter a world where they could not follow them, control them, or even know what they were doing. Many legends relate a fear that the wife could be having a sexual affair with an animal, or with another shapeshifter, and the husband would never know. There are many legends where husbands go to great lengths to try to prevent physical shifting, try to force cures, and try to prevent women from going into the wild once transformed. Many of these legends ended tragically, either with the death of the wife, or with the wife leaving to become an animal permanently. Chinese folk wisdom mentions that there can be no happy marriage between a man and a werefox, because the man can never be happy unless he can control his wife, and know what she is doing at all times, and the werefox can never be happy unless she can periodically turn into a fox and go out into the wild.

If it is true that a pregnant shifter cannot experience physical transformation, it would certainly appear in the literature as a way to prevent shifting. It does not. It is hard to imagine, however, how this could happen, and many modern shifters who have thought about it have concluded that such a shift would endanger the unborn child. I have found no folklore about miscarriages provoked by physical shifting. How it may happen is a question worth exploring. It is at least possible, in the cases of wolf-sized or larger animals, that the physical body of the animal might be carrying a human fetus. But it is unlikely, at least in an advanced pregnancy. A wolf normally has five cubs weighing a pound each, so carrying a full-term human child would be quite a strain. Bears have tiny, helpless cubs, and it would be even less likely for them, even though they are bigger. And it would be quite impossible for a fox. Some have suggested that the fetus also transforms, but, for various reasons, I think this is unlikely. It is certainly impossible in the case of bird shifters and crocodile shifters who don't even have wombs!

Many people wonder what happens to shapeshifters when they are killed in animal or half-animal form. Do they change back to human form? According to legend, for a dying shapeshifter to change back to human form at death is rare. Although there is some evidence of it in legends, most shapeshifters killed in animal form simply remain as dead animals. In a few rare cases, however, shapeshifters in human form assumed animal form at the moment of death. In some legends, this happened to people whom no one suspected of being a werewolf, on their deathbeds. It was a great shock to their families. Do shapeshifters killed in the process of transforming change back to human form at death? The legends relate that this is rare. If a shapeshifter is killed while transforming, in most cases, the corpse remains in that transition state.

When someone touches the body of a physical shifter during transformation, they sometimes suffer burns. Occasionally, scorch marks are left on floors as well. This is due to the kundalini. The kundalini is a kind of power surge that relates to the chakras and to *chi*. This and other phenomena connected with physical shifting lead me to believe that the process of physical shifting is related to kundalini energy. Those who wish to experience physical shifting may learn much of value by studying yoga and kundalini with an experienced teacher.

In fact, many shifters believe that spontaneous combustion can occur when a physical shift "tries" to happen, but somehow goes awry, although all those who experienced spontaneous combustion are not necessarily shifters. Spontaneous combustion also has much in common with the kundalini, and is probably a rare result of some malfunction of it. In fact, some cases of spontaneous combustion were probably just ordinary people experiencing a badly misfiring kundalini, and not shifters.

Another strange phenomenon occurs when a physical shifter shifts while clothed. The clothes are sometimes mysteriously shredded, even though the animal body does not shred them by expanding and tearing them during the change. They are often shredded to bits. This problem appears to be most common in instantaneous shifters.

Sometimes, more rarely, a shifter's clothing partially "melds" to the body during a physical shift, with part of it actually turning into the hair and skin of the animal body. Parts of the cloth, and any hard objects, like buttons or zippers, become painfully embedded in the flesh, unchanged. This also seems to be most common in instantaneous shifters. This phenomenon is also found in legends. In fact, many legends warn, without quite saying why, that it is very bad for a werewolf to shapeshift while clothed. The warnings are so strong and so frequent that they can hardly refer simply to the possibility of clothing being ripped, dirty, or lost. Some accounts actually describe buttons or pieces of cloth partially embedded in the skin. These are not accounts of berserkers in costume, because, in some cases, the shapeshifters are killed and found to still have the parts of clothing embedded in their bodies.

One of the most famous of these cases happened in 1808, in the province of Kalmar in Sweden. It involves a benevolent werewolf, who was killed accidentally by a neighbor who mistook him for a real wolf. The mistake was discovered when the wolf was skinned: "When the dead wolf, a huge beast, was skinned, a shirt was discovered inside the wolfskin. A woman identified the shirt as one she had sewn for her soldier husband."[11] This phenomenon may sound unbelievable, but it should be remembered that etheric matter and ectoplasm can be formed into clothes as readily as into a body, otherwise all our ghosts would be naked!

The etheric body, especially when separated from the physical body, does get its shape partially from our beliefs. Since most ghosts spend their lives clothed, subconsciously thinking of clothing as pretty much part of their bodies, after death, they just seem to generate ectoplasmic clothing to go with their ectoplasmic bodies. This kind of phenomenon can also be seen in ghosts who smoked constantly during life. Their ghosts often gen-

---

[11] From Daniel Cohen, *Werewolves* (New York: Penguin, 1996), pp. 46–47.

erate the smell of tobacco, constantly, subconsciously, and uncontrollably. This is because they were so strongly associated with tobacco smoke during life that, on a very deep level, they feel that it is part of themselves. It therefore becomes a characteristic of their ghostly bodies. In the same way, people projecting a ghostly manifestation of their etheric body, or even engaging in regular bilocation (not bilocation shifting, but normal bilocation), will almost always produce a body that is clothed.

Etheric matter, under the right conditions, can form many things. Many objects have a corresponding etheric "ghost" object that can, under certain conditions, be "phased out" into the etheric. This explains why clothing, on rare occasions, can partially meld to the animal body during a physical shift. It also explains the existence of "ghosts" of inanimate objects, such as ghost trains. Legend also reports that a few sorcerer-werewolves could fully transform their clothing into the animal body and back, so that they did not end up somewhere human and nude. This reflects a controlled and practical use of the same phenomenon.

In most cases, however, it is uncomfortable for modern physical shifters to "confuse" their clothing with their body during a change. It is quite painful to have pieces of cloth, buttons, or zippers embedded in your body. For all these reasons, if you do wear clothing, it should be extremely loose-fitting and without buttons or zippers. Wear a huge T-shirt, or cut a head-hole in a blanket and wear it like a poncho, with nothing underneath, or simply wrap yourself in a blanket.

PHENOMENA MISTAKEN FOR PHYSICAL SHIFTING

Before I conclude this chapter, I should discuss what physical shifting is *not*. Some phenomena, under certain conditions, can be mistaken for physical shifting, and it is important to know how to distinguish them from true physical shifting. Visions and experiences with astral shifting or apparition shifting, if extremely intense and vivid, can often seem like a physical shift to those experiencing them, though it won't seem like a physical shift to anyone watching. This is why I always ask those who claim to be physical shifters if they have any witnesses. If a physical shifter has shifted enough times, sooner or later someone will see a transformation, or see them running around as an animal, or see a lot of circumstantial evidence of physical transformation.

This witness is usually a family member, friend, lover, or roommate. Often, the witnesses are frightened and unsettled by what they have seen, and a fair number allow fear and prejudice to make them into ex-friends or ex-lovers. Many try to force the physical shifter to get cured or to submit to an exorcism. They may even, in some cases, try to kill the physical shifter in animal form. Prejudice and fear of the strange and unknown can make people do horrible things, even to their loved ones. For this reason, many of those who have been physical shifters for many years live alone, often on their own land outside of town, and share their secret only with a few very close friends.

Another distinguishing feature of physical shifts, especially useful in cases where the shifter hasn't transformed enough times to have witnesses, is the symptoms that are associated with the shift. Physical shifts have particular characteristics and symptoms associated with them. In some cases, these symptoms are fairly mild, but all or most of them are usually present in real physical shifts.

Shifting, combined with out-of-body travel, especially etheric shifting or apparition shifting, is sometimes mistaken for physical shifting by the person experiencing it. The person feels a strong, detailed, and physical sensation of being in the body of an animal. The person may be wandering around in familiar places in this form, and it may seem much like either a physical or a bilocation shift, especially to one who strongly wants to believe that he or she has experienced a real transformation into animal form. The cases most likely to be mistaken for physical shifting are cases of apparition shifting, where the apparition is so strong that it is close to the physical in some ways. The apparition may leave wolf pawprints, or greasy and foggy wolf noseprints on windows, or even, in some cases, shed hairs that are physical and that remain when the shifter is entirely human. I have heard a number of stories of these kinds of phenomena that border on being fully physical. They are much more common, in fact, than true physical shifting.

If shifters wake up and find their beds full of shed wolf fur, or find muddy wolf pawprints in the kitchen after being in a dimly remembered trance, they may jump to conclusions and decide that they have experienced a true physical shift. It is more likely, however, that they simply experienced some paranormal phenomenon that approached physical or bilocation shifting. I know this, because I've come across many reports of other people witnessing such phenomena, when no physical change occurred and any wolf apparition produced, even if it did leave footprints, was ghostly and transparent.

When trying to judge whether a physical shift really occurred, ask yourself a few questions. First, were you fully conscious throughout, or did you experience all this while in a strange trance? It is not unusual for physical shifters to remember their experience as dreamlike and have some holes in their memory of it, but real physical shifters almost always have a fairly clear memory of the change itself and the events immediately following. If you cannot remember actually changing into an animal, and the whole experience is exceedingly dim, then you probably didn't experience a physical shift, even if you managed to generate enough shifting-related paranormal phenomena to leave footprints or hairs.

If there is some physical evidence, always suspect berserker powers or other shifting-related paranormal phenomena first. Compare the details of it to the details of berserker phenomena and other shifting-related paranormal phenomena. If you find a close match of characteristics, don't suspect physical shifting. It is easy to get quasi-physical effects from advanced berserker powers. One of the classic mistakes Westerners make when dealing with magic is to try to divide everything into "real" and "not real," "physical" and "not physical," "mundane" and "supernatural." In reality, there is a continuum from one to the other; the two categories are intertwined. Many paranormal events combine the fully and the quasi-physical, straddling the borderland between them and producing effects that Westerners are unable to place squarely within either category. This baffles them and often causes them to try to discount the paranormal experiences altogether. Non-Western cultures are more in tune with the reality of how the supernatural operates, however, and they know that these phenomena straddle the borderland and produce results that have some characteristics of the fully real and some of the fully ethereal.

Compare your experience to the typical symptoms and side-effects of physical shifting and/or bilocation shifting (whichever is more appropriate for the experience that you had). If you experienced typical physical-shifter symptoms and side effects, then suspect physical shifting rather than lesser paranormal phenomena. Check your body. While you were "changed," did you look down at it? What did it look like? Did you look at yourself in a mirror? Did you feel, lick, or touch your own body? If you simply "felt" an animal body around you in incredibly clear detail, but did not look at or touch it, then suspect a very clearly felt "phantom animal body," instead of physical shifting.

Even though some paranormal phenomena imitate the characteristics of physical shifting, it is fairly easy to tell the difference. Those confused are usually those who want to believe that their dimly remembered trance experiences were really physical shifting. Real physical shifting is quite dramatic. Once you have experienced it, you are generally quite sure that it truly happened.

CHAPTER 6

About Shifters

I n previous chapters, I defined shifters as people who actually "become" an animal through astral shifting, mental shifting, dream shifting, apparition shifting, physical shifting, or some other type of shift. Shifters also have additional defining characteristics. For instance, many people can induce an experience of astral shifting by following certain techniques during meditation.[1] This does not mean, however, that they are true shifters. They have merely experienced a part of the magic of shapeshifting. The astral body shapeshifts very easily, and many who are not shifters can experience astral shifts.

True shifters must enter a condition where the animal side (which in normal people stays deep within the subconscious) simmers on the surface of the subconscious, cannot be banished for long, and rises to the surface on its own every so often. Shifters have a strong, and usually permanent,

---

[1] Some very good instructions for how anyone can experience an astral shift are included in Felicitas D. Goodman, *Where the Spirits Ride the Wind* (Bloomington & Indianapolis: Indiana University Press, 1990) pp. 128–140.

connection to the animal within. In shifters, the inner animal is not merely something that they are able to invoke sometimes; it has become a part
of them and tends to invoke itself. All shifters also have a second etheric
body in the form of an animal that manifests in various ways, such as in
feelings of "phantom limbs." Shifters experience shifting energy.

There are two ways that people become shifters. They may be born
with a strong potential to develop these abilities and simply do, in a way
similar to people who have hereditary psychic abilities. In other cases, they
learn to become shifters and invoke their inner animal into permanent
wakefulness through their own efforts. Both of these methods appear in
legend. Every primitive or native culture reports two types of werebeasts:
the natural type (usually hereditary) and the artificial type (induced by
magical practices). It is only in the doctrine produced by the church in the
Middle Ages that this view was contradicted. In *The Beast Within: A
History of the Werewolf*, Adam Douglas states:

> The present day Banyang . . . have a rich and complicated belief
> in a variety of were-animals, which they call *babu*. Although the
> Banyang occasionally report seeing actual physical transforma-
> tions of humans into animals . . . most hold a much more spir-
> itual notion of what a were-animal is. Among the Banyang,
> someone is said to "own" a were-animal. The property is envis-
> aged as a spirit-double of that person, capable of being sent out
> at night. . . .[2]

This is the notion of werebeasts encountered in just about every primitive
or native culture. It is also very close to the view held by modern shifters,
even those who have never dug deeply enough to uncover the folklore
behind medieval werewolf trials. Modern shifters hold a very different
view of themselves than that portrayed in Western cinema, or in treatises
on lycanthropy written by Christian theologians or modern psychologists.

Both modern shifters and native societies, such as the Banyang, view
physical transformations as part of being a shifter. More important, and

---

[2] Adam Douglas, *The Beast Within* (London: Chapmans, 1992), p. 21.

more pervasive, however, are the non-physical qualities intrinsic to being a shifter. Being a shifter is dependent upon having a spirit-double in the form of an animal—possessing an animal's spiritual essence, as well as a second etheric body in the form of an animal. This "spirit-double" manifests in various ways, such as being clearly felt as a "phantom body."

Speaking of the Banyang, Adam Douglas states:

> Opinions differ as to how the were-animal is to be acquired in the first place: usually it is said to be passed on from parent to child; others state that were-animals can be purchased, or that special herbal medicines must be prepared before the were-animal can be assimilated.[3]

This is the view held by most native societies, as well as by modern shifters. In medieval legend, shifting was frequently thought to be hereditary, even though the church tried very hard to get people to believe that lycanthropy was brought on only by making a deliberate pact with the devil.

The notion that lycanthropy is hereditary is found in every culture. The Greeks believed the family of Antœi, from Arcadia, to be full of shapeshifters.[4] The town of Blois in France was supposed to have more werewolves than any other town, so that anyone who had a last name associated with hereditary lycanthropy, and who also lived in Blois, was simply assumed to be a werewolf by everyone else.[5] There are also supposed to be shapeshifters from the hereditary line of Vaudois.[6]

Legend tells of entire clans that were riddled with hereditary shapeshifters. One of the most famous is the Neuri, a nomadic people who lived in the area that is now Poland and Lithuania, around the river Bug. It is no coincidence that this area of Poland and Lithuania, long after the disappearance of the Neuri, is one of the areas in Europe where shapeshifting folklore is most common.

---

[3] Adam Douglas, *The Beast Within*, p. 21.
[4] Montague Summers, *The Werewolf* (Secaucus, NJ: Citadel Press, 1973), pp. 138–139.
[5] Elliot O'Donnell, *Werewolves* (Hertfordshire, England: Oracle Publishing, 1996), p. 128.
[6] Elliot O'Donnell, *Werewolves*, p. 128.

It is ridiculous to assert, as the church did, that all werebeasts are evil. Just about every native culture holds the belief that werebeasts can be good or evil. The modern stereotype of a ravening beast driven by a bloodlust for human flesh is entirely untrue. Even in the few cases where werebeasts have killed people, they were usually deliberately planned killings of the werebeast's enemies, not "helpless bloodlust" killings of the kind portrayed in modern movies and novels. Adam Douglas says:

> Were-animals of the Banyang are not regarded as uniformly evil. Different were-animals are understood to have different potentials for good or evil. Nevertheless, the owner of a were-animal may find himself in difficulties even when his were-animal is not consciously used by him for malign or selfish purposes.[7]

This view is more in line with the actual events of werebeast folklore than with the church doctrine and the later stereotypes. Werebeasts were rarely evil, but often got into trouble. They were commonly suspected of killing livestock, using their abilities to steal things, spying on people, or frightening them.

Modern ideas about werebeasts tend to focus only on the physical shifter, perhaps because of modern movies and novels. Folklore includes many of the other types of phenomena, however, that are also associated with the modern shifter. There is quite a lot of folklore about bilocation and mental shifters. Perhaps the best example of this is the Scandinavian berserker, but there are many others. From many different cultures and places, we have descriptions of mental shifters compelled to spend time wandering in the woods at night. In urban areas, they hung out in graveyards, because graveyards were the only semi-wild place available. The ancients tell us mental shifters may be recognized by their eyes, which develop something of a wolfish look, along with keen night vision and a sensitivity to normal daylight. Their thirst is great, and so is their appetite. They often have many scratches on their legs from running through the bushes in the dark.

---

[7] Adam Douglas, *The Beast Within*, p. 21.

Descriptions of actual modern mental shifters (not the examples of "clinical lycanthropes" that modern psychiatry likes to hold up, who are merely insane people) from modern folklore support this. In her investigations into the weredolphin folklore of Brazil, Candace Slater found similar traits assigned to people who were slowly being converted into weredolphins, but who had not yet started transforming. They were struck by strange cravings; they ate enormous amounts of food, especially raw fish. The urges came upon them most strongly at night, when they were apt to wander. They developed a strong desire to go down to the river at night.[8]

Folklore also includes references to astral shifting. Many of these take the form of shamanic "journeys to the spirit world," but in animal form. We don't hear much about these in medieval folklore, probably because we hear so few accounts from the werewolf's point of view, and only the werewolves themselves would know about such spirit-journeys in animal shape. However, we still have folklore about astral shifting, especially the cases recorded in anthropologist's records of the beliefs of modern tribal peoples.

There is one particularly famous case of astral shifting. This was part of the confession of an accused werewolf named Theiss, in the town of Jürgensburg in Livonia in the year 1692.[9] This case was particularly famous because, as in many Eastern European werewolf beliefs, the werewolf depicted had characteristics very different from the werewolf stereotype that had been built up by that time. The inquisition tried to get Theiss to confess to the standard devil-worshipping foolishness, but he refused to do so, and astounded his accusers with very convincing defense that werewolfism was a good thing. Theiss called werewolves "the dogs of God" and claimed that they fought against witches and demons in battles

---

[8] Candace Slater describes a woman in danger of becoming a weredolphin: "Often, her skin will develop a peculiar, soapy texture, and a pronounced fishy smell, and she will display an inexplicable desire to go down to the riverbank." *Dance of the Dolphin* (Chicago: University of Chicago Press, 1994), p. 96.

[9] Livonia, though having few famous werewolf trials, is very much the center of werewolf folklore in Europe, having many more cases than places like France. Therefore, Livonia's view of werewolves and the views of Theiss are probably much closer to what a real shifter truly is.

conducted during spirit-journeys.[10] Nor was Theiss the only Livonian werewolf making such claims of both shamanic spirit journeys for the good of the people and of werewolves being on the side of good. This appears again and again in Livonian werewolf legends.[11]

ASIAN TRADITION

Skinwalking is also mentioned in folklore. Some cultures even have references to shifting energy and how it works. In Europe, the people telling werebeast legends didn't understand the phenomenon, but in Asia, most people understood that shifting was linked with *chi*, and that energy had to be built up and assimilated before one could become a physical shifter. Asian legend outlines ways to become a shifter with much more understanding than is generally found in European legends. Doctors of herbal medicine, particularly if old and wise, were said to have enough wisdom and knowledge to become physical shifters themselves.

Various "illegal" (bad karma) ways of building this energy were outlined in legend, such as the shapeshifting maidens who waylaid Samurai knights for sexual encounters in the forest. Using their esoteric knowledge, at the moment of the Samurai's orgasm, they stole all of his considerable *chi* and, to his horror, started transforming on the spot. The Samurai suddenly found himself clasping a furry woman, changing more and more, even as he watched and struggled to disengage himself.

Modern Asians know much more of the truth of shifting and how it operates than most Westerners. I was surprised at the amount of knowledge some Chinese-American friends had on the subject of *kitsune*. They described the *kitsune*'s state as being intertwined with both destiny and

---

[10] Adam Douglas tells us "Theiss said that he and the other Livonian and Russian werewolves, both male and female, went out on three nights of the year, on St. Lucy's night before Christmas, on St. John's night, and on the night of the Pentecost, and . . . battled with the devil and sorcerers . . ." Later, he describes how "Theiss regards himself as something of a shamanic figure: he travels in animal-shape to the other world . . ." *The Beast Within*, pp. 151–152, 154.

[11] Douglas gives the case of a werewolf imprisoned at Riga in the 16th century, and cites the Livonian treatise on lycanthropy written by Gaspar Peucer, which also mentions werewolves fighting against evil sorcerers. *The Beast Within*, pp. 152–153.

with the flow of *chi*. I did not expect ordinary, modern Chinese-Americans to know so much about the subject. I thought their people had forgotten about those old legends by now, just as Westerners have.

THE DEMOGRAPHICS OF SHAPESHIFTING

People with "animal medicine" are abundant, shifters are more rare. I estimate that there are approximately fifty people with animal medicine for every shifter. Sometimes people with animal medicine develop into shifters, but this is rare unless they seek it. The vast majority of shifters are mental shifters who experience an occasional dream shift or astral shift. I estimate that less than half of all mental shifters also have berserker powers, although many have experienced rare one-time occurrences of such powers. A few shifters sense shift or possession shift. Very few can physically shift, bilocation shift, or apparition shift.

Bilocation shifters may be more common than I believe, since many shifters have had one or two experiences that sound like bilocation shifting. There is, however, no evidence to prove whether these were truly bilocation shiftings or merely astral shiftings, vivid visions, or even etheric projections of a ghostly animal body. I prefer to err on the side of skepticism, so I count bilocation shifters as those few who have substantial evidence and who could prove their cases. It is entirely possible, however, that many of the others may be bilocation shifters as well.

It is also possible that physical shifters are more common than I think, but for a different reason. Physical shifters tend to be quiet about their abilities. In most cases, they tell only trusted friends.

Some believe that nearly every mental shifter eventually becomes a physical shifter, given enough time. This doctrine holds that all of us will eventually "mature" into physical shifters, even if this occurs many years after our first mental shift. I believe this is wrong, because there are many accounts of mental shifters who never developed into physical shifters, such as the Norse berserkers.

I estimate somewhere between 75 and 80 percent of all shifters that I've known are wolf shifters. Cat shifters are the second most common, and they may be even more common than I believe, because they are more solitary and secretive, joining packs less often, staying quiet about themselves. Bear shifters are the third most common, but they also tend to a solitary lifestyle, and so may be more common than I've observed. The fourth most common are the fox shifters, although most fox shifters are in transition and soon mature into some other species. Whatever their relative numbers, the wolf, bear, fox, and cat are definitely the top four species in modern shifters. After them, various kinds of bird shifters seem to be most common. It is hard to tell what species is most common after bird shifters, although there are certainly a great variety of species beyond that.

Race, Gender, and Ethnicity in Shapeshifting

In most movies and novels, werewolves are depicted as white males. Females and other races hardly ever appear as werewolves in fiction. This is not at all like shifters in real life. In fact, more shifters are female. This is also consistent with shapeshifting folklore. There is more folklore about female shapeshifters than about males. The most violent legends, however, almost always concern males. Since compilations of werewolf folklore spend most of their time discussing the most violent cases, we get the impression that werewolves are male. This perception dominates Western ideas about werewolves, generating a perception of the werewolf as a nasty, beastlike, and violent male. There have been some very famous, though misled, anthropological theories about "why all the werewolves were male and the witches were female."

The most famous violent werewolf cases were reported in France, and French folkwisdom claims that all werewolves are male. However, there are a few famous female French werewolves, such as Clauda Gaillard and Perenette Gandillon. Moreover, if we research more deeply, a curious fact comes to light. French folklore reports two separate categories of "people who periodically turn into wolves." One is the *loup-garou*, the "werewolf"—usually violent, almost always male, and associated with a peculiar type of werewolf cult unique to France. The other is the *lupin*[12] (also

---

[12] Montague Summers, *The Werewolf*, p. 237.

sometimes spelled "lubin")—usually female, usually hereditary in origin, and known for their cowardice and timidity. Lupins were always crying, and ran away from any human who happened to see them in their transformed state. Most influential werewolf literature ignores the lupin, and concentrates on the loup-garou.

In Portugal, on the other hand, almost all werewolves were female. Interestingly, whenever a culture believes werewolves to be female, werewolf legends almost entirely concern benevolent werewolves. Whether someone becomes a shifter or not is partially dependent on the same sort of sensitivity and reactions to the paranormal world that makes many women into psychics, sensitives, or witches. The female is closer to the cycles of Earth and Moon, and every type of paranormal current. Just as there are more female psychics, faith healers, and witches, there are more female shifters. Cultures that have traditionally had more male shapeshifters are also those with extensive werewolf cults that barred female membership, such as the werejaguar societies of South America. Even in these cultures, however, where folk wisdom credits werewolves with being male, there are always a few legends involving female shapeshifters—and always a small number of hereditary shapeshifters.

Of the hereditary shifters that I have known or heard of in America, almost all fit into three major ethnic categories. The most common is the American Indian. Many hereditary shifters have a parent or grandparent who is part or fully Native American. In one case of a hereditary wolf shifter, the person discovered he was a shifter long before he discovered that he was adopted, and part Native American. Furthermore, his Native American relatives had chosen the last name of "Wolf" for themselves, back in the days when the American government was trying to force last names on all the Native Americans.

The second most common ethnic category is Caucasian, and especially Scandinavian. Historically, Scandinavia has had an usually large number of shifters. Scandinavians have retained their hereditary ability to produce unusually large numbers of shifters, even to the present day.

The third ethnic category is Asian, or part Asian. A lot of shifters have Oriental ancestry. It should be remembered that the Orient has traditionally generated quite a bit of shapeshifting folklore, as well as a better understanding, on average, of the phenomena involved. It should also be remembered that China and Japan are unique in that werefoxes outnumber all other species, including werewolves. To become a physical shifter while still in the fox stage is rare. This implies that Asians must have great shifting knowledge in order to accelerate the development to this point.

There are also a fair number of Hispanic shifters. Historically, Spain was the area in Europe with lowest incidence of werewolf legends, but most Hispanics in the Americas have some American Indian ancestry. I have also known a few African American shifters, but not very many. I think it is likely that there are many more (after all, Africa is full of shapeshifting legends, even today), but that they just don't frequent the packs with which I've had contact.

Contrary to movie stereotypes (even the movies know that Eastern Europe is a hotbed of werewolf folklore), I have known very few American shifters of Eastern European origin. It is true that there is a great concentration of werewolf legends in that area, and probably a great deal of hereditary potential. Perhaps few people from that area emigrated to the United States, or perhaps they just don't frequent the packs with which I am familiar.

Despite these racial and ethnic patterns, a person of any race can be a hereditary shifter. After all, there is no race, no people, that is entirely devoid of shapeshifting folklore. And, of course, artificial shifters can be of any race as well.

Whites are the race with the least potential for hereditary shifting. Europe has the lowest concentration of shapeshifting folklore in the world. England, Spain, and France have relatively little, with shapeshifting folklore concentrated mostly around the edges of Europe—Portugal, Ireland, Scandinavia, Eastern Europe, Wales, and Greece. Even when shapeshifting folklore appears in England, France, or Spain, it often involved people of different ethnic origins, such as Gypsies or Celts. Thus it is no wonder that the Western world has developed a skewed view of what shapeshifters are and what they stand for.

PHYSICAL CHARACTERISTICS OF SHIFTERS

Shifters tend to have a number of unusual physical characteristics, such as strange eye color. The most common eye colors in shifters are blue and green—brilliant or unusual shades of those colors. There are many shifters who have unusual eye colors, such as hazel, gray, black, and yellowish- or reddish-brown. Shifters are often described as having a strange "look" to their eyes, hard to describe, yet distinctive and easy to pick out once you've seen it a dozen times. This odd "look" is mentioned in countless legends. Sometimes the eyes are unusual in more concrete, definable ways, as in the Welsh legend of a weresnake whose eyes were sometimes blue, sometimes gray, and sometimes green, and always with a peculiar sparkle to them.[13]

It is very common for shifters' hair or eyes to permanently change color at puberty. Shifters often have eyebrows that meet in the middle, or eyebrows of strange shape, as many legends relate. Some are born with these eyebrows, while others develop them very slowly over time. Shifters may have long ring fingers, so that the ring and middle fingers are of the same length, a characteristic that is also related in many legends. Similarly, wolves and cats sometimes have middle toes the same length as the fourth toe.

Many wolf shifters start to go gray at a young age. This is not premature aging, just a graying of the hair. Since most wolves have gray fur, this, like many shifter characteristics, makes their human bodies just a wee bit more wolflike. Wolf shifters are not usually the well-muscled "supermen" described in so many werewolf novels. They tend to have a typical body type—lean, long-limbed, loose-jointed, and scrawny looking, like a wolf. This body type is described in many legends.

Other species of shifter also have their own characteristic look and body type. Hereditary shifters are most often born with these body types, while artificial shifters tend to slowly develop them over time, although they may never change much. Legend relates that, especially over time, the animal form often left its mark on the human form in subtle ways. In Asia,

---

[13] Frank Hamel, *Human Animals*, p. 175.

werebadgers were recognized by their very long torsos, small reddish eyes, skinny long limbs, and the bell-like tone of their voices. Werefoxes were recognized by their large eyes, rounded ears, high cheekbones, and wide mouths.[14]

Bear shifters are often large, stocky, broad-limbed people, often muscular or fat. Fox shifters, at least those that are permanent fox shifters, and not just moving through this phase to another species, are small, short people, frequently even scrawnier than wolf shifters. Cat shifters tend to have a "gymnast" look about them. Many are fairly muscular, though not "stocky," so much as lean and muscular. They often have large eyes. Bird shifters frequently have a distinctive hook-shaped nose.

Female shifters, especially those with high shifting energy, tend to have menstrual periods that are light, and the cycle may be longer than one month. This is an example of how their bodies become slightly more like an animal's. Most animals don't menstruate, and the female reproductive cycle of most species is longer than a month.

One misperception about shifters is that they are very hairy. This is not generally true. The only shifters I have known who were hairy were those who strongly identified with their hair as a substitute for fur, who were always wishing they had more of it. These hairy shifters became more and more hairy over the years, almost as if their minds were influencing their bodies. It is true, however, that shifters often have one or two very small patches of hair growing in odd places. Legends also relate this, some claiming that werewolves have patches of hair on the palms of their hands, and many other strange places, even on the underside of the tongue!

In a few cases, I've found shifters with even more odd physical appearances. An extremely small number of shifters have characteristics such as fangs, yellow eyes, pointed ears, or small, stubby tails. In most of these cases, the characteristic was inherited, and all other family members that had it were also shifters, neatly marking them all.

---

[14] Frank Hamel, *Human Animals*, p. 100.

In one case, I came across a man with yellow eyes and fangs whose grandmother had them as well. It was part of his family lore that this characteristic showed up every so often and was known as "the mark of the coyote." Nor was this just a fluke mutation. There was something paranormal about it. This man got his fangs filed off to look like normal teeth, but they eventually grew back. He had to keep switching dentists, because, after a while, the dentist got suspicious. In a few of these cases of extremely odd physical characteristics, the shifter was not born with the characteristic, but developed it very slowly over years. Some also claim that they came upon these characteristics suddenly, as the result of a physical shift gone wrong.

Many shifters have some slightly unusual physical characteristics. The weirder characteristics are more rare. Average shifters have no discernible traits that mark them as "werewolves." Nevertheless, many shifters have a thousand tiny things about them that distinguish them. Shifters often have an "aura" of "something weird" that even normal people can sense somewhat. Many have a certain look to their faces that is hard to describe, perhaps not stemming from outstanding characteristics, yet very easy to recognize once noticed.

Shifters often look much younger than they actually are, because they are full of *chi* and shifting energy and vitality. When psychics "scan" a shifter, especially a physical shifter, they rarely figure out that the person is a werewolf, but they always describe the person as a big ball of energy. This "high energy" sometimes generates other weird, even somewhat paranormal, side effects. Some shifters frequently have TVs, computers, and radios mysteriously misbehave or even black out when they get near them. Electricity seems to be attracted to some shifters. Many have received severe shocks from stray voltage. Many shifters with high shifting energy are storehouses of static electricity, frequently giving or receiving painful shocks to people or just about anything they touch. An unusually high percentage of shifters have been struck by lightning.

Behavioral Characteristics of Shifters

Shifters also have behavioral characteristics in common. They seldom live completely within the mainstream of human society. They can never quite conform to the popular crowd, and, even if they can, they often choose not to do so. Shifters find the social rat race is meaningless and empty. This does not mean that they don't have friends. They often have lots of friends, but they are rarely "in" with the "in" crowd. There is always an invisible boundary between shifters and non-shifters. Shifters are in the human world, but can never be completely part of it. They always have one foot in the animal kingdom, but they can never be completely part of that either.

Shifters have a different body language from that of normal humans. They often find themselves using mannerisms that are similar to the body language of their species. These mannerisms are almost always present in a hereditary shifter from very early childhood. They don't replace the human mannerisms—rather both sets of mannerisms are used. Humans often misinterpret is body language. These "hybrid" mannerisms show up in dozens of subtle ways. Since earliest childhood, I've had the tendency to bite off food, such as carrots or very tough meat, with the teeth at the side of my mouth, far in the back, instead of using my front teeth, as most people do. My mother constantly told me this was bad table manners and tried to correct me. I honestly tried to develop a habit of biting things off with my front teeth, but it never felt "right." In fact, I was well into my adulthood before I conquered this persistent habit. I never associated it with being a wolf shifter until many years later, when I read in books that wolves always shear off tough meat by biting with their specialized side teeth. The animal shows through many subtle ways like this, even when shifters themselves don't associate the habit with "being an animal."

In shifters, perhaps the most common overlapping body language is the human smile and the animal showing of teeth. Humans smile, showing their teeth, in happiness. Animals show their teeth when upset, frightened, or angry. Shifters do both. When I am happy, a smile comes to my face as a natural expression. When I'm very upset or angry, I show my teeth. Smiling is accompanied by a happy expression in the rest of my face. When I show my teeth, it looks very similar to a smile, but is subtly different in the way my lips are held, and how the smile combines with the upset expression in the rest of my face. It has always mystified me that normal people can't tell the difference.

Nearly every shifter has had this experience. I have tried for years to suppress showing my teeth entirely. I have largely succeeded, but when I am upset enough, it still happens. It is as difficult to suppress as any other natural facial expression.

Showing my teeth in a situation when smiling would be inappropriate causes difficulties. People think I am "smiling" on purpose, which makes them suspect me of some strange motive. Showing my teeth during a nasty argument with a friend makes the friend think that I'm making fun of him or her, or that I am enjoying the argument. Once, on learning of the tragic death of a friend, I was very upset and cried while showing my teeth. Despite the fact that it was evident I wasn't happy, my friends still wondered why I was smiling. It is clear why werewolves have always frightened people and earned bad reputations. Shifters are subject to the same fears and prejudices. They are always inadvertently causing misunderstandings that breed suspicion and mistrust.

Shifters have many other mannerisms reminiscent of their animal heritage. They often walk with a peculiar, animalistic grace, sometimes so pronounced that all their friends talk about it. Many wolf shifters have a long "loping" stride, reminding people more of wild panthers than canines. Those shifters with high shifting energy often find themselves walking digitigrade (without their heels touching the ground). Shifters tend to have average or better than average eyesight, though there are still nearsighted shifters, especially among bear and wolf shifters. These individuals depend on and notice their other senses much more, however, even if they are not among those shifters with "heightened senses." Some shifters tend to touch or brush lightly against objects as they pass. This makes them appear somewhat vision-impaired, but they are not. It simply reflects an instinctive desire to have a tactile knowledge of their environment, not just a sight-based knowledge. This is similar to the way animals use whiskers and also often brush against objects. Many hereditary shifters have had this mannerism since early childhood, and have been scolded by their mothers for getting their clothes dirty by brushing against things, or for constantly touching "germy" surfaces.

Shifters often find sitting unnatural. Most hereditary shifters are more comfortable when crouching on chairs or sitting on the floor. Once, I stayed with cousins who were fanatical about not letting anyone put their feet on a chair because that would make it dirty, even if the feet were recently cleaned and clad in clean socks. I had never before paid much attention to my habit of crouching on chairs, but at the end of some weeks I could hardly believe how miserable this was making me. The worst of it was that I was not even allowed to sit on the floor, because it would make me dirty. Shifters are often happier sitting on the floor than in chairs. Many enjoy sleeping on the floor. Many have, from earliest childhood, slept curled up in a ball, as animals do. Many even turn around three times before going to sleep. I myself go to sleep stretched out, like ordinary people, but when I wake up, I'm curled up in a ball, just like a cat or dog. This has been going on since infancy, since long before I had any inkling that I was a shifter.

Shifters have a tendency not to talk much. Instead, they do a lot of nonverbal communicating, using body language, gestures, and expressive noises, like happy sighs, grumpy "hhhrrrrumpfs," and thoughtful or questioning "hmmmmms." Shifters are also more likely to hum or sing softly to themselves, especially when alone, just to express their moods. Nonverbal communication is very important to shifters, as it is to animals. Contrary to stereotypes, shifters don't go around howling, barking, or growling, at least not when they know other people are around, except during very deep mental shifts or during rare moments of extremely strong emotion. I have heard stories of shifters who lost control and growled at muggers, even though they did not make animal noises in their everyday life.

Many shifters find themselves strangely attracted to strong, nasty smells, such as skunk or rotten meat, even while their human sides are repelled. If wolves find a nasty smell, they roll in it until they smell just as bad. Shifters also have unusually sensitive necks and are unusually aware of anyone touching their necks. It is often uncomfortable or even frightening for them to be touched on the neck, unless they deeply trust whoever is doing it. This is because the neck is the place that an enemy or predator tries to bite, to most easily kill an animal. All animals have evolved a deep and instinctive desire to protect their necks. Humans seem to have lost this instinctive fear, but shifters retain it. It can be difficult for shifters to convince their girlfriends or boyfriends that nothing is wrong, when they get nervous while "necking." Many also become nervous if anyone touches them while they are eating, and many eat quickly, bolting their food.

Shifters age at the normal human rate and enjoy a normal lifespan. Part of them, however, feels that they should age at the animal rate. For most species, this would mean reaching old age at the age of 8 or so. Hereditary shifters often feel very mature and adult at 5, and feel very old by age 8 or 10. Many feel ancient beyond belief when in their teens. This being "out of sync" with other kids is something that hereditary shifters go through, and it causes anguish and loneliness in childhood. Shifters are also unusually affected by the aging and death of pets.

In many novels and movies, animals are terrified of shifters. This is far from the truth. Animals often have strong reactions to a shifter who is about to shift, or who is manifesting phantom limbs, because there is a strong current of paranormal energy playing about the shifter at these times. This can disturb animals in much the same way that even a friendly ghost can, or in the way that excessively loud sounds can disturb them. It is also true that cats fear wolf shifters who are manifesting a lot of wolf nature, while dogs fear tiger shifters, and other big cats who manifest a lot of feline nature. On the whole, however, shifters are animal magnets. Most animals like them a lot; they are unusually successful in getting strange or even wild animals to like them.

Shifters are likely to be unusually aware of wildlife. Many glimpse animals hiding in the grass every day. Normal people may go weeks or months without seeing mice. Shifters are likely to see raccoons at the edge of the yard late at night, or deer slipping into the woods on the next hill, or a dozen different things that are usually well hidden by the time normal people finally look at the right place. Shifters often feel as if normal people are walking around half-numb and barely aware of their surroundings.

HEIGHTENED SENSES

Shifters often enjoy heightened senses. When a shifter with low shifting energy experiences heightened senses, it often happens in conjunction with mental shifts, but it can also happen independently of any shift. In shifters with high shifting energy, heightened senses can be present most of the time, although they may also come and go, or get much stronger during mental shifts.

Heightened smell is the most commonly reported heightened sense. Shifters are very disturbed by smoke; amazingly few are smokers. Many will drop friends who smoke, just because the smoke makes them uncomfortable. A few with high shifting energy can distinguish people by smell, even blindfolded, and can occasionally follow scent trails that are only a minute old.

When I was a teenager, and had the high levels of shifting energy associated with teenage shifters, my friends talked about how I always knew when they sneaked up behind me, and knew who it was without turning around. I could smell them when they came within a few feet of me, and could identify them by their individual smell. I never told them how I knew. It wouldn't have done any good, because they wouldn't have believed my sense of smell was that good, and would have been terribly offended if I had said, "I can smell you coming."

Heightened hearing is also reported—not only hearing well, but hearing into the ultrasonic and subsonic ranges. Many of these phenomena can be attributed simply to a heightened awareness of the senses we already have. It is amazing how modern humans ignore their senses, almost as if they prefer to be partially deaf and blind. Some heightened awareness can be attributed to hearing, seeing, or smelling partially through etheric animal ears, eyes, or noses. For example, when you hear extremely high-pitched noises that only other shifters hear, you may notice that the sound is slightly "tinny," or sounds far away. This is a hall-mark of something heard with the etheric ear. Clairaudience and sounds heard during etheric travel often have these qualities. In this case, it comes from hearing partially with animal etheric ears.

I also believe that, in some cases, the inner ear physically becomes a little more wolflike over time, and can physically hear higher-pitched nois-es than the normal human ear. Televisions, computers, high-voltage lines, and many machines can make very annoying high-pitched noises. In one case, a wolf shifter who was an electrical engineer was miserable at his job because of an electrical component that made loud noises so high in pitch his coworkers couldn't hear it. Since he was somewhat skeptical about his own "werewolf" nature, he brought in sound equipment to verify that the noise existed. It did exist, but had a high decibel level. He fixed the prob-lem by replacing the component with one that didn't make the noise. I have heard that other shifters have used sound equipment to verify the existence of the high-pitched noises. Some can hear the devices that send out high-pitched sounds to drive away rodents and cockroaches. I know shifters who won't patronize certain stores that use these devices.

SHIFTING ENERGY

Shifting energy is the basic underlying component in most shifting phe-nomena. All shifters have shifting energy, even if they don't know quite what it is. Shifting energy is similar in "feel" to the energy we call chi or prana, but it relates specifically to shifting. Sometimes shifts "burn off" shifting energy, so that you have to build it up again before another shift. Sometimes a shift leaves you at the same level as before the shift. One way to help avoid "burning off" your energy is to avoid shifting too often. Most shifters build up shifting energy slowly with time, storing large quantities of it through activities like "prowling." Most can fully recharge themselves from even a great depletion within a month or two.

Shifters characteristically have huge appetites. It takes a lot of food, especially protein, to maintain shifting energy and the animal etheric body. The etheric body is partially of this physical world and needs some physical nourishment. Shifters often consume appalling amounts of food without gaining weight.[15] They also have a deep thirst,[16] particularly right after any mental shift. I myself have drunk about two gallons of water a day since my early teens. Shifters who are unable to get as much food as they want generally see their shifting energy decrease. This is useful, because if you want your shifting energy to decrease, eating less is one of the surest ways to achieve this, although you should be careful not to overdo and cross the border into anorexia. This shifting-related appetite is usually referred to as "the hunger" by shifters. "The hunger" fluctuates with the phase of the Moon, usually reaching its peak around the Full Moon.

High shifting energy will usually cause regular mental or astral shifts. High shifting energy may cause mental shifts accompanied by strange effects that border on physical shifting (such as eye-color changes), or it may cause various paranormal nonshifting side effects. If all other conditions are right, high shifting energy may also cause physical shifts, but that is more rare. High shifting energy feels much like regular shifting energy, but is more intense. It often feels as if every cell in your body is trying to stretch and change. It feels like heat, like itching, like pressure. It can feel as if your body is going to explode if it doesn't physically change. Despite this, however, nothing bad will happen. It can be very frustrating and can get you worked up, but it does you no actual harm.

With high shifting energy, when the energy reaches its peak in the cycle, usually near a Full Moon, it can vividly feel as if tiny worms are wriggling just underneath the surface of your skin. This feeling is often accompanied by the most curious involuntary twitching and writhing of

---

[15] This characteristic of modern shifters is also found in many legends, as in the legend of the "varou" of Guernsey: "The 'Varou', now almost entirely forgotten . . . is allied to the 'Loup-Garou' of the French, and the 'Were-Wolf' of the English, if, indeed, he is not absolutely identical with them. He is believed to be endowed with a marvellous [sic] appetite, and it is still proverbially said of a great eater 'Il mange comme un varou'." Montague Summers, *The Werewolf*, p. 204.

[16] The prodigious thirst of shifters is mentioned in many of the legends as well, particularly in the legends of mental shifters. There is also some lore that somewhat contradicts this, by saying that werewolves are scared to death of water and will not go near it, and cannot shed tears, but I believe these are old-wives tales that are confusing witch lore (witches are said to fear water and are unable to shed tears) with werewolf lore—particularly since very many legends strongly associate werewolves with water, especially in transformations while swimming.

the skin, as if something underneath were pushing it. Some shifters say that this is caused by fur trying to grow, and marks the beginning of a physical change. If werewolves experienced this, and if they saw fur pushing out of or sliding back in their skin during physical changes, it is no wonder that a superstition arose that werewolves had fur on the underside of their skin. Many superstitious peasants have dissected werewolves trying to find this fur, but none has ever been found.[17] This fur is etheric and temporary in nature, and does not exist in the human form except during a change.

Some shifters learn how to consciously reach out at will and affect their own shifting energy and the shifting energy of others. These shifters are often called "catalysts," and can force a mental shift in almost any other shifter. Those who are good at it can help inexperienced shifters with their mental shifts. The catalyst plays an important role in a pack, and can determine how fast and far pack members progress in their development. From studying shapeshifting legends, I believe that catalysts played a major role in ancient packs of physical shifters, and were able to accelerate a shifter's development much more than modern catalysts, as well as reverse the development of pack members who were deemed "unworthy." If this is true, it is yet another reason why there were so many physical shifters in former times, and so few now.

When two or more shifters get together, everyone's shifting energy interacts and augments through an involuntary catalytic action. This is one of the reasons why shifters tend to gather in packs. Legends from the Middle Ages suggest that some werewolves could not physically change except when with their pack, probably because they could not generate enough shifting energy alone, or could not manipulate it well enough to cause a physical shift. The interaction of shifting energy when shifters get together can cause some strange effects, however. Some stories tell of shifters who have never been around other shifters, and who go to a large gathering of shifters for the first time and are suddenly thrown into an intense brief, mental shift, sometimes howling involuntarily.

---

[17] As in the case of the lycanthrope of Pavia, in Montague Summers, *The Werewolf*, pp. 160–161.

Even the presence of just one other shifter can have a disconcerting effect. Once, I was waiting on a long line in a public place. I noticed a man very close to me in line who was giving off strong cat shifter "vibes." I decided to watch him, and perhaps talk to him to see if I could pick up any clues as to whether my perception was right. In this case, I got much more than I expected. I could feel my own shifting energy interacting with his the whole time, increasing his energy significantly, mine just a little. I noticed he had striking green eyes that, as I watched him, slowly turned from green to green-brown and finally lightened to a pale gray with no trace of green. During this time, he became more and more restless and showed other signs of fighting a mental shift. His friend kept asking him what was wrong, and he kept giving noncommittal answers. I have no idea why I affected him so much, I can only speculate that maybe he was close to a mental shift anyway, and my presence just pushed him over the edge.

HEREDITARY AND NATURAL SHIFTERS

What is it like to be a shifter; living in a modern society that doesn't believe in shifters? If you are a shifter, you already know. For the rest, imagine that you are a member of a group that is generally unaccepted in society, such as gay people. Now imagine that you are back in the 1950s; this is not only unacceptable, but really shocking and seen as a form of mental illness. Little information is available on your condition, and you are confused, or frightened, or even ashamed about it.

Through life experience, however, you come to understand that, contrary to the official view, you are not evil. In fact, you are truly healthy when you make peace with yourself and embrace your true nature. Even though society thinks differently, you also come to understand that your "condition" is a part of you, something that can't be "cured." You also find that you are not limited merely to the action that society considers your "defining feature" (such as physical shifting for shifters, or homosexual sex for gays), but rather that you are part of a lifestyle, a way of being that is intertwined with all that you do in subtle ways. Shifting is not something you do, it is who you are.

Just as people can be gay in every fiber of their being, and yet never have experienced homosexual sex, they can be werewolves in every fiber of their being, right down to the roots of their souls, and never have experienced a physical transformation. Even if you are one of the few who have experienced a physical transformation, being a werewolf is much more. It is a way of life and a way of being, not just something you do on occasional Full Moons. When you become a werewolf, the biggest changes happen to you on the inside first, and these remain the most important things, whether or not you someday become a "real" werewolf and experience physical changes.

Many of us hope that, in the same way that gay people have gained a measure of acceptance and understanding, someday shifters will also gain a measure of acceptance and understanding, that someday at least the mental/spiritual/lifestyle aspects of shifting will be understood somewhat by society. It may be too much to ask that society believe in even the possibility of true physical shifting. Yet I do hope that, someday, society will become reasonably tolerant of the fact that physical shifting is a part of shifter beliefs, just as society has accepted the fact that Christianity believes in "impossible" things, such as miracle healings, and that people—at least the Son of God—can rise from the dead.

Artificial shifters, of course, discover what shifters are long before they themselves become shifters. Hereditary shifters have to figure it out and find other shifters on their own. Most hereditary shifters realize they are shifters sometime between age 12 and 16. Hereditary shifters experience many symptoms from birth or early childhood. A few natural shifters show so many signs from birth that you almost wonder why their parents didn't realize the truth.

Natural shifters are usually shifters for quite a number of years before they find packs of other shifters. I've even known of a few cases where they did not find other shifters until they reached old age! I was quite lucky and unusual in finding other shifters while I was still a teenager, and I stumbled onto an entire pack in my early 20s, a pack that knew of other packs, some of whom knew of yet other packs. When shifters first find other shifters, they often feel as if they have been raised among another species their whole life, and have finally found their real family! It is a great and wonderful emotional shock, a life-changing experience. Many shifter packs are close-knit and act as families, many call their fellow members "pack-sisters" and "pack-brothers." Eventually you realize, however, that fellow shifters are simply people, unusual perhaps, but full of individual foibles, tendencies, and personality types. As older shifters say, eventually you realize that you don't necessarily want to be friends with other shifters just because they are shifters. Beyond their shifter kinship with you, they may well be personality types that you wouldn't choose for friends, or perhaps even types you would normally dislike.

After reaching this point, you come down off of the initial high of finding other shifters and start being more discriminating, associating with fellow shifters with whom you share more of a bond. In some cases, you may not join a local pack, but rather a pack spread out over a larger area that communicates by phone, letter, and e-mail. This type of spiritual "support group" is more satisfying to some, especially since it allows them to follow their own individual paths as shifters. There are also "lone wolves," who prefer to follow the shifter path alone. Many "lone wolves" do, however, prefer not-entirely-human company, and fill this emotional need by becoming involved in furry culture.

When a person becomes a shifter, both hereditary and artificial factors are involved. Although there are more and more artificial shifters out there, many shifters have at least some hereditary potential. If they look back in their family tree, they can find a grandparent or great-grandparent that had shifter characteristics who passed them on to aunts, uncles, or cousins in an easily traceable line. It is common for shifters to have one or more siblings who are also shifters, or who are people with strong animal medicine. I've known many cases where two or three siblings were shifters. I've also had a few shifter friends "come out of the closet," only to have a sibling admit that he or she had always felt somehow "werewolfish" as well. Hereditary potential isn't everything, but it can help a lot. Shifters with a hereditary potential develop more advanced powers, such as berserker powers, more easily.

It is said that shifters with high enough hereditary potential either become physical shifters or die trying. For this reason, a high hereditary potential can be a liability. Fortunately, most decide to do something about their block before it gets too bad. Sadly, however, many shifters are led to believe that fighting their "werewolf nature" is the road to sanity, and some only fight it more when faced with these problems, creating a vicious cycle. Since so little information is available about shifting, it is fortunate that few have such high hereditary potential. The more hereditary potential you have, the more likely you are to become a shifter without doing anything to encourage it, sometimes even a physical shifter.

There are other things that can cause you to become a shifter. People who were physical shifters in a former life have strong potential to become shifters in this one. Those who are experiencing their first human incarnation always have strong animal medicine, and some of them are shifters. Those left alone for long periods with dogs or cats when they are toddlers tend to absorb so much animal influence that they develop strong animal medicine and sometimes become shifters. Those who encounter some kind of shifting spirit when they are very young can be permanently impressed by the experience and become mental shifters.

Although you may have a certain potential to become a shifter, what you experience in life, especially when very young, seems to determine, at least partially, whether you actually become one or just end up with a special connection to animals. Having a familiar as a child, and having access to open land, especially at night, really helps. There are a few people who have always lived in the city and never had pets or access to animals, who suddenly develop into shifters later in life when they first get pets or move to a more rural area. I believe these people are hereditary shifters who never had a chance to develop into shifters when young, because they were so isolated from animals and nature.

Natural shifters start by becoming aware of characteristics that are very different from what normal humans experience. They become acutely aware of these characteristics, because these are what alienates them from normal human beings. By age 7 or 8, most shifters have figured out these characteristics are somehow related to their lifelong "kinship" with animals, but few figure out what they really mean at this age.

Some shifters have the knowledge of their power creep up on them over the course of many years, and some realize it fairly quickly, perhaps with the help of some major event or turning point. In one case, a wolf shifter first became aware when he was a boy and tried to include a friend in his favorite game: sneaking out at night to the nearest wild area, a grave-yard, and "letting the wolf come out," becoming a wolf mentally. He real-ized then for the first time that not everyone did this. Many of us go through a time of denial. It is even possible to deny to yourself that you are a shifter when you go through many mental shifts and berserker phe-nomena. Some physical shifters remain in denial, and refuse to believe in their own experiences.

When children experience significant side-effects and symptoms, adults often view this as fairly normal, because children are expected to play and pretend, mixing fantasy with reality. Their identities have not really solidified yet. Many normal young children display some pseudo-shifter characteristics as they incorporate animal play and characteristics into their lives. What is seen as merely cute play and normal behavior in early childhood is seen as childish or pathological if it extends into the teenage years and beyond.

Shifters who had visible part-animal characteristics in childhood are mystified when everyone else is able to leave these things behind as mere play. The characteristics are such a deep, strong part of them, however, that they cannot get rid of them if they try. Just as a child with homosex-ual tendencies learns to start hiding them as their peers settle into sex roles, shifters learn to hide their shifter characteristics as they get older, becoming ashamed of them, and spending many sleepless nights wonder-ing what it all means. Most shifters figure out that they are shifters long before any possibility of a physical shift (although I've run across a few supposed cases of physical shifters who become aware after their first phys-ical shift). Shifters usually acknowledge their own nature before they meet other shifters.

Most shifters have a strange fascination with shapeshifting from child-hood, though they may not identify this as "a fascination with shapeshift-ing." This may first manifest as a recurring envy of dogs and cats, a wish to have their abilities, or a desire to break away from being human and live a different life. Many children have feelings like this (especially the wish to be a bird), but natural shifters experience them strongly, persistently, and often. Natural shifters feel as if they have been cheated of their rightful due. They feel severely handicapped by being human, because they observe that animals have greater abilities in almost every area.

The first time a natural shifter reads a book about werewolves, it is often a deeply moving, even spiritual, experience. They feel a deep kinship with these creatures, even though they don't identify with the violent parts of the legends. A part of them "knows" that werebeasts don't go around eating people and wreaking havoc. These feelings are mystifying because they wonder why the stories and legends provoke such strong feelings of identity and kinship, while prompting a rejection of most of what these creatures are supposed to stand for—cannibalism, violence, perversion, and cruelty. Many natural shifters, while reading their first book of werewolf legends, have actually started shaking from emotions welling up.

Most natural shifters have strong, strange reactions to seeing any sort of transformation on TV, especially if the transformation is into an animal, even if the special effects are bad. These reactions tend to be especially strong in people with strong hereditary potential, and in younger people. After you've seen many of these fake transformations, you get somewhat used to them and they affect you less. These reactions often include a strange feeling of excitement. In more severe cases, they include tingling sensations running up and down your body, chills, and uncontrollable shaking. Men report sexual excitement in these episodes, but few females report this.

For many shifters, this is the start of a long and largely fruitless search for a part of their souls, pursued through reading and collecting werewolf and shapeshifting books, fiction and non-fiction, and collecting movies and other werewolf fan material. Hereditary shifters instinctively feel such a kinship with fictional accounts that they often get very deeply involved in this "werewolf fan" lifestyle. This is usually only a phase, however. They become disillusioned with werewolf fandom, because the answers they need are not on the outside, but within. The world of werewolf fandom may stimulate something deep inside, a deep soul-need, a mystical recognition of what shifting truly is. But it cannot satisfy that need. Satisfaction can only come from within. If what you seek is not found within, you will never find it.

SHIFTER PACKS

Many packs keep in touch with other packs or find new members by being part of an organization that attracts other shifters. One such organization is the furry movement, but I've also heard of packs forming within environmental groups dedicated to saving wolves, and in wolf and wolf-hybrid owner's organizations. Sometimes, the larger organization knows about these subgroups of shifters, and sometimes the other members of the organization don't have a clue. This is similar to the way in which organizations such as the Renaissance Faire and the Society for Creative Anachronism (SCA) serve as a networking and meeting arena for many magic workers, neo-Shamans, witches, Wiccans, and neo-Pagans. Some shifters manage to meet up with other shifters outside of any group. Some just find themselves to have a deep kinship with certain people, make friends with them, and eventually discover that they are shifters as well.

In one case, a wolf shifter met a fellow wolf shifter working in the same office building, because he heard that she got in trouble several times for using company resources to print pictures of wolves from the Internet, and had once growled at a boss who told her to stop doing it. I met two shifters, total strangers who were just walking down the street giving off "werewolf vibes," and who, to my utter surprise, singled me out and started talking about wolves. Many shifters claim to recognize other shifters, at least when the other shifter has high enough levels of energy. There are many small packs that don't know about any other packs. The reason that I know about them is that these packs frequently stumble onto a "network" of packs, and the small pack will talk about how it existed for many years without knowing any other packs existed, fearing that it was the last group of shifters in the world.

Packs usually get together in a wilderness area, in an out-of-the-way state park, or at the home of a shifter who lives in the country. If these meetings can be held monthly, they are often on the night of the Full Moon. If they are held only once a year, or a few times a year, they may be camping trips that last as long as two weeks. A lot of "animal" games will go on—mock fighting, tag, and hide-and-seek. Shifters compare and test their senses of smell and hearing against each other, and talk about shifting for hours. Often, they sleep most of the day and are awake all night.

Some packs are into costuming as a way of connecting to the inner animal. This practice is called "skinwalking." Some individual shifters are very involved with costuming as well, even joining organizations devoted to costume making. Since many shifters feel like animals trapped in human bodies (or at least a half-animal half-human creature trapped in a human body), they do the same thing that women trapped in men's bodies do: they dress the part in order to express their souls. Many shifters say that nothing helps them connect to their inner animal more than dressing up in an animal costume. This is simply a modern version of "skinwalking"—the ancient practice of dressing in a "wolf skin" (often made of cowhide cut to imitate a wolf) without actually shapeshifting.

Although many shifters swear by it, many deplore skinwalking. They say it is a distraction from better ways to contact the inner animal. I have seen it work in different ways for different shifters, or even for the same shifter at different points in life. Sometimes skinwalking opens a gate to the inner animal as nothing else can, allowing shifters to put aside their human identity and let themselves truly be animals. At other times, skinwalking can be a distraction from the real work.

There are a number of things to look for when choosing a pack. One is to be aware of the age of its members. When you find a pack of teenagers, that pack will probably not be good for you. Teenagers are immature, and teenage shifters are extremely emotional. Even if you are a teenager yourself, try not to join a teenage pack. Try to join a real pack, or be satisfied with being a "lone wolf." Conversely, if you find a pack where all members are in their 30s or 40s or older, this pack will probably be good for you. Older pack members are wiser. Even in a very young pack, older shifters are a good sign, a source of wisdom and stability.

Watch for any sign that the pack is a "cult." Cults can be dangerous and unhealthy, and some packs have degenerated into cults. One of the most common and obvious signs of a pack being a cult is if it expects or demands that members indulge in "sex rites" or "sexual magic." This is nothing more than an excuse for the leader to seduce new members. Another sign that the pack may be a cult is if it has only one leader. Packs, unlike human organizations, tend to be democratic. As in a wolf pack, leadership is usually shared by two or three "alphas"—and shared amazingly equally. Some packs, especially very large packs and cat-shifter packs, are so loose and unorganized that they have no leaders. Cults, on the other hand, tend to have only one leader.

If you are unsure about any pack, trust your instincts and learn how to recognize cults. Larger packs are usually benign, but they nearly always have some "black sheep" or unsavory characters in their midst. As long as you steer clear of such people, you should be safe. The largest packs are often recruiting grounds for various smaller packs, and a few of these smaller packs are cults, looking for new and gullible members. Another warning sign is about money. No real pack needs money. You can certainly be expected to contribute food at the meetings, and perhaps even carpool local members to faraway meetings, but any "membership fees" or requests for money should be treated with suspicion.

One of the worst scams I ever heard of involved a man who was reportedly setting up a commune for shifters. He needed a lot of money for this. He also claimed to be doing research on tissue samples from shifters, and to be on the verge of discovering the scientific basis of physical shifting. Then he claimed to have run out of money for his research and asked for donations. He hinted very strongly that, as soon as he completed his research, he would be able to make any shifter into a physical shifter. Many shifters believed in him and made donations. The commune never materialized, and neither did anything else. As soon as he had as much money as he thought he could get, he disappeared.

It is fairly common for several shifters to live together. Sometimes, there is nothing like living with other shifters to teach you about shifter nature. Most of the shifters I've known who have done this say it was an amazing educational experience, and recommend it highly. In a number of cases, shifters have used this living arrangement to give them the courage to "come out of the closet" as shifters. When one shifter tries to admit to family and friends that he or she is "some kind of werewolf," the results are often disastrous. At best, they think the shifter is joking, but more often they fear either demonic possession or insanity, regardless of how normal the shifter seems. Nothing seems to revive people's fears and beliefs in the demonic as much as learning that "werewolves" really exist.

When a group of shifters comes out together, people are far less likely to think them insane. Instead, they may see it as a joke, or as a bunch of weirdos, or, at worst, as some kind of New Age cult. Unlike the case of the single shifter, people are likely to listen a little more deeply to what is being explained. Instead of fixating on, "He thinks he's a werewolf," they listen and start to understand that they are hearing about a philosophy involving part of the soul being an animal—the notion of an animal trapped in a human body. The group can give its members help and moral support through this period, and the strength of the group can help convince people that whatever is going on is certainly not insanity.

The worst cases of discrimination happen when family and friends know that something weird is going on, but don't know what. Perhaps they see some berserker powers or other paranormal effects at work, and they freak out. The paranormal causes a lot of alarm in people, and makes them jump to all sorts of conclusions. If you are thinking of coming out as a shifter, I recommend having them read this book. Even if they don't believe in the paranormal, or magic, or physical shifting, the parts of this book that don't involve the paranormal will help them understand some of what is going on.

Teenage shifters in particular tend to have a hard time coming out. They are still living at home, under the supervision of parents, when their shifting is most turbulent. They are involved in the process of integrating their child and adult selves into a final adult persona. This is a heavy load on top of dealing with integrating the animal and human selves—like normal teenagerhood intensified, as if normal teenagerhood weren't already bad enough! Teenage shifters need a lot of love and support. Parents tend to become alarmed at any side-effects that they happen to see, and may send the shifter to either a psychiatrist or a priest. They often try to force the shifter to kill the animal part of themselves. This is not only impossible, it is like asking them to cut off their own arm. I have known too many tragic cases of teenage shifters running away from home, contemplating suicide, or isolating themselves from family once they move away from home. I've also known a number of cases in which the family disowned shifters because they saw some berserker or other paranormal powers.

If you are the parent of a shifter, you need to love and accept your child without trying to kill the animal part of his or her soul. Shifters need your support. Keep an eye on them, help them through the bad parts, steer them away from any bad shifters or cults they may encounter, and help them find good shifters if necessary. You also need to address your own feelings. You may be afraid of them because you yourself have had some dormant animal medicine or shifterism within you that you've been taught to fear and fight.

CELEBRATIONS

Perhaps the urge to celebrate, to have special holidays set aside, is a human instinct, for it is something found in every culture. Every group has at least one holiday unique to it. Those who are involved in particular cultures, religions, or other groups often feel a need to have particular holidays set aside especially for them. Those involved in modern Wicca, Neo-Shamanism and Neo-Paganism, as well as those involved in the study of the paranormal, feel the need to celebrate their special lifestyle with holidays such as the Winter Solstice, Samhain, Candlemas, or esbats.

Shifters also feel the need to celebrate their special lifestyle with holidays, even though only a tiny percentage of shifters consider "shifterism" a religion, or anything like a religion. One of the most natural times for shifters to celebrate is, of course, the Full Moon. But Full Moons occur too often to fully satisfy the need for a truly special holiday. Shifters want some other holiday that occurs less often and is, therefore, more special. Many shifters celebrate Halloween, a holiday that celebrates "monsters," the powers of the wild and the night, and the paranormal. Moreover, Halloween is very centered on costuming, on "becoming" something else. It is therefore a time when shifters can engage in public skinwalking, and even let out a bit of their animal behavior, without being condemned or ostracized. They can be more their true selves, even in public, and celebrate what they are. This is a very precious kind of celebration for those who have to pretend to be human and hide their true selves in public all year.

Halloween is also particularly appropriate for shifters because it is a time when the veil between worlds is thin, especially between this world and the spirit world. Shifters are walkers between the worlds—this world and the spirit world, the human world and the world of animals, the world of physical truths and the world of mystical truths. In fact, shifters can never fully enter any of the worlds between which they walk. They always straddle them. Unlike some, shifters are always between the worlds, bridges of a sort, channels, connections, ambassadors.

Many shifters feel that Earth Day is a particularly appropriate time to celebrate being shifters (but not with public skinwalking, of course!), because they feel very connected to Earth, her animals, and her environment. They are often environmental activists, trying to save what little of our wild home and wild cousins remains. Shifter-oriented Earth Day celebrations include private gatherings to celebrate being shifters, and environmental activism, especially that oriented toward saving one's own species.

There are also lesser-known holidays that are oriented toward shifters. There is ample evidence that ancient shapeshifters had their own special holidays and celebrations. There are the legends of the annual celebrations atop Mount Lycaeus[18] in Arcadia in Greece, during which at least one person was said to be "chosen" and changed into a wolf. There are tales of the lakeside werewolf festivals of the Arcadian werewolves, in which youths who were of age experienced their first transformations while swimming across the lake. Legends speak of the famous Christmastime beer-cellar break-ins and drunken celebrations of Prussian werewolves. In Scotland, werecats congregated in large numbers in certain old castles at certain times of the year. Huge gatherings of werebeasts

---

[18] Also called Mount Lykaion, and in modern times called either Mount Diaphorti or Mount St. Elias. There are two peaks to the mountain. The higher peak is called Stephani; the lower is where certain Arcadian ceremonies were held. It is still crowned with the ruin of the temple of Zeus Lycaeus. The temple ruin is about half an hour's climb from the shrine of Saint Elias.

have been described atop Mount Brokken in the Hartz Mountains in Germany. There is also a well-authenticated case of a gathering of were-horses in Blocula, Sweden in 1669.[19]

The most famous Neuri shapeshifters held a special festival once a year that resulted in some of them remaining in animal form for either three or twelve days (accounts vary on this). Many of these festivals happen either on the holiday that we now call Halloween, on the Winter Solstice, or during February. Even after these "pagan" celebrations were suppressed and faded away, we still have reports from Europe of shapeshifters being especially riled up on both the Winter Solstice and during February.[20]

I and many others have also noticed a tendency for shifters to be particularly active during the Winter Solstice (for a short period) and during February (for a longer period). These heightened energies are apparently a deep characteristic of shifters, and are not related to any knowledge of this tendency in ancient shifters, for they occur in many who know nothing of the ancient legends. One pack with which I was associated called February "weird month," although its members seemed ignorant of the connections with ancient legend. It is a time of strange dreams and social tensions, during which the animal side is both more awake and more unpredictable.

One appropriate holiday for shifters is Lupercalia, the ancient Roman holiday in celebration of Lupa, the she-wolf who was said to have suckled Romulus and Remus, the mythical founders of Rome. In Western culture the she-wolf has long been the symbol of all the positive wolf qualities. Lupercalia, as shifters celebrate it, is not just a celebration of the wolf, it is a celebration of the connection between wolf and human, especially in its most positive sense. It is a celebration of the wolf who mothers human

---

[19] Frank Hamel, *Animals* (New York: University Books, 1969), p. 111.

[20] Countless ancient authorities recognized the connection between lycanthropy and February. Montague Summers cites two: "*This malady*, saith *Avicenna*, troubleth men most in February, and is now-a-days frequent in Bohemia and Hungary"; also "Altomari . . . agrees that the disease is at its worst in February." *The Werewolf*, pp. 41, 45. Sabine Baring-Gould cites another: "According to Marcellus . . . men are attacked with this madness chiefly in the beginning of the year, and become most furious in February . . . living . . . in the manner of dogs and wolves." *The Book of Were-Wolves* (London: Senate, 1995), p. 9.

beings, lending them some of her powers and qualities. Young men who wish to be werewolves celebrate a symbolic marriage with a statue of the she-wolf during Lupercalia. Lupercalia is celebrated on February 15th, not coincidentally a time that is the height of wolf mating season, a time when wolfish energies are at a very high point. While many readers are more familiar with Lupercalia as involving the sacrifice of a dog and some goats, and various fertility rites, this festival can also be used by shifters.

My wolf spirit guide gave me a chant or song for opening and closing any type of Lupercalia celebration. It is a song in honor of the she-wolf, symbol of all the good qualities of wolves. It may be best, if using this in your own celebrations, to intersperse the song with joyous howls.

Opening Chant

Mother Wolf, lend us your strength, for we are weak.
Mother Wolf, lend us your senses,
*   for we are dull toward the world around us.*
Mother Wolf, lend us your shape, for we wish to walk
*   between the worlds, to be two in one, to be shifters.*

Closing Chant

Mother Wolf, thanks for your strength,
*   for we are strong as the wolf.*
Mother Wolf, thanks for your senses,
for we have truly been aware.
Mother Wolf, thanks for your shape,
*   for we have walked between the worlds,*
*   we are two in one, we are shifters.*
Mother Wolf, may you ever inspire us to reach beyond our humanity.

7

How to Become A Shifter

Traditionally there are two ways in which people become shifters—heredity and practice. In modern shifter cultures, these types are called "natural" and "artificial" shifters. Hereditary shifters are born with varying potentials. Those with low potential may not even become mental shifters unless they have the right kinds of experience. Those with average potential will probably become mental shifters while young. Those with high potential have a good chance of becoming physical shifters, sometimes even without encouraging it. There are a few natural shifters who are not hereditary—some who are experiencing their first human incarnation, a few who were shifters in a former life, and a few who have just always been shifters, but no one knows why.

Artificial shifters are those who become shifters later in life, usually as a result of their own efforts. At first, the shifter movement consisted almost entirely of natural shifters. Artificial shifters were thought to be natural shifters who were simply confused about their origins. Few other members of the shifter movement took them very seriously. Shifter doctrine, promoted by most of the gurus within the movement, claimed all shifters were hereditary, that existing shifters could strengthen their abilities, but that ordinary people could not become shifters. Nor could shifters be "cured."

That has all changed. Although it still appears that natural shifters can't truly be cured, we now know that artificial shifters certainly do exist. There are examples of apparently ordinary people becoming shifters, but most who become shifters start out with at least some animal medicine. As the shifter movement grew and developed, it came to include more artificial shifters as better techniques and increased knowledge combined over time. Shifters take time to develop their powers.

The information and techniques in this chapter are for people who wish to become shifters, and for shifters who want to become stronger, more regular shifters. The same practices and techniques that may turn an "ordinary" person into a shifter will, when used by someone who is already a shifter, tend to strengthen them. Even though shifting has much to do with the supernatural, you need not follow a magical path or know how to "do" magic to enhance your shifting potential, especially if you have natural powers.

There are shifters who have progressed all the way to physical shifting without doing anything even remotely like a magical ceremony. Most of this chapter is concerned with more ordinary ways of connecting with your inner animal and enhancing your abilities. These ways may seem less glamorous and more tedious, but they are the foundation of everything else. Practicing fancy magical techniques, without a foundation, is nearly useless. It is as if you sent in a great résumé and then showed up at the job interview looking and acting totally disreputable. I have included a section on purely magical means for those who wish to use it, but it should be used as a supplement to the rest of the work. Magical techniques can be great catalysts, but it is ridiculous to expect magic to do everything. Magic is not a "shortcut," even though the word "magic" has become a euphemism for "easy."

If you wish to become a shifter, the first step is to cultivate your own animal nature. If you are already a shifter, strengthening your own animal nature will strengthen your shifter qualities. The cultivation and strengthening of the inner animal is a valuable technique for both. There are other techniques, however, such as those that strengthen the qualities of shifting within a person. There are also techniques that relate to specific shifting talents, and those aimed at strengthening things that promote shifting, or that are necessary for shifting.

If you are not a shifter and wish to become one, I give you a word of warning before you proceed. You must be serious in your intent, approaching this path in a way that is mature and well thought out. It does not pay to be sloppy when dealing with deeper and higher forces. If you do become a shifter, your inner animal will be more active and rise to waking consciousness more often and more completely. Since the inner animal is part of the subconscious, part of the instinctual, primal self, you will have to deal with issues relating to your subconscious.

This process is one from which much good can come, but it is often a painful and frightening process. This is especially true for people living in modern society, who have been taught to beat down their subconscious and totally suppress it. Many people are often quite frightened of their subconscious, and if they try to make friends with it, they will be forced to deal with years of suppressed desires, fears, and complexes. This causes some people to believe that the subconscious is bad, and that they are justified in ignoring and suppressing it. This often becomes a self-fulfilling prophecy and creates a vicious circle.

If you become a shifter, you will have to deal with your subconscious, and you may not like it. If you become an integrated shifter, you must not only deal with your subconscious, but also partially merge with it, which is even harder. If you wish to follow the path of a shifter, you should be ready for all this. Popular psychology calls this dealing with the "shadow," and you do need to know yourself when you take this path.

The techniques outlined in this chapter are very effective. The first step on the path of a shifter is the hardest. The techniques outlined in this chapter can help, although it may take time and, for some, it may not work at all. There is one thing you can do, however, that is much more effective than any technique that can be learned from a book. Many who aspire to be artificial shifters become "apprenticed" to someone who is already a shifter, someone who can show them the ropes, and show them how things are done. This can be much more effective than just picking up techniques and then trying them on your own. It is somehow easier to "birth" your animal side with help. Something seems to "rub off on" you simply by being apprenticed in this way. In shifter culture, those who have had help in becoming shifters often refer to those who taught them as "Mom" or "Dad," in much the same way that shifters casually call pack-mates "packsisters" and "packbrothers," because the shifter who teaches is sort of a parent to the new artificial shifter, the new being that was "birthed." I've even known of cases where a couple of "generations" were produced, and the newest generation referred to the original teachers as "Grandma" or "Grandpa."

To become a shifter, you must be a person with strong "animal medicine." If you wish to become a shifter and do not have strong animal medicine, you need to gain it as your very first step. Animal totemism is a topic already covered adequately in many New Age books, to which you can refer. If you already have a strong empathy with animals, you are halfway there. Becoming a shifter will be much easier for you.

CULTIVATION

One of the most basic techniques is called "cultivation." Cultivation involves deliberately acting like the species of animal that you are, in order to strengthen your bond with it. Natural shifters do this automatically. They do not need to try to deliberately act like their species, it is simply a natural part of them. If they do practice cultivation, however, it can bring more animal magic into their lives.

Cultivation may be done in subtle ways that are worked into your everyday life. You may try to be more suave and concerned with your appearance if you are a cat-shifter. Or you may get down on all fours and meow. This is not a mental shift, though to the outside observer it may appear to be one. On the other hand, cultivation may trigger a real mental shift on occasion. Moreover, some shifters may retard their progress by cultivating the wrong characteristics. For instance, I have known people who tried to cultivate a wolf nature by being cruel, aggressive, and domineering. Since these are not truly characteristics of the wolf, however, these people made no progress.

There is also another problem that occasionally crops up with cultivation. Once a shifter has bonded with a particular species, they almost always realize which species they are fairly quickly. In some instances, however, they may refuse to admit to themselves what species they truly are, and may go on trying to cultivate another species. It is particularly common for women to try to distance themselves from the wolf species, thinking it too masculine and wild—"The Big Bad Wolf." These women often decide that they are cats or foxes, or domestic dogs. They try to ignore their true wolf nature and cultivate the other species. This misdirected cultivation can slow progress and cause problems, particularly during mental shifting. There is also a feeling that often builds up in those who persistently cultivate the wrong species, a desire, deep down, to strangle a real animal of the mistaken species. If you ever feel this, you are pursuing the wrong species.

Connecting with animal magic is a process that never ends. It is done regularly, almost by instinct. Animal-related activities and ways of being are attractive and pleasurable for shifters, and they just naturally fall into these ways unless they purposely hold back. Being part animal has become a part of who and what you are. If you become a shifter, this will one day be true for you as well. Until then, find ways to deliberately connect to your inner animal.

If you already have high shifter potential, becoming a person with strong animal magic will soon result in your first mental shifts. If you have low shifter potential, you'll need to do some more work before you experience your first mental shift. This work should be specifically oriented toward attracting the magic of shapeshifting into your being.

BUILDING YOUR SHIFTING ENERGY

There are several things necessary for shifting, or that help promote shifting. One of the most basic is called shifting energy. Shifting energy is a kind of paranormal energy, an energy of the higher planes. It doesn't seem in exist in people unless they are shifters. Exercises specifically designed to build shifting energy will occasionally turn normal people into shifters, especially if these practices are pursued diligently.

Shifting energy feels and behaves much like *chi*. In fact, it is probably just another variety of *chi*. Activities that build *chi* also build shifting energy. Yet there are other things that specifically build shifting energy, without necessarily building *chi*. To build shifting energy, you first need to work the basics, the foundation, into your lifestyle. These basics build both *chi* and shifting energy. If you choose to neglect these basics, don't expect to make much progress with the fancier techniques.

- Eat the freshest food you can get, and make sure your diet consists of unprocessed foods, such as fruits, vegetables, and unprocessed meats.
- Eat a large breakfast and a light supper.
- Learn correct, upright posture. Do not practice it in a stiff way, however, but learn to have perfect posture while relaxed.
- Get fresh, outdoor air every day and every night.
- Let the Sun and Moon shine on you often (but stay away from excessive sunbathing).
- Learn to breathe properly, with deep, nourishing breaths, not the shallow breathing most Westerners use.
- Set aside some sacred space, some time alone every day.
- Exercise, especially walking and stretching, a little every day.
- Avoid drugs, tobacco, and caffeine when possible.
- Avoid anything more than moderate alcohol, and avoid excessive sex, pleasure-seeking, or overeating.
- Wear loose-fitting clothing, of natural fibers like cotton, when possible.
- With your doctor's approval, fast once a month for two or three days, drinking plenty of water during the fast, plus a little fruit juice or vegetable broth.
- If you have any major stress in your life or any major health problem, get rid of it if possible.

You do not have to do all these things perfectly, but you should make a reasonable attempt to work as many of them into your lifestyle as possible. In a shifter, the basics will build shifting energy and *chi* at the same time. Whenever *chi* is increased in a shifter, shifting energy is increased, but things that specifically increase shifting energy won't necessarily increase *chi*.

When you try to build both *chi* and shifting energy, it is helpful to know the signs of high *chi* levels. If *chi* is high, shifting energy probably is at average-to-high levels for a shifter. If *chi* is not high, shifting energy is probably low.

A person with high levels of *chi* has more energy and vigor than most people. They tire less, seem to be under less stress, and tend to be optimistic about life, looking forward to the new day when they wake up in the morning. If they get cuts or bruises, they heal faster than most. People with high *chi* are invigorated by the cold, and are comfortable in less clothing when it is cold. People with high *chi* are often "people magnets." They seem to attract an unusual amount of interest, even when there seems to be no real reason for it. They also seem to be more memorable. They tend to stick in people's minds, even if the meeting was brief and they did nothing noteworthy.

There are many ways to build *chi* beyond these basics. Every system of magic has similar theories about *chi*, and similar systems for teaching how to build, sense, control it, and even use it to cause paranormal phenomena. Many modern books on magic, from wicca to Western ceremonial magic, tell of ritual objects or spells being "charged." They usually mean charged with *chi*.

One of the best systems for building *chi* and learning to use it is the Eastern discipline of *chi-gong*. Many cultures have similar systems, but I believe that *chi-gong* is a better and more complete system that any other. Those shifters interested in building and manipulating high levels of *chi* would do well to study it in detail.

Shifting energy is very like *chi* in many ways, yet different from generic *chi*. It seems to exist only in shifters, not in any ordinary people, not even in animal people. All people have *chi*, but only shifters have shifting energy. It seems to be associated with the second etheric body that shifters possess, and seems to be particularly strengthening to this second etheric body, much more so than generic *chi*.

In the early stages of becoming a shifter, the second etheric body tends to be weak, undeveloped, even to have parts missing. But as time goes on, this body tends to become more "solid," stronger, better defined, and more vigorous. Those with stronger animal etheric bodies are more likely to experience the "higher powers," such as berserker abilities or even physical shifting. Long-term exposure to high levels of shifting energy seems to be the main thing that strengthens the animal etheric body.

Although shifting is much more likely to happen when shifting energy is high, astral shifting, sense shifting, dream shifting, and bilocation shifting are the least dependent on it. In fact, these four types often have very little to do with shifting energy. Mental shifting, on the other hand, is quite noticeably affected by high or low levels of shifting energy. When shifting energy is high, mental shifts are much more likely to occur, more likely to be deep or to last a longer time, and more likely to be accompanied by berserker powers. Physical shifting is absolutely dependent on very high levels of shifting energy.

Levels of shifting energy tend to cycle through high and low points. This cycling is strongly affected by the cycle of the Moon. Most of the time, shifters have their highest peaks of energy at the Full Moon, with smaller peaks at the New Moon. A high peak can occur at some other time, depending on various factors, but most occur at the Full Moon. Shifting energy is affected by both mundane and paranormal conditions. Mundane conditions that can boost shifting energy are being in the wilderness and being around companion animals. Paranormal conditions that affect it include the Full Moon, or having a vision of your animal spirit guide.

Some shifters seem to be particularly receptive to shifting energy and they can quickly replenish it, no matter how often they deplete it. If you are a shifter, you know exactly what shifting energy feels like, even if you've never labeled it as "shifting energy." It is a presence, a pressure, a tension, a "humming" of energy, everywhere in your body. If it is high, it makes you feel very good and yet full of uncomfortable tension at the same time. You are always very aware of when it is high or low. If you have trouble sensing your shifting energy or telling when it is high or low, then it is probably very low.

The best and most basic way to build shifting energy is called "prowling." When you prowl, you go out in the wild, usually at night, and wander around enjoying yourself, while letting out some of your inner animal nature. You may stalk fenceposts or the shadow of a bush, dig holes, secrete yourself in some place and watch raccoons and deer pass by, run and leap for the sheer joy of it, rub your back against trees, and generally behave in ways natural to your shifter side. In order to prowl effectively, you need a wild place that is very safe, secure from anyone who might watch you, and available for frequent use. Prowling is the most basic way to build shifting energy, everything else is merely a supplement. One of the things that hampers shifters is that they are unable to find a place suitable for prowling.

Shifters can only handle a small level of shifting energy at first. If they build above that level, the excess will soon drain away on its own, or be burned off by a shift. As time goes by and they progress on the path, they find themselves able to handle higher levels of shifting energy comfortably. At some point they will be able to comfortably hold within the high levels of shifting energy necessary for berserker powers or physical shifting. This progression in the base level of shifting energy is linked with the cycle of integration. As you go through more integration phases successfully, your usual level of shifting energy, as well as the highest level of shifting energy that you can handle and retain, will increase. The stronger and more defined your animal etheric body, the more shifting energy you can handle. It may be that shifting energy is actually stored in the animal etheric body.

Many shifters fall into the trap of trying to accumulate huge amounts of shifting energy. They think that it alone is the key to progression on the path of a shifter. The truth is that shifting energy must be assimilated properly to do much good. Trying to retain a lot more than you can handle can lead to odd symptoms and bad side effects. Some shifters feel ill all the time. In many cases, the shifting energy finds other ways to discharge itself. The shifter may feel the energy leave them, then suddenly a door slams by itself, or something falls off a shelf.

In rarer cases, shifters may develop involuntary pyrokinetic abilities. In every case, this fire has been green in color. If shifters stubbornly persist in this condition—deliberately retaining more energy than they can handle—they sometimes develop symptoms where the body begins to fail in strange, inexplicable ways. They may develop severe vision problems, or various organs may stop working properly. Their doctors can tell that real, physical things are wrong, but they can find no cause or cure. In some cases where shifting energy is kept deliberately too high for many years, the shifter's hair may grow in as a new color every few months.

Conditions like these need not be endured. Those who experience extreme side effects of excessively high shifting energy are simply those who have gotten themselves into their own mess. Excess shifting energy can always be "earthed" or "grounded" naturally. Many methods for earthing excess energy are outlined in various New Age and paranormal books. One very good method is to lie belly-down on the ground, and try to visualize sending the energy into the earth, until you feel that it is gone. Some people like to discharge the energy by holding a large, rough rock on their lap and sending the energy into it.

Teenage shifters often have abnormally high levels of shifting energy. It is ancient and universal knowledge that puberty and the teenage years often bring high levels of all sorts of psychic energy, and often temporary, uncontrollable psychic powers, as in the teenager who produces poltergeist phenomena.

In teenage shifters, this tendency often manifests as shifting energy that is uncomfortably high, and that tends to recharge quickly whenever it is depleted. Teenage shifters often experience berserker powers that die out once they become adults. It is also common to hear adult shifters claim that, during their teenage years, they were regular physical shifters, but then stopped entirely and haven't been able to reclaim that ability. This is mostly due to high levels of shifting energy, although I suspect that the childlike openness and faith that young people have may also have something to do with it. Teenage shifters are also prone to having shifting energy "feed" their emotions, so that they become too strong and disruptive. For these reasons, it is particularly important for teenage shifters to pay attention to their level of shifting energy, and to know how to earth it.

There is another technique that can help shifters who suffer from the side effects of high shifting energy, an overactive inner animal, or frustration at being unable to move forward on the path of a shifter. This technique is to employ a cure for melancholy. Under the ancient system of Western medicine, which is different from modern medicine and very much connected to the paranormal and astrology, they diagnosed those who suffered from this condition as having an overabundance of melancholy. In this sense, melancholy does not refer to being sad, depressed, or brooding (its modern meaning). It refers rather to a particular pattern of paranormal energies, a pattern that was formerly thought to be caused by too much "black bile." Those who suffer from various circumstances connected with shifting often find relief by following ancient "cures" for melancholy, especially the use of certain herbs.

The condition of melancholy can result from a build-up of problems connected with shifting. It is not just a side effect, as some have thought, nor is it necessarily a problem to be "cured." Many of those who suffered from a strong buildup of paranormal powers only partially under their control, such as witches and psychics, were diagnosed in the past as melancholic. Some of the so-called symptoms of melancholy, however, are actually a difficult, but necessary, part of being connected to the paranormal worlds in certain ways. Shifters who "cure" themselves of melancholy often find their shifter nature somewhat weakened or inhibited. Cures for melancholy should only be used in the more drastic cases, and only to "bleed off" excessive side effects.

FINDING YOUR INNER ANIMAL

The inner animal seldom belongs entirely to one species. In many people, it may lean toward one species, or manifest mostly as one or two species, other aspects having little to do with the active part that rises to the surface. My inner animal manifests almost entirely as wolf. My nature was fairly canine to begin with and, years ago, I entered a phase in which my inner animal "solidified" as wolf. Originally, I was a fox, as are many shifters. Before I was even a mental shifter, I was connected to several species of the little animals of field and forest. I do not consider myself a "polywere," but I do have occasional astral shifts into species other than wolf, and I can still feel elements of other animals present, latent, deep within my inner animal. These other aspects manifest mostly as subtle characteristics within my wolf self or as totem animals. Many shifters likewise have a number of animals other than their main species manifest, either as totem animals, or in very minor or occasional ways during shifts. Astral shifts are particularly prone to bringing forth multiple-species shifts. If you experience astral shifts or dream shifts into multiple species, don't consider yourself a polywere. This is quite common. If you have two or more distinct mental animal sides that manifest in mental shifts, then you are a polywere.

If you do not yet have a species, one will come to you. It may not be your favorite, but you should accept it and allow your natural inner animal to manifest. If you fight this process, you will get off to a bad start on your path as a shifter. This first animal may be one of the little ones of field and forest. In a few years, you may find yourself switching species. You may spend awhile as a rat, for instance, then switch to otter.

If you succeed in becoming a shifter, you will probably soon switch to fox, or to one of the other common shifting species. As you continue on your path, you may stay with your original shifter species, you may switch to another, or you may enter a phase of rapidly switching species or accumulating several at a time. Whatever you go through, at some point you will "solidify" as just one species. In very rare cases, this does not occur, and these shifters are called "polyweres." In most polyweres, one animal is still dominant. Extreme polyweres are often those who deliberately prevent themselves from solidifying as one animal, refusing to move forward on the true path of a shifter.

If you are having trouble becoming a shifter in the first place, the best animal to cultivate is the fox. The fox is often a gateway to the world of shifting. An incredible number of shifters spend a brief phase as fox-shifters when they first began experiencing mental shifts. Animal people who are manifesting fox often develop into shifters eventually.

Some shifters are afraid of their shifter nature, and suppress it horribly for many years. In some cases, this severely weakens their inner animal and, when they finally decide to embrace their true nature, they find it has faded to almost nothing. In these cases, they often get an excellent resurgence of their shifter nature if they deliberately cultivate fox. Regardless of what species you may be, cultivating fox represents going back to the beginning and getting a new start on the path.

MENTAL SHIFTING

If you are not yet a shifter, you need to become one in order to experience mental shifts. If you are a shifter, mental shifts simply happen. They can often be suppressed or delayed, but causing them at will is a rare skill. Some people use certain techniques to provoke mental shifts, but these do not work for everyone. One is to imagine a large transparent form of yourself enveloping your human body, then imagine it slowly changing into a large transparent animal form. Many shifters have learned to grow phantom animal ears at will, by imagining them on their head extremely vividly until they appear. This often causes a mental shift.

Some mental shifts are linked to a certain emotion, causing the shifter to shift whenever they manifest that emotion strongly. For example, some shifters experience mental shifts whenever they get really angry. They can often provoke a mental shift by deliberately trying to experience that emotion, although I think it is an unhealthy practice to encourage any connection between mental shifts and a negative emotion like anger.

Many shifters are able to provoke mental shifts by creating the right conditions, such as being outdoors in a wild area on the night of the Full Moon. Some can cause mental shifts just by opening up to the animal side. Some find that cultivation often provokes mental shifts. If they get down on all fours and meow or howl, their animal side starts rising within them.

ASTRAL AND DREAM SHIFTING

In order to practice voluntary astral shifting, you must already have the ability to astral travel. For involuntary astral shifts, no ability is really necessary. When it happens to you, it simply happens. Most astral shifts, however, are induced.

In fact, many people who aren't even shifters can do astral shifting. The astral body is very malleable, especially when it is separated from the etheric and physical bodies. A very vivid "guided visualization" of shapeshifting, if done intensely and with feeling, can cause your astral body to shift to an animal shape, even if you are not a shifter. You may go into a trance or dream with a thought at the forefront of your mind that you will shapeshift as soon as you leave your body. This often induces astral shifts once you are deeply under. If you astral travel, and remain lucid and aware, simply try to shapeshift during your journey.

Dream shifting, which can be very important, is similar to astral shifting. Dream shifting often includes powerful teachings or important information about your path as a shifter. During a dream shift, you may be an animal for the entire dream, or you may be in midform, or you may go through the act of transformation in your dream.

Dreams are important because they are a type of trance state that everyone experiences, easily and often. The trance state is important to any spiritual or magical path. It is one of the most important ways of directly sensing other realities, which, in turn, is quite helpful in learning to affect those other realities. Once you learn how to enter a trance state, it becomes easier to reenter it. For most people, however, learning to enter a trance state in the first place is very difficult. The next best thing to a trance state entered while awake, is the trance state that is called dreaming.

You may say: "But I don't remember my dreams," or, "I don't dream." You do dream. Everyone dreams. To have longer, richer dreams, and to remember your dreams well, is to bring you closer to integration with your subconscious selves, as well as to teach you enough about the dreaming trance state that it becomes easier to learn other trance states. To learn to dream better, and remember those dreams better, first make sure you get adequate sleep. Most people don't get enough sleep. The best way to get adequate sleep is to apply the following test: Do you often wake up naturally before the alarm goes off? If your answer was "no" or "never," you need more sleep.

Another very good way to remember your dreams is to drift slowly from a sleeping state to a waking state. If you are dreaming when you wake up slowly like this, you will certainly remember your dream. Even if you are not dreaming at the time you wake up, your dreams from earlier in the night will be more likely to drift into your consciousness. For further help in learning to dream, try reading books on lucid dreaming, dream imagery, and dream interpretation.

Many shifters learn lucid dreaming in order to deliberately shapeshift frequently in their dreams. Another way to experience dream shifting is to say to yourself that you will shapeshift, or imagine shapeshifting, and let your thoughts dwell on it, as you drift off to sleep. Those who dream shift frequently find that it increases their shifting energy, strengthens their animal etheric body, and helps with integration. If you are having trouble of any sort on the path of a shifter, you can often discover what path you should take by deliberately provoking a lot of dream shifting.

SENSE AND BILOCATION SHIFTING

It is tricky to give instructions for sense shifting. Most of the time, it simply happens. When I have successfully done it on purpose, I've reached out with my mind to the mind of the animal and connected myself to it with invisible cords of magical energy. This is difficult and requires concentration and finesse. You can learn to sense shift by paying close attention to exactly how it feels when you experience a spontaneous sense shift, analyzing the subtle currents and connections of energies. As in biofeedback, once you know exactly how it feels to do something, you have a fair chance of doing it again on purpose.

I have little information on how to bilocation shift. There are few bilocation shifters, and many of them don't know exactly how they do it. Bilocation shifting is not dependent upon shifting energy, and the animal etheric body does not necessarily have to be strong. Bilocation shifters "borrow" the etheric body of their animal spirit guide. In fact, many report that the animal spirit guide simultaneously occupies the body that is formed, and is in partial control of it.

There is evidence in legend that bilocation shifting was once taught, and was a power more easily acquired than physical shifting. In the days of legend, bilocation itself was much more common. Perhaps those who already knew how to bilocate found it simple to learn bilocation shifting. In the future, the art of teaching bilocation shifting may be recovered, and bilocation shifters will become more common.

I recommend that those who wish to learn bilocation shifting also learn astral travel, astral shifting, etheric travel, and etheric shifting. If you experience apparition shifting, you are close to bilocation shifting. Bilocation shifting is simply apparition shifting with more solidity to the apparition thus formed.

PHYSICAL SHIFTING AND LETTING GO

I have talked to many physical shifters about learning to physical shift, and they all agree on the basics. Though individuals may have their own particular concentration techniques to help smooth the way, the basics are the same, even according to those who have never met each other. Most discovered these basics by a combination of experience and instinct. Few physical shifters learned them from another physical shifter.

Before trying to physically shift, there are some requirements you need to fulfill, or it simply won't work. You need to have a strong, well-developed animal etheric body. This animal etheric body must be "dense" enough to support physical matter, or physical shifting cannot occur. You also need to have a very high level of shifting energy, not just at the "peaks" in the cycle, but even at ordinary times. You need to be one of those shifters who can support a base level of shifting energy that is higher than that with which ordinary shifters are comfortable. These are the symptoms to look for:

- A humming, pushing, pressure, and tension within your body that feels both very good and uncomfortable;

- A strong increase in this feeling near the Full Moon, your body feeling as if it will burst, your skin twitching and feeling as if many tiny worms are wriggling just beneath the surface;
- Frequent eye color changes or skin turning gray or white during mental shifts;
- Heightened animal senses that are often or always present;
- An incredible appetite near the Full Moon;
- Sharp rises of fear mixed with excitement just at the beginning of some mental shifts;
- A building pressure that frequently makes you feel as if your skin will split open if you don't shapeshift.

If you have all these symptoms, you are definitely ready. If you have most of them, you are probably ready. If you have few of them, you are probably better off working on other techniques until you become truly ready. If you have none of them, don't even bother trying.

Once you are ready, there are certain basic techniques to best provoke physical shifts. Most of these are adapted from techniques that caused physical shifters to experience their first physical shift, accidentally. To physically shift on purpose, many simply note what caused their accidental shifts, and put themselves in the same conditions and mindset to provoke it again.

The one great key to physical shifting is "letting go." Merely having high levels of shifting energy and a strong animal etheric body may be enough to give you berserker powers, but more is needed for a physical shift. For a physical shift to be triggered, you must "let go." When I speak of "letting go," I am not speaking of giving full reign to all your petty desires, or of being aggressive or sexual, or of letting "the beast," as it has been imagined in Western culture, loose. I am speaking of an altogether different, more sacred way of "letting go."

To "let go" in this way, you must learn to release energy on a deep level. Letting go in the right way involves a lot of faith and trust in yourself, and love and acceptance of the animal portion of your being. For people living in our modern age, it can involve emotional change and questioning your beliefs. If you manage to let go in the right way, and when you have enough shifting energy, you will physically shift. If you are an integrated shifter, you will experience a classical physical shift. If you are not, you will experience an instantaneous physical shift.

Learning to let go is very simple in essence. Once you have acquired high enough levels of shifting energy, go out to a safe and secure wild area on nights of the Full Moon. This should be a place where you feel secure, even at night, and where you know that you will be alone and unobserved. This is important, not just to prevent any embarrassing moments, but to give you a deep peace of mind that will help you let go and change more easily.

The best time for this is from about 10 P.M. to midnight. Once you are in the right place at the right time, undress, or wear extremely loose clothing with no metal or hard plastic parts (no buttons, no zippers). If the weather permits, it is best to be completely nude. Nudity is the natural state of all animals, and highly conducive to bringing forth your inner animal. Moreover, there can be nasty problems associated with physically shifting while clothed. The most obvious is that human clothing does not fit animals, and you may become tangled or strangled in it, or rip and ruin it, or be unable to get it off and end up muddying and soiling it beyond belief. (Just imagine the state your clothes would be in if you dressed your dog in them and let him loose in the woods for a few hours.)

When appropriately attired (or un-attired), wait for a physical shift to occur, and try to let go so that it can occur. As a person with high levels of shifting energy, at this point you'll probably feel your inner animal awakening and stirring in the late night, Full Moon, and wilderness that stimulate it. Feel the pushing pressure of high shifting energy, your body feeling as if it will burst if it doesn't physically shift.

If something happens while you are waiting that brings you near the brink of physically shifting, you will probably feel a sudden great panic rise within you, and not want to continue. This panic is similar to attacks of cold feet before marriage. The groom wants very badly to get married, has planned and anticipated it for months, yet, when the wedding is right there, staring him in the face, he is suddenly scared to death and can't exactly explain why.

The secret of properly letting go is being able to let go of both your feelings of desiring to change, and your panic at doing so, long enough for a physical shift to occur. As long as you are trying to shift, or fighting the shift, it won't happen. You must separate yourself from both your desire and your panic. You must let go of both your desire and your fear. Zen teachings, which teach us how to truly banish desire and fear, may be of great help. True letting go doesn't involve suppressing or ignoring your fear and desire, but truly letting go of it, as in the Christian spiritual practice referred to as "Let go and let God."

There is a very old, wise part of you that knows exactly how to physically shift. Most physical shifters have the ability to physically shift from the animal form back to the human form at will. This is because the animal part has a supremely great ability to let go, and is very close to the subconscious, which knows exactly how to shift. Instantaneous shifters are usually limited to just a few hours in animal form anyway, but they can often purposefully turn back to human before their time runs out.

For the physical shifter in human form, it is a much different matter to change to animal form. In order to physically shift, the ego-centered, very human part of you must step aside, stop fighting for control, and simply let your instinctive, primal self steer you through the shift. It is the only way. It is both incredibly simple and almost impossibly difficult. For those living in the modern age, it is harder than it was in previous ages. If there is one thing that our culture teaches us, it is not to let go. But it can be done.

The process of letting go is often compared to learning to gain more control over bodily processes that are partially or fully under subconscious control. In this way, biofeedback and letting go are similar processes, and a shifter wishing to learn how better to let go may benefit by studying biofeedback.

Physical shifting has been compared to sneezing, another function that is more under subconscious than conscious control. If you feel a sneeze coming on and panic or try to stop it, you probably won't sneeze. If you feel a sneeze coming on and try to sneeze, you probably won't sneeze. If you feel a sneeze coming on and just let go, however, leaving your instinctive self in charge, you'll sneeze. In order to sneeze, you must let go. Of course, it is much easier to sneeze than it is to physically shift, but the basic process of letting go is much the same. Many physical shifters compare the process with trying to urinate while someone you feel uncomfortable around is watching you (as when you can't produce that sample for the doctor!).

What happens when you have high shifting energy, high enough to physically shift, and you try this program for letting go? You wait, nude in the woods, and probably have a number of close calls during which you either panic, or try to take control, or both, and ruin it. You may find you are at the brink of physical shifting a number of times, but desire or fear well up and stop the physical shift from occurring. In actual practice, you almost certainly won't physically shift the first or second time you try this. Going home after ten minutes won't help you at all. Each night you try this, wait for a couple of hours, or until the weather sends you in, whichever comes first, and you will greatly increase your chances of success.

ELEMENTS OF PHYSICAL SHIFTING

1. High Shifting Energy;

2. Integration;

3. Ability to Let Go;

4. Access to Wild Area.

You'll get cold, stiff, bored, and frustrated. Chances are, you'll go out again and again before the first success and, even then, you may make many more attempts before your second success. Some shifters succeed quickly, but most start off slowly and gain few successes until they have been at it for awhile. Some have a block against letting go, and can go without success for a couple of years or more. For them, it would be more productive if they worked on self-healing and spiritual growth first to get rid of their block. Waiting in the woods will do them little good until their block is gone. Most shifters find, when they try to let go, that personal issues come up. They have to deal with these issues in a satisfactory way in order to succeed at letting go. The most common issue that arises is "Why do I want to physically shift?" This is an important question to deal with, and dealing with it honestly helps a lot in learning to let go.

The level of shifting energy necessary for physical shifting generally causes you to desire shapeshifting with the same intensity with which a young man desires to experience sex for the first time. It can be rather intense! But it is an instinctive desire, and many shifters haven't fully thought out their real motivations, fears, and the accompanying responsibilities. It is important not to ignore those questions. You need to think them out in detail, looking beyond instinctive desire and honestly questioning your motives and expectations. Do you expect that physical shifting will be fun? Are you expecting to use your physical shifting to do "neat" immature things, or to further your human purposes? Do you expect it to be a "trip," like getting drunk? Are you afraid of it? If so, why are you afraid? Are you expecting it to be an escape from real life? Are you ready to deal with the side effects and responsibilities of physical shifting? Do you want to physically shift only if things go your way? How do you feel about descending to an animal level of stupidity? Will you be able to accept physical shifting for what it is, or will you be unhappy with the usual sort of physical shift? Will anyone see you wandering about as an animal in the wild area you've chosen, and if they do, will they shoot you?

If you have not deeply thought of these issues and responsibilities before, then you are probably not approaching the idea of physical shifting from a mature point of view, and are probably not ready for it. About half of the shifters that I've known who tried this exercise decided that they were not yet ready to physically shift. Other issues come up as well, when you try to let go. When you go nude into the woods on a Full Moon and wait to physically shift, it really stimulates your animal side. Your animal side starts pointing out things to your human side that it doesn't exactly like. Not dealing with them will not prevent physical shifting, but dealing well with them can lead to an easier time with physical shifting, and it can lead you toward integration.

It can be very hard to accomplish this integration. A few shifters, especially those raised by mature and capable parents, become integrated rather easily and early in life. Others become integrated through lots of hard work. Simply aging and becoming more mature and wise can often eventually bring integration. Physical shifting is a spiritual journey of personal growth more than anything, even if you never become integrated. Approach it first from that perspective, and it will go well.

Physical shifters of the classical type have additional difficulties with the process of letting go. In order to complete their physical shift, and not have it reverse in the middle, they must remain in a state of letting go for the entire length of their change, which may last minutes. This is a fairly long time to keep yourself in exactly the right state of mind. This is especially true since, all the while you are experiencing a physical shift, something alarming and disconcerting is happening, especially your first time.

When a classical shifter slips out of the right state of mind at some point in the middle of a shift, the shift simply slows and then stops, and the body starts changing back to human form. If the shifter manages to achieve the right state of mind again before reaching human form, the shift will once again reverse its course and the shifter will change into an animal again. It is possible for a shifter who is experienced and in control to purposely go back and forth in the middle of a shift repeatedly, or even to "stall" at some point in the middle and run around half-changed for a while. I don't recommend trying this, especially for beginners, because it can mess up your shifting and lead to problems.

Here is an experience common to classical shifters, especially for the first physical shift: Walking through a small wooded area at night, probably on or near a Full Moon, they feel the symptoms of an immanent physical shift but don't really pay attention, merely thinking that they are feeling really good. When they start growing fur, or perhaps even later, when they start having significant changes in their shape, they notice it, look at themselves, and see that they are partially transformed. They may watch themselves slowly changing for a little bit, until their mind recovers and it really registers with them. Then they panic and think, "Oh no, what's happening to me?" At this point, the change reverses itself, the fur starts sliding back into their skin, and they return to human form. By the next day, they may even have convinced themselves that they imagined it all—until more changes happen and they end up with too much evidence to ignore.

Very rarely do classical shifters ever complete their first physical shift. It is almost inevitable that very soon after they notice it, they will go into a panic and return to human form. Even if they don't panic immediately, they will probably panic when they lose their balance and fall over, or when their clothes start strangling them, or when they cut their tongue on their fangs. It is best, when experiencing the classical type of physical shift, to sit down, lie down, or get on all fours early in the shift, before you fall over and hurt yourself. (If you are experiencing instantaneous shifting, it is best to sit down or lie down before the shift, because you won't have time during it.) A body that is part way between human and wolf, and in the process of changing, just wasn't meant to be balancing on two legs, especially when it's not used to it. In movies and novels, when werewolves wander around and do all sorts of things in midform, it just isn't very realistic. You should also keep your mouth open when shifting. Wolves have twice as many teeth as humans, and the big upper and lower fangs, as well as many other sharp new teeth, often thrust out of the gums rather suddenly, before the mouth has grown quite large enough to hold them all. By keeping your mouth open and your tongue out of the way, you can avoid cutting your tongue and lips.

There are a number of tricks to keep from panicking or trying to take control. The most effective is simply to have experienced so many classical physical shifts that you are completely used to them. There are other tricks that are more accessible to the beginner. One is to watch yourself change in a full-length mirror while trying to play the role of a detached, but curious, observer. Try to forget that it is your precious body that is experiencing all these strange things. Just lie back and enjoy watching your change. Don't think too much, and don't worry.

When you observe yourself changing in a large mirror, you can see most of your body at once, and see what is happening easily. This is less frightening than feeling all sorts of strange things and glancing from one body part to the next to keep track of what is going on. It also helps you think of yourself as an observer. Because you can see exactly what's happening, it increases your curiosity and interest in the change, an attitude that can stave off panic and promote letting go.

Another trick is to distract yourself during the change, so you don't start thinking too much and worrying. Some classical shifters always shift while exploring the woods. They keep themselves moving and exploring throughout the change to distract themselves and to help the change along by stimulating their wolf self with the outdoors, though there are also many reports of how difficult and unwieldy it can be to move around while half-transformed.

One thing that will not help is an audience. You are much more likely to start worrying if someone else is watching you change, and probably judging you as well. If you want to prove to your best friend or spouse that you are a physical shifter, and are determined to change physically in front of them, it is best not to attempt this until you have a fair amount of experience, so that worries and complexes don't build up around physical shifting and end up robbing you of your ability. You should also try to prepare others for the shock to make sure they don't panic and shoot you. Don't try to change from human to wolf in front of them. It is very difficult to get into this delicate state of mind if someone is watching you. It is far easier to appear to others in wolf form and then change to human, than it is to change from human to wolf. Remember, however, that you as a wolf may not feel it is important to change back in front of some human just to make a point.

Another shortcut that some physical shifters use to let go is to enter a deep trance state or practice self-hypnotism. This can involve some danger and should only be attempted by those who are properly experienced. Even so, the results are usually quite disappointing. One danger is that this trick, especially if self-hypnotism is involved, is likely to produce only a powerful vision that can seem like a physical shift, especially if the subject has never experienced real physical shifts. This is especially likely if the person desires physical shifting very much, or isn't approaching the practice in a mature manner, or is not a person who truly has the necessary requirements to become a physical shifter. Moreover, this technique only helps in letting go, so you must have all the rest of the prerequisites for it to truly produce a physical shift. If it does produce a physical shift, the results are often disappointing. Shifters usually remain in a deep trance state for the rest of the shift. This often leads to memory holes, and makes them feel disconnected, groggy, as if their brain were stuffed with cotton during their time in animal form. In short, it is a very unsatisfying experience, even when it does work.

Alternatively, someone else may hypnotize the shifter and guide them through their physical shift. This produces the same kind of disappointing experience that other trance states produce, but it does have several advantages. Someone who is not shifting themselves is guiding the shift, which may make success more likely. Moreover, there is a witness who can readily distinguish whether you really experienced a physical shift or just a powerful vision induced by hypnotism. It can also lead to a greater self-confidence and feeling of well-being about physical shifts, and make it more likely that you will be able to experience physical shifts the natural way, without trance or self-hypnosis.

OTHER TRICKS FOR SHIFTERS

There are also a number of mundane tricks that increase the likelihood of having a successful physical shift that have nothing to do with letting go. Try to have as many things as possible "just right" for shifting—work at night, under a Full Moon, for example. Stimulate your animal side—work outside, try to think like your animal, walk on all fours, for example.

These conditions are not absolutely necessary for a physical shift. Physical shifts can happen indoors, in broad daylight, and far from both the Full and New Moons. But the more of them you can invoke, the better chance you have. For some, the problem in achieving a physical shift is not in letting go, but in getting to the "brink," the time when the shifting energy peaks. These conditions—being outdoors under a Full Moon—are likely to push you to the brink if you have really high levels of shifting energy. There are some who become skilled in stimulating the inner animal, getting all the conditions right, and forcibly pushing themselves to the brink more often than would naturally occur. This gives them many more chances to properly let go and experience a physical shift. Some can bring themselves to the brink a dozen times on a good night.

STEPS TO PHYSICAL SHIFTING

1. Have symptoms of High Shifting Energy;

2. Wait in a Wild Area;

3. Reach "The Brink";

4. Let Go.

One secret to making physical shifting easier is to fast for a day before your attempt. Having an empty stomach makes physical shifting much more likely. The irony here is that, for someone with high enough shifting energy to physically shift, "the hunger" is nearly impossible to resist around the Full Moon. Another thing that helps is to have very little material in your bowels. Make sure your diet includes plenty of fiber. For some reason, foreign matter inside the human body, such as food or fecal matter, is somewhat inhibiting to physical shifting.

Another technique that helps physical shifting is to stay perfectly still until the shift has completed. This is irrelevant for instantaneous shifting, for the shift is over so quickly that you don't really have time to move. For classical shifting, it can be very important. Moving around too much during a shift—especially quick, sudden movements or brushing against things—tends to slow down the shift or sometimes even reverse it.

Physical shifts should be done in the dark. Physical shifting is a process in which the body becomes partially like ectoplasm, so that it is possible for it to change. Grayish or white ectoplasmic smoke may even spill out of the body and cling to the skin during the change. All ectoplasm is very sensitive to bright light. In most cases it will actually dissolve in bright light. This is why séances are most often held in the dark, or in dim light. This is also why, in legend, werewolves who shift during the day most often crawl under a bush or descend into a cellar to change. I've heard stories of physical shifters who started to shift, who turned on a light because they wanted to watch the change, only to have the change immediately reverse itself, sometimes painfully. Mediums who are generating ectoplasm with a light turned on also sometimes report pain.

Once you are able to physically shift, it is important to know how to do so more easily and regularly. One way to accomplish this is to find some food and eat it while you are physically shifted into animal form. Assimilating this real food somehow strengthens the animal form, and "anchors" it to reality a bit more. When you return to human form, and it again becomes an etheric body, it will be stronger. Your next physical shift will also be easier, because the animal form will pass from an etheric to a physical state more easily. Remember these facts when trying this trick: cats and wolves have great difficulty digesting vegetable matter—in fact, it can make them sick. Bears and foxes digest many types of vegetable matter just fine, especially fruits. If you make your new body sick, it will actually weaken your etheric form.

Chi-gong can also contribute to better physical shifting. Fortunately, you do not have to be a chi-gong master to better control your physical shifting. If you are already a physical shifter, you need not be more than an amateur at chi-gong to gain more control. The large center of *chi* near your second chakra strongly affects physical shifting. A lot of activity takes place in this *chi* center right before and during a physical shift. For instantaneous shifters, this can manifest as horrible cramps and gut-wrenching nausea. For classical shifters, it can manifest as a very alive, flushing, elastic "warm chill" that spreads out from this area to the whole body.

Chi-gong can't, on the other hand, make you able to physically shift. But it can drastically reduce your dependence on stimuli. Average physical shifters need to have everything just right, stimulating their animal side extensively, for a physical shift to occur. They cannot physically shift indoors; they must be outdoors. It must be night. They must stimulate their inner animal by dwelling on certain thoughts and feelings. Anything that interferes with these conditions is likely to ruin the chances of a physical shift that night, or even that month. Even if they have the ability to let go fairly well, shifters may need to have everything else right in order to bring themselves to the brink.

Moreover, average physical shifters may lose their ability entirely if separated from the wild areas where they can prowl and feel safe and secure. More than any other type of shift, physical shifting is deeply connected to the land and dependent upon prowling. Every physical shifter I've known had some private wild land to which they had easy access, and they made use of this area by prowling regularly. Average physical shifters prowl in human form many times for each time they do so as an animal. Many who thought of this ability as a permanent part of themselves, almost stopped shifting altogether when they moved to a city. Chi-gong allows shifters to physically shift without going through such a delicate balancing act each time. Serious shifters, whether close to physical shifting or not, would do well to learn the techniques of chi-gong.

PROGRESSING ALONG THE PATH

Developing higher levels of shifting energy and a strong etheric body, becoming better integrated, and learning better shifting techniques and "higher powers" requires that shifters progress along the path by learning lessons. As you traverse the path, you will experience many new things, both hardships and wonders. You must go where the path truly leads you and learn the lessons that are presented. If you want to experience only the wonders and not the hardships and painful lessons, you will not progress on the path. The path of a shifter is a wondrous path, utterly unlike many others available in life. Yet it asks you to learn some hard lessons, face difficult truths, and, above all, truly know yourself. If you resist the lessons presented, you may find yourself unable to make progress toward integration, stronger connections to the inner animal, and acquisition and improvement of the higher powers. In fact, you may regress. Nothing in this chapter will do you much good if you stubbornly resist the lessons presented along the path.

To progress on the path of a shifter, you must have right intentions in your heart. You must not want to shift for selfish, petty, or indulgent purposes. While it is perfectly okay to enjoy being a shifter, you should truly love and respect all aspects of the process, not just lust after "neat" abilities. You must not let shifter goals consume you. They should be merely part of the path, part of a way toward enlightenment and wholeness. Too many shifters lust after "the Holy Grail" of berserker powers or physical shifting. While it is natural to want these things, they should be only a part of the path, not an all-consuming goal. That part of the path most often ignored is the gradual joining of human and animal, conscious and subconscious. The animal-mental side is often pushed to the back, feared, or considered too stupid to be useful.

Too many shifters want to receive the animal body, but reject the animal mentality. They want full human intelligence at all times, combined with berserker powers or physical shifting. The animal within, however, is an important part of progression on the path, and you are unlikely to receive the higher powers if you don't progress properly. You must learn to acknowledge the animal mentality as a valuable, wonderful, instinctual, and wise part of yourself. You must court it, dance with it, and merge with it, making its unique and wonderful powers and viewpoint more accessible to your conscious mind. You must learn to respect and love it fully for what it is. Remember, it is the animal side of yourself, dwelling mostly within your subconscious, that has all the keys to what you want most from shifting. The conscious, ego-centered part of you can only obtain these keys by learning to merge with the animal side, integrating your consciousness.

This dance between your human and animal self is much like the romance between a man and a woman—the man representing the ego-centered, more conscious, human side, and the woman representing the animal side, more connected to the subconscious. Men tend to be interested mostly in certain aspects of the woman: her body, her beauty, and having sex with her. Women reject these requests unless and until they are satisfied that the man is interested in more, and that he fully appreciates and loves her as a person. The man mostly wants sex, but the woman wants a real relationship. If she is courted properly and shown a genuine interest in and appreciation of her nonsexual qualities, she will eventually agree to sex. The romance will blossom, the woman will give the man what he needs, the man will give the woman what she needs, and the two will join their purposes and powers, to the advantage of both.

Thus it should be between the animal and human sides of a shifter on the true path. If shifters want only the more dazzling aspects of shifting, not wanting to enter into a full-blown relationship with their own animal self, they are unlikely to progress on the path. If they lust after the higher powers, but feel it burdensome and unenjoyable to let out their animal side—for prowling in the woods, or for subtle integration of its qualities into their everyday human persona—they will be unlikely to get those higher powers. To be a shifter, you must joyfully accept the whole package and be willing to live it as a spiritual path and a lifestyle. There is no such thing as a weekend werewolf.

All the physical shifters that I know approach shifting in a similar way. They are all mature, quiet, thoughtful, and humble people who tend to enjoy life. They tend to approach shifting in a spiritual way, in an attitude of joy, acceptance, and satisfaction with what they are. Most of them say that physical shifting is irrelevant to the path of a shifter, that it is merely a side effect of getting to certain places on the true path. They are all people who very much enjoy and revel in the nonphysical aspects of shifting. If you can't fully immerse yourself in these nonphysical aspects, you can't get to the physical aspects. A werewolf is not defined by the physical transformation into wolf. The physical transformation is merely an occasional side effect of already being merged with the wolf within.

The attitude of physical shifters toward physical shifting tends to be that, if the totem bestows its physical form on you, it's okay; if it does not, it's okay. You need to be at peace with what you get out of shifting, not focused on what you don't. The most important part of being a shifter is to experience it and live it, to revel in being part animal, and having your animal part available, even if at the back of your mind, all the time. You must respect and honor the animal part of yourself, not expect or demand things from it, or think that it "owes" you anything. It is, after all, a part of you. Whatever it does to you, you did to you, so how can you be unhappy with it, unless you don't truly know yourself? If you cannot be happy with how much of a werewolf you are right now, and enjoy it and accept it for what it is, then how can you possibly handle and enjoy being even more of a werewolf? One must come before the other.

CONCENTRATION SHIFTING

There is another type of "physical shifting" that I should mention. "Concentration Shifting" is not true physical shifting, as the changes that occur are extremely small and temporary. Concentration Shifting is more in the class of minor paranormal effects that are sometimes associated with shifters. Instantaneous shifting needs only high shifting energy and "letting go" to accomplish a physical shift, doing away with the need for integration by using lots of shifting energy. With enough energy, you can even do away with the need for "letting go," although the result is often a very sorry excuse for a physical shift, and can be very unpleasant. This process requires such huge amounts of energy that you cannot actually hold it within you for any length of time. It must be used as soon as it is obtained, or it is lost. The levels of shifting energy involved in instantaneous shifting are about as high as can be held and maintained for even a brief amount of time, and even that makes instantaneous shifters very sick and uncomfortable. The levels required for concentration shifting are too high to hold for any more than the briefest time.

In order to generate enough shifting energy, you must have fairly high levels to start with. You also need to draw lots of energy from an outside source—for instance, a large moonstone. You may be generating it yourself by using yoga techniques or kundalini exercises, by some visionary technique borrowed from shamanism, or by the formal raising of "power" within a ritual circle. Whatever the source, you need very good "energy channeling" and visualization skills, and a good bit of practice, for this process to succeed. To cause concentration shifting, you must channel all of the energy into just one body part, such as a finger, while vividly visualizing that part changing into, say, a wolf's toe. If this works, the part changes, very slowly and with intense pain, for as long as the energy holds out and your concentration remains intense.

This method has a number of problems and dangers, however. One problem is the pain. Shifters who have done this all report that the pain in extremely intense, almost as if every cell is being burned, or cut apart and put back together. This may, in fact, be exactly what is happening.

Moreover, there is never enough energy to go very far. If you concentrate on a larger part, the energy is stretched very thin and runs out much faster. If you concentrate on the whole body, the energy isn't strong enough to do anything. Even when concentrating on a tiny body part, I have never heard of anyone going farther than just a partial transformation of that part. Yet another problem is that the process tends to burn out all your shifting energy, so that you are left with very low levels. If used often, it tends to "wear out" your shifting energy, so that your energy starts burning itself out more easily, even in the normal course of things.

When the energy runs out, the part immediately returns to human form most of the time. One problem, however, is that it doesn't always return to human form, especially if you do this a lot, or if you manage to get the change to go very far. In all the cases I've known, the fur always fell off or pulled back into the skin, but the hand, or whatever, retained its new shape. One man I knew managed to badly deform both his hands and feet with repeated tries to shapeshift by this method. His thumbs shortened and the joint changed, so that he no longer had opposable thumbs. His hands also developed somewhat toe-like fingers. His feet became partially digitigrade and very long, so that he couldn't fit them into any shoes well.

A lot of shifters get inspired by this method. They often believe that, if they just practice more, eventually they'll be able to fully change their whole body. Some go off on great searches for more and more energy to "feed" the process, and some reportedly end up descending into black magic and vampirism trying to get ever more energy. All of this is a dead end. No amount of practice, refinement, or energy will ever allow this process to be true physical shifting. Even if, by some great source of energy and lots of practice, you did manage to fully transform by this method, you would probably either end up badly deformed, or permanently transformed into an animal. What, then, is the use of this process? It is good for only one thing: convincing yourself, or others, that actual physical changing can and does exist. As long as you never take the change too far, and don't do it too often, you shouldn't end up with any problems worse than the horrible pain that you endure during the change. Especially for shifters in doubt of themselves, there is nothing quite so precious as real, physical proof that what you are striving for is not a delusion. Since this process is much easier to learn than either instantaneous or classical shifting, it is much more available as a means of proof. I have known of several "gurus" who gained a large following among shifter groups based on nothing more than their ability to demonstrate this power to others occasionally. At least one of these gurus was dispensing "wisdom" about shifting that was little better than nonsense.

THE GREAT CYCLE

One of the major, universal patterns in the path of a shifter is called "the great cycle." The great cycle has three stages: change, integration, and transcendence (see figure 3, page 202). Each of these stages leads to more self-knowledge. Every shifter goes through this cycle many times while on the path. Difficulty with one or more of them is a common impediment to progress. Shifters must be ready to accept change, to become what they were not before, to recognize and bring forth parts of themselves that were buried, to change as people, to let old beliefs and ways of doing things die so that the new patterns can emerge. Change is often one of the hardest and most painful spiritual lessons, but it is only the first step for a shifter. Shifters must learn to change their very selves, to put on the new and take off the old.

CLASSICAL SHIFTING
High Shifting Energy +
Integration + Letting Go =
Slow, Gradual Full
Transformation.

INSTANTANEOUS SHIFTING
Very High Shifting Energy +
Letting Go = Fast, Volatile
Full Transformation.

CONCENTRATION SHIFTING
Extremely High Shifting
Energy + Focus on One Part =
Partial Transformation
in One Part.

Change by itself is of little use. You can learn to bring forth the pure animal mental state, and let it fully overwhelm you in a deep and spectacular mental shift, but this is of limited use, from both a practical and a spiritual viewpoint. To truly grow as a person, to make this ability into an

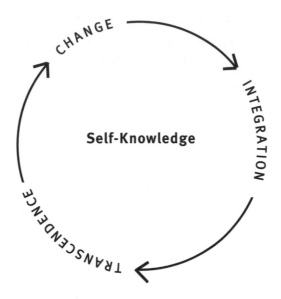

Figure 3. The Great Cycle is the natural, cycling, progression of the most important processes that are part of the path of being a shifter. The three lessons of change, integration, and transcendence all lead to self-knowledge. The shifter who resists these lessons, or is uninterested in them, is unlikely to progress to the higher powers.

accessible tool, you must integrate it into your self. You must not just learn raw change and fragment into a thousand powerful, yet separate pieces. You must take this change into yourself and merge with it, become a new, integrated whole—the best of the new and the old combined.

This is of limited use as well, however. To truly use this process to move closer to inner peace, spiritual awareness, and enlightenment—to use it fully—you must learn transcendence. You must learn how to look at the whole process from God's viewpoint, to step back and see how the true, eternal soul is revealed by the process of change and integration, to see how, in a sense, there never was any change or integration, for it was always there, always a part of you, from the beginning. From the perspective of transcendence, change and integration are merely a shifting dance through which you see glimpses of your true self. You merely looked within in the right way, and thereby changed your point of view of yourself.

The self, per se, remains the same—eternal. To proceed to the next step as a shifter, you must learn to transcend the change and integration stages, and move beyond them.

Those who have difficulty with transcendence can often ease their passage by working with herbs of immortality, in a magical sense. Herbs of immortality relate to the energies of infinity, forever, above, transcendence, the divine, the void, pure love, long life, and the mysteries of birth, death, and reincarnation. Be careful in working with them, for some relate so strongly to the mysteries of death that they are deadly poison! Some herbs of immortality are chervil, cinnamon, heather, honeysuckle, life-everlasting, mistletoe, pennyroyal, periwinkle, primrose, and tansy.

Once you have transcended the stages of change and integration, along comes another change. You take the next step, and the great cycle continues. Every shifter goes through this cycle many times, experiencing many types of change, integration, and transcendence. You must learn to recognize the cycle, embrace it, and anticipate it.

THE MAGIC OF SHAPESHIFTING

There are a number of purely magical techniques related to shapeshifting. So far, I have outlined only the more mundane, everyday ways to advance along the path of a shifter, ways that many people do not think of as magic at all. These "hermetic" means, being mostly of the mind and soul, are not usually thought of as magic at all by those who encounter them. There are aspects of shapeshifting, however, that are more connected with the ritual, physical tools, and ceremony of magic.

The magic of shapeshifting is very close to nature. With a few exceptions, it has nothing to do with the type of ceremonial magic that requires tools and the formal raising of a circle. It has much to do with meditation, spirit journeys, the "fairy" and nature realm, divas, shamanic magic, nature magic, and attracting certain energies into your life. There are certain simple tools and practices that can bring more of the magic of shapeshifting into your life. Certain herbs, colors, symbols, and gemstones are conducive to the energies of shapeshifting, or tend to attract the energies of a particular species (see Table 1, page 204).

Table 1. Magical and Spiritual Correspondences of Shifting.

CATEGORY	STRONG	LESS STRONG
General	Female, Darkness, Rhythms, Passion, Instinct, Duality	Strength, Dragons, Kundalini, Life/Death/Life Cycle
Stones	Moonstone, Silver, Bloodstone	Rose Quartz, Amber, Opal, Pearl, Cat's-eye, Iron, Ruby, Cinnabar,* Chrysoprase**
Symbols	I-Ching Hexagram 49, the Rune *Algiz*, the number 9	Symbols associated with your species
Herbs/Plants	Ash, Wolfsbane, Dragon's Blood, Mythical Moonflower	Foxglove, Catnip, Oak, Camphor, Willow, Asafoetida
Colors	Pine Green, Black, Silver	Red, Light Blue
Astrology	Cancer, Moon, Neptune, 8th house, Nadir, South Node	Taurus, Gemini, Leo, Pluto, Sun, Saturn, sometimes Mars
Elements	Fire, Water	Earth, Elements associated with the species you are
Direction	North, West	Directions associated with the species you are
Senses	Smell, Touch, Spatial sense	Any sense that is unusually strong in your species
Season/Time	Fall, Full Moon, From 10:00 P.M. to Midnight, Winter Solstice, Friday	Summer, New Moon, Dawn, Lupercalia, Halloween
Saints	St. Christopher	St. Francis, St. Jude, St. Patrick
Places	Mountaintops, Rocky gulches, Springs	Small streams, Lakes, Good habitat for your species
Goddesses & Gods	Freya, Sekhmet, Brigit, Anubis, Lupa, Oya	Apollo, Diana, Loki, Gaia, Pan, Artemis

*Cinnabar is poisonous, even to the touch, for it often exudes mercury, a toxic liquid that poisons slowly by causing brain damage. Handle only with the most extreme caution.

**Chrysoprase is most useful for increasing an understanding of the magic of shapeshifting, learning to control the energies invoked, and for long-term increase of shifting-related powers. It is best to wear it as an amulet, especially during periods when you need more help than usual or are trying to progress on the path of a shifter.

Before I go on, I should stress that the techniques outlined in the first part of this chapter are more important than the techniques you are about to read. You should focus your efforts and concentrate on them. The magical techniques are powerful tools. With the possible exception of a few that are very powerful in the hands of a competent magic-worker, however, none of them will do you any good unless you have mastered the basics. The basics are the foundation. Without a foundation, how can you build?

Too many shifters look for some "magic key" that will make physical shifting simple. They search for a physical shifter to bite them (which doesn't work), or for just the right herbal unguent (which doesn't work), or to drink water out of a wolf's footprint (which doesn't work).

Those looking for shortcuts look to ceremonial magic as well. People tend to think that, just because magic can do some supernatural things, it can make a miracle fall into their lap on demand. But magic just doesn't work that way. It can occasionally produce very spectacular supernatural occurrences, but it does so only in accordance with its own rules. Moreover, magic is a lot of work. It is never a shortcut. With or without magic, there is no way to make a miracle happen. There is no free lunch.

Nothing, except perhaps the most powerful magic in the hands of a great magician, or the occasional fluke accident of being "chosen" by destiny, can suddenly make one a physical shifter without going through the basics. There are a few people who have become physical shifters very quickly, breezing right through the basics. I have a feeling that these may be people who had learned the basics already in a former life. I haven't known anyone who managed to use magical techniques to "shortcut" to physical shifting, but I have known quite a few who've tried to use magical techniques to take a giant step in their advancement along the path. In all of these cases, if the magic worked, the shifter didn't deal well with the effects. They were simply not ready for that stage yet. That was why they hadn't gotten there on their own. Once there, it did them no good, and they often regressed. If a shifter manages to advance by magic alone, it can do damage to the psyche, which has not been prepared by the basics.

If it is true that great magicians of the legendary past could make ordinary people into physical shifters without the basics, this may explain some of the nasty werewolf legends. The psyche cannot handle this transition easily. It is a good thing that in modern times it is so hard, and takes so long, to become a physical shifter.

MAGICAL HERBS

Wolfsbane is perhaps the most famous herb associated with shapeshifting, and with werewolves in particular. This herb has long had an association with wolves, werewolves, and dogs, partly because it is extremely poisonous, and was put on arrows to kill wolves and other "vermin" beasts that would not be consumed. Wolfsbane should always be handled very carefully. It should *never*, under any circumstances, be eaten or used internally. If used externally in a salve, extreme caution should be used, since it is one of the few poisonous herbs that can be dangerous even when used externally. It is perfectly safe, however, to use the herb in magic if you never touch any part of the plant. For instance, you can meditate near the living plant, or keep a dried sprig of it in an amulet.

Wolfsbane is most commonly known by other names, such as aconite and monkshood. There are a number of varieties of it, with various different flower colors. Those who use the magic of color may want to choose a variety with a particular flower color for their magic. Wolfsbane is difficult to find because of its poisonous nature. If you wish to use it, you will probably have to purchase it from a flower catalog (where it will be listed under the name "monkshood") and grow it in your own garden. As with all poisonous plants, take measures to keep kids and pets safe.

The legends about wolfsbane seem almost contradictory. Some say that wolfsbane was used to turn people into werewolves, and to cause shapeshifting in people who were already werewolves. It is commonly listed as an ingredient in legendary recipes for "werewolf salve." Yet some legends say that it was used to cure werewolves, and that werewolves were repelled by it. People grew it around their houses or kept dried bunches of it hanging from the ceiling to protect them from werewolves.

How can wolfsbane be said to both cause and cure werewolves? Any herb or substance that is used to magically attract a certain energy can also be used to control that same energy. Wolfsbane is an herb that works with shapeshifting energies, not just to attract them, but to control them and to work with them in more complex ways. If you want it to repel and inhibit werewolves, it can do that just as well as encourage or attract them.

Wolfsbane also has other energies associated with it that explain the repulsion of some werewolves. It is known to give protection from evil, which is why it is used so often to consecrate sacred blades used in ritual. Presumably, if a particular werewolf is linked with black magic, wolfsbane might indeed repel it. Wolfsbane is thus an excellent herb for a wolf shifter to use magically. It can both attract what you want, and repel what you don't want.

Foxglove is another herb associated with shapeshifting and especially with foxes. Foxglove is also associated with the fairy and deva kingdom, and with spirit journeys to the underworld. Foxglove and wolfsbane should not be used simultaneously unless the shifter is in the process of moving out of the fox shifter stage and into the wolf shifter stage.

Foxglove and wolfsbane "oppose" each other's energies and the two herbs do not work well together. Foxglove has a capricious and carefree energy that is opposed by the somber, serious, and "adult" (in astrological terms, "Saturn") nature of wolfsbane. Folklore, in fact, claims that foxglove is an antidote for wolfsbane. Foxglove is also a poisonous herb, and should never be eaten or used internally for any reason. It is beautiful and can easily be found for sale at nurseries and in garden catalogs.

Dragon's blood is an herb associated with animals in general, the paranormal element of fire, and the build-up and increase of magical power. When dragon's blood is combined with other magical shapeshifting practices, it makes them much more potent. If you have a special moonstone that you use for shifting, anoint or consecrate it with dragon's blood.

The herb most often found in shapeshifting lore, even more than the famous wolfsbane, is moonflower, or mariphasa. This is, in all likelihood, a mythical herb. No one has ever identified a known species of herb with this legendary herb, although it is possible that it exists but is rare and yet to be identified. It is the flower, and not the whole plant, that is especially infused with shapeshifting magic. It was said to work its magic when plucked and then worn or carried on the person as an amulet.

Descriptions of the moonflower from many areas and cultures are surprisingly similar. It appeared in a number of colors, tended to grow in low-lying and especially swampy areas, and could only be found in the deepest wilderness. It often grew in areas known to be haunted or places where the veil between this world and the next was thin. It had a very peculiar, sticky sap, and a strange, sickly, heady odor.

The ash tree has a very long history of magical lore associated with it. It appears not only in shapeshifting lore, but in magical lore in general. Like wolfsbane, the ash has strong magic for protection from evil, and was often said to magically repel evil shapeshifters, as well as vampires, evil ghosts, and malefic astral entities. Like wolfsbane, it also has the magic of great energy and the raising of power. In some legends, it was used to invoke shapeshifting magic, particularly in the famous Russian ceremony for becoming a werewolf.[1]

A very good way to use herbs for the magic of shapeshifting is to plant a "sacred garden" and go there to meditate near the live plants. Since shapeshifting has such strong ties to the natural world and nature magic, it is best to make this small garden as natural as possible, perhaps in a small clearing deep in the woods, near a spring or source of water. The garden should remain secret, if possible, as other people may contaminate it with their energy, and with the influence of civilization. Try to choose a place where people almost never go.

Some herbs are used in magical salves. Herbal salves were used in witchcraft and shamanism for all sorts of purposes. Herbs or other substances were selected for the qualities the magical practitioner wanted to invoke then converted into a substance that was easily mixed into a base of fat or vegetable oils, such as a tea, tincture, or mash. Sometimes the herbs were burned and their ashes mixed into the base of fat or vegetable oils. As in homeopathy, these salves tended to be fairly dilute. The salves

---

[1] Montague Summers, *The Werewolf* (Secaucus, NJ: Citadel Press, 1973), pp. 109–110.

were then used to anoint ritual objects, or in some cases, the body of the magical practitioner. The herbs, embedded in salve, conveyed their magical qualities to the object or person.

If you decide to use shapeshifting salves in your magical practice, select your herbs for the energies you want most. Books of shapeshifting lore have many different recipes for shapeshifting salves, because true magic-workers tailor their formulas to their own needs, or create them from scratch. If you decide to use a formula from a book, at least do a little research to find out what energies the herbs are invoking, and then decide whether these energies are compatible with your purposes. Always include at least one herb that protects against evil, since ceremonial shapeshifting magic can sometimes invoke powerful, dangerous energies.

You should research the mundane qualities of these herbs. Many of them are poisonous. Some are psychedelic and may help astral travel or open up communication with your own more subtle senses. Even though most recipes include such ingredients in very dilute form and authorities say that they are harmless when used externally, you should still find out which herbs are dangerous, and how they are dangerous. There is no excuse for blindly using some poisonous preparation out of some arcane tome. If you do decide to use dangerous herbs, be sure to use dilute preparations such as a mash of the leaves diluted in a great deal of fat. Never use the oil of any herb. Even nonpoisonous herbs can become toxic when mixed with an oil. If you do use poisonous herbs, prepare and store them in clearly marked containers that will never be used for edible food. If you are unfamiliar with the terms and operations of herbal preparation, you are certainly not ready to make herbal salves and you should gain experience and knowledge of herbology before proceeding.

I recommend against using dangerous herbs, since it is quite possible to invoke similar energies with preparations of nonpoisonous herbs. Dangerous herbs are safe when used correctly in salves used to anoint ritual objects, and they are not to be used on the body. Ritual objects that have been anointed should still be handled with great care until the salve has dried and flaked off. Shifters who make shifting salves often use vegetable shortening as the base, warmed right before use.

Shifting salves are most often used to anoint ritual objects involved with invoking shapeshifting energies, such as a wolf belt or an amulet. When the body is anointed with shifting salve, it is usually to help induce astral or bilocation shifting, rarely physical shifting. When used to induce physical shifting, it was usually used in conjunction with a shifting belt. More often, just the shifting belt was anointed, not the body.

MAGICAL COLORS

Colors are often associated with the magic of shifting, and with the energies of various species of animal. Black and a dark rich ("forest" or "pine") green are most closely associated with the magic of shapeshifting. Many shifters wear necklaces of black and dark green stones. Some feel that the necklace connects somehow to their shifting energies. Others have no idea of the magic involved, but just wear the necklaces because they are pretty. In a thousand little ways like this, shifters are led to the right path by their instincts, even when they don't know what is going on. This affinity for black and green shows itself in other ways. Many shifters have a wardrobe with an unusual amount of black and forest-green clothing. Many decorate their houses in these colors, or own black or dark-green cars.

The color green symbolizes growth, creation, change, fertility, nature, and love. Forest green is particularly symbolic of nature in its full ripeness and maturity. The color black symbolizes protection, sobriety, creation, fertility, maturity, and the darkness out of which all life comes. Black also symbolizes "Saturn" energies that take a long time to ripen, but are extremely powerful when they do, much like the true way on the path of a shifter. Black is serious and symbolic of the wisdom and power of the old. It is the color of the richest soil, whence all life comes. It is also the color inside eggs, wombs, and seeds, where life starts. Black symbolizes change and the destruction of the old, so that the new can arise. If you think about these qualities of black and forest green, you can see why they invoke the qualities of shapeshifting so strongly, especially when used together.

Some colors invoke the essence of a certain species. For an example, red is very much a "fox" color. The systems of many cultures assign certain colors to certain species, along with "directions" and other qualities. Not all systems agree on these colors, but they tend to be similar. A shifter interested in better invoking the magic of a particular species would do well to study one or more of these systems in detail.

MAGICAL ELEMENTS

Most of those interested in the paranormal have heard about the Western system of classifying energies and qualities into four "elements" that correspond to nearly everything magical or mundane. These elements act in ways that resemble earth, air, fire, and water, so are named after them. The elements of fire and water both have much to do with the magic of shapeshifting, especially when invoked together. Many ancient recipes, spells, charms, or ceremonies for shapeshifting invoke the elements of water and fire.

Water and fire are both malleable and changeable, in ways that earth and air are not. Real water and fire continually shapeshift, reforming themselves—water to fit its container, fire just dancing and reforming on its own. Water and fire together are also potent agents of change and transformation, for water is creation and the life-giver, and fire is great energy and destruction of the old. In studying the astrological birth charts of natural-born shifters, I have found that they are usually dominated by water and fire signs.

Shifters have to go through processes and lessons connected with the elements of fire and water. The element of water is strongly connected to the subconscious, emotions, intuition, and femininity. Shifters on the path find that, in order to progress, they must absolutely make peace with their subconscious and learn to work in partnership with it. They must learn to acknowledge and deal with their emotions better than others. They also find that it is essential to develop their intuition and learn how to rely on it.

Males find that they must confront issues relating to their own inner femininity. A surprising number of male shifters are gay or bisexual, but few female shifters are. Most male shifters who manifest higher powers are somewhat feminine in their manner. This does not mean their masculinity is impaired, it may be very strong. They have merely mixed into it a number of balancing female traits, the kind of traits that the men's movement is trying to legitimize.

Shifters must learn to deal with many fire-related issues in order to progress on the path. The element of fire is connected to passion, energy, courage, the physical body, and driving forces. One of the prime lessons of fire is the proper use of energy. Use it well, and fire can give you tremendous energy from just about any source. Use it badly, and, like fire, you will "burn out." The energy will be consumed in a brief, powerful flare, and then be utterly unavailable for quite some time. Shifters often find these energy patterns in their lives. They must learn to use them well, or they will get stuck in a cycle that consists of being "burned out" most of the time. If they learn this lesson, they will have lots of energy available continuously, as from a well-fed fire.

The element of fire is connected strongly to passion. Shifters often find that, in order to progress, they must learn to deal with passions of all sorts. They may have inappropriate passions connected with mental shifts that they must learn to work past. They may lose control because of anger, as in the legendary berserker. Shifters often have unusually strong sexual passions. They must learn to deal with them in a positive manner, neither suppressing their sexuality in an unhealthy attempt to control it, nor letting their sexual appetites lead them into inappropriate activities.

Fire is strongly connected to courage, as well. Shifters often find that they must learn many lessons relating to fear, and they must muster up the courage to confront these fears. Fire is also connected to the physical body. Shifters find that they must take very good care of their bodies, keep in good shape, and keep their intuition in tune with their bodies' needs. Fox shifters often have many fire-related lessons to learn, because foxes are strongly connected to fire energies.

Water and fire together symbolize the two polarities of the universe. They are two opposites, like yin and yang, and generate enormous energy when mixed the right way. Any practitioner working in the Western system would do well to work fire and water into shifting-related rituals or magical workings. Many old charms for becoming a shapeshifter involve swimming across a lake, drinking from a lycanthropic stream, or even rolling in a puddle.

The element of earth has only occasional relations to shapeshifting. The element of air has even less to do with it—in fact, it is often opposed to it. Air is the element of the conscious intellect, the ego, the mind apart from instinct and intuition. Air is an element that often connects us too strongly with the human mode of being and thinking, blocking the path to the animal self.

I have found that one of the most effective and simple ways to work with the elements to invoke shapeshifting is to use water and fire herbs on a daily basis. The simplest way is in an herbal tea. Herbs associated with the element of water are frequently recognized by their "cooling" taste and effects. They grow near water, and are often the same herbs used to treat fevers or lung problems—mints, licorice, willow, lemon balm, or watercress. Herbs of fire are frequently recognized by their "heating" effects, their "hot" taste, and the vigor sensed on tasting them. Some fire herbs are basil, ginseng, cumin, borage, and cinnamon. Work with water and fire herbs on a daily basis to help you along your path of shifting. Find some water and fire herbs that you like, and drink tea made from them every day (assuming, of course, that the particular herbs you choose are non-poisonous). Vary the amount of "water" and "fire" tea you consume, according to how you feel these elements are working within your own nature at the time. Let your body tell you how much you need.

MAGICAL STONES AND CRYSTALS

Moonstone is the stone most often associated with shapeshifting. Some legends say that anyone can become a werewolf by carrying a moonstone that has been inscribed or charged in a special ritual. I haven't known any who tried that, but I have known shifters who agree that moonstones really help their shifting. Many consider moonstones to be more effective than wolf belts or any other magic tool.

For many shifters, simply having a moonstone nearby (the bigger, the better) boosts shifting energy and increases an awareness of the inner animal. Some shifters actually draw shifting energy directly out of a moonstone, in a matter of minutes, and use this energy to produce effects that they could not otherwise produce. A moonstone used like this becomes very depleted, and needs to be fully recharged before it can be used again. The best way to recharge a stone is to bury it in the ground for a couple of weeks.

Moonstones come in a number of colors. The most common kind is a milky white, but they are also yellowish-white, creamy orange, silvery gray, blue, and brown. Some shifters use specific colors of moonstones for specific purposes. The silvery-gray moonstones relate best to wolves. Since wolves are usually gray, this is a case of magical correspondence. In much the same way, I expect that orange moonstones are particularly in tune with red foxes, and that brown moonstones are in tune with brown animals.

Moonstones have a "flash," like a cat's-eye, that crawls over the surface when the stone is rotated. According to ancient lore, this "moon flash" is supposed to be brightest when the stone is fully charged, and dullest when the stone is depleted. It is also supposed to be brightest near the Full Moon and dimmest near the New Moon (all other things being equal). The larger the moonstone, the better, even if it is not the "right" color and is unpolished. If you want a small moonstone as an amulet, however, it may as well be the color you prefer and polished.

There are a number of other stones and crystals of note, among them rose quartz. An ancient name for rose quartz is "wolf stone." Many wolf shifters own a large rose quartz, and most don't quite know why. Amber, sometimes called "lynxstone," is used in some rituals of lynx-totem medicine. Legends say that it consists of solidified lynx urine (it is really petrified tree sap). Cat's-eye stones have always been strongly associated with cats. The term "cat's-eye" actually relates to many stones. Other stones, including sapphire, can be cut to show the cat's-eye effect. Even glass can show this effect and can have a little of the magic of the cat's-eye. The stone most often called cat's-eye is tigereye. Tigereye is usually yellow, orangish, or reddish. The blue variety of tigereye is called "hawks eye" and is useful for bird magic. Many cat shifters wear cat's-eye rings.

Another stone connected with shapeshifting is turquoise. Turquoise, however, does not promote shapeshifting. In fact, it inhibits it. Shifters should diligently avoid turquoise unless they are in a phase where they are having great difficulties with shifting and need to dampen their shifting energy. I have been unable to find any legends about the anti-shifting quality of turquoise, but the history of turquoise suggests that it may be inimical to shifters. Turquoise is an ancient treatment for melancholy, and is also said to "keep away wild beasts." The Navajo are one of the few Native American societies that consider werewolves evil, and they use turquoise extensively.

Turquoise has been used all over the world for psychic protection. Shifters do not have trouble with any other stones that are used for psychic protection, even more potent ones like jasper. I have used many different stones for protection in my spiritual practice, and have never run into the same trouble as I have had with turquoise. Turquoise seems to be particularly opposed to shifters.

MAGICAL SYMBOLS AND TALISMANS

One of the symbols associated with shapeshifting is the I-Ching hexagram number 49, "Ko" (see figure 4, page 216). This hexagram has long been associated with shapeshifting, transformation, molting, and an animal's skin or a bird's feathers. Animal skin is an ancient, universal symbol of the shapeshifter. The skin is the symbol of the outer body or form, which the shifter can put on and take off. The caul, or embryonic birth sack, is also a symbol of the shapeshifter, a symbol of the skin, and of the other shadow-self, the subconscious. Legend says that shifters are born with the caul still covering their head. Cauls taken from animals, especially horses, and in some cases the shifter's own caul, preserved from birth, have played an important part in some shapeshifting magic and ritual. Some folklore states that a child will be able to understand the language of animals if their caul is offered to the wildlife right after birth. Serious shifters should study the lore associated with the I-Ching hexagram 49 and meditate on its meaning. It is a powerful shifter's amulet.

49

50

Figure 4. I-Ching Hexagrams 49 and 50. The I-Ching is an ancient system of divination and magic that first started in Asia. One of the fundamentals of this system are the symbols for yin – – and yang ——. These two are combined to form many different symbols, in trigrams, hexagrams, and other formations. The symbols of the I-Ching are best known for their use in divination, but they are also used in other forms of magic. Various trigrams are associated with the elements, and with other things such as wind, mountains, lakes, mother, and elder brother. The trigrams combine to form hexagrams, with their energies and correspondences interwoven in intricate ways. Many of the hexagrams are believed to have special energies or powers associated with them, and it is common for them to be worn as amulets to attract that kind of magic. Hexagram 49 is intimately associated with shapeshifting energies. Hexagram 50 is also of importance to shapeshifters, for it corresponds to the next step in the Great Cycle, integration. Integration is just as important as shapeshifting. Note that hexagram 50 is simply hexagram 49 upside-down. These two energies truly complement each other.

Another useful symbol that promotes integration is the I-Ching hexagram 50. It comes right after 49 in the cycle, showing that integration truly is the next step after change. Symbols of integration should be used during periods when you are doing only integration. For example, if you are wearing hexagram 50 as an amulet for integration, this will work best during a period when you are also not wearing any amulets for attraction of more shapeshifting magic.

Another symbol strongly associated with shapeshifting is the Norse rune *algiz* or *eolh* (see figure 5, page 217). This rune also makes a good shifter's amulet. The runes have long been used for magic and divination, and each rune is a potent symbol of a particular type of energy. Those who have heard a little about rune magic often think it is a superstition based on the awe with which illiterates approached writing. This is not true. The runes were symbols of magical forces, and used in magic long before they

Figure 5. Runes and bind runes. The ancient rune alphabet of pre-Christian Europe was not just used for writing. The runes were believed to symbolize more than mere letters and sounds. They were part of the sacred pattern of the universe. Various runes were believed to have certain types of magic and energies associated with them, and runes were used in many ways—in divination, to cast spells, or to wear as amulets. The rune that is believed to draw shapeshifting magic to itself is called *algiz* (sometimes called *eolh* or *secg*). Its most common form is pictured here, but sometimes the junctions are rounded, and a few cultures (notably Icelandic and Gothic) write it upside-down.

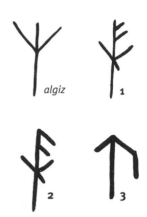

Bind runes can also be made, combining two or more runes according to traditional rune magic techniques, in order to strengthen the shapeshifting energies or attract particular types of magic. Above are several bindrunes I made myself. The rune numbered one, made from algiz, fehu, and laguz, is for artificial shifters, or for attracting more shapeshifting magic into your life. The rune numbered two, made from algiz, laguz, and ansuz, is for hereditary shifters, or for strengthening what shapeshifting magic already exists within you. The rune numbered three, made from tiwaz and uruz, is for attracting the magic of integration and moving past blocks on the path of a shifter.

were ever used for writing. Modern rune magic uses both the written meaning of runes and their more ancient symbolic meanings.

The rune algiz has many energies associated with it, not just shapeshifting. Of the twenty-four runes of the elder *futhark* (the purest, oldest runic system) algiz is one of only four runes that symbolize animals (*fehu*, *uruz*, and *ehwaz* are the others). Algiz is one of only two runes that symbolize wild animals (the other being *uruz*). Unlike any of the other four animal runes, algiz symbolizes two different species, the swan and the elk.

Algiz is also associated with the mythical *valkyrjur*, shapeshifting spirit-beings who often used swan-cloaks to change into swans. It also relates to the mythical divine twins, Alcis, who are often portrayed in ideographs joined at the head, assuming a form much like the most ancient form of algiz. Twins and duality are often a symbol of the forces involved in shapeshifting. Being joined at the head depicts two bodies/one soul, the condition of a shapeshifter. Algiz is a symbol of the strengthening and build-up of energy. Like many other things connected with shapeshifting, it is also a potent symbol of psychic protection. Algiz symbolizes the rainbow bridge of Norse myth, the mythical pathway that connects the lower realms, the earthly realm, and the higher realms. It is part of the path of a shifter to traverse this bridge, to become whole by connecting with the power of being animal (the lower realms) and using it to assist on the journey toward enlightenment (the upper realms).

The number nine is often found in shapeshifting rituals. The magical numerology of the number nine has much in common with the magic of shapeshifting. In legend, groups of shapeshifters often numbered nine. Nine years is a particularly symbolic time, especially for wolves, because nine years is a full wolf life. Captive wolves may live to almost twenty years. More rarely, wild wolves may also reach that age. However, when wild wolves die, it is almost always at age nine. Their teeth wear out at about that age. Shifters should research the mystical meanings of nine and meditate on them.

TIMING YOUR SHIFT

The phases of the Moon, day and night cycles, and seasonal cycles are important to shapeshifters. Every shifter with a significant level of shifting energy is aware of the cycle of the Moon. Shifting-energy levels tend to peak around the Full and New Moons. Any magical practice to enhance shifting has its best results when done at one of these times.

The day/night cycle is important to shifting since every shifter's inner animal (except extremely diurnal species, such as eagle shifters) is awake and active at night. This is especially true in the hours between 10 P.M. and midnight when most legends tell of physical shifts happening. Around midnight, shifting energy peaks. After that, the activity of the inner animal slowly decreases, until sunrise. At sunrise, it dramatically decreases to a normal daytime level within a few minutes. Many werewolf legends relate that the change back to human happens exactly at sunrise. I have often awakened at three or four in the morning, feeling perfectly rested and ready to start my day. Then, as soon as the Sun came up, my wolf mental side subsided, and I felt dead tired.

An unusually large number of shifters were actually born on the day of the Winter Solstice. One old legend claims that those born on Christmas Day will become werewolves. Christmas Day falls near the winter solstice. Natural shifters also tend to be born under a New Moon. The student would do well to research the full astrological meaning of a New Moon birth.

MAGICAL SKINS AND COSTUMES

At some point, those interested in the magic of shapeshifting wonder about the legends of wolf skins and swan cloaks and other animal hides used for shapeshifting. What is really behind these legends? Is there truly any magic in an animal hide? As in most magic, the superstitious assign all the power to the object, while in truth it resides in the magic worker. The object is only a tool. Many people get the idea that wearing a wolf skin somehow allows them to connect better with the collective essence of all wolves. In truth, most wolf shifters, if they have a strong connection to their animal at all, are horrified and sickened at the idea of wearing a wolf skin. Wolves are their species as much as humans are, and it would be like skinning a human and wearing the skin.

This is found in legend as well. Many "wolf skins" in legend were not made of actual wolf hide, but of cow hide, cut and dyed to resemble a wolf. There are words for "werewolf" that refer to cowhide or cow hair. Moreover, there are many legends about "werewolves" that seem to be describing humans in costume. These probably describe shifters practicing the magic of skinwalking, dressing up as an animal in order to more fully "become" it and be in tune with it.

When in costume, it's easier to drop your inhibitions and let the inner animal come out. Having "assumed" an animal on the physical plane it is easier for its mental side to emerge. The costume is a potent signal to your inner self and to the universe that you are trying to become an animal. Skinwalking is closely related to the magics of mask wearing and painting the body to look like an animal. It is not the substance of the costume that

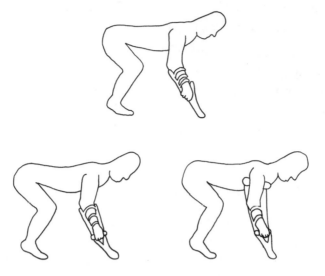

Figure 6. Leg extensions. Leg extensions are like very short crutches. They are strapped onto the arms to help you run on all fours in a natural and easy way. Leg extensions even out the fact that human legs are too long and human arms too short. They are commonly used in the movies when a human in costume has to act as some sort of four-legged creature. Shifters sometimes use leg extensions to allow them to bond more with the inner animal self. Always remember, leg extensions can be dangerous, particularly if you slip at high speed and end up plowing your face into the ground! If you do make or purchase leg extensions, be careful, start out slowly, and try to make sure the ground you are practicing on is not too hard.

---

matters to a skinwalker as much as its look and function. Modern skinwalkers wear acrylic fake fur and get spectacular results.

In making a costume and wearing it, the magic is increased by the thought and intent that go into the act, rather than how realistic the final result looks. For this reason, it is better to create your own costume. Some shifters make four-legged costumes with devices called "leg extensions" to allow them to easily run on all fours (see figure 6). The skin, or outer covering, is very symbolic. It symbolizes the body in which all souls are clothed. When you put on a costume of an animal, you symbolically put on its body. You transform symbolically.

In some legends, the skinwalker shifts mentally and displays the powers of a berserker. Such a person can make a big impression on the locals as "a real werewolf," without any physical shift actually occurring. I do want to emphasize, however, that for modern shifters, the art of skinwalking is not used to make the locals think a werewolf haunts the neighborhood woods. In fact, most shifters would be horrified at any such sighting, because they want to keep their existence and activities secret. In the legends, there is evidence that skinwalkers felt the same way. They were not dressing up to "put on a show" or create legends, or spook people, but as part of a practice similar to the practice of cross-dressing. They were skinwalking for themselves, not for anyone else.

"Curing" a Shifter

Having covered the basics of both mundane and magical ways to become a shifter or to strengthen your shifter nature, it is now time to address the opposite question. How do you "cure" a shifter, or inhibit or weaken shifter qualities and characteristics? Indeed, can a shifter even be cured? The ancients often asked this question, and legend is full of failed attempts. It is rare to find an actual cure in legends. In fact, folk wisdom doesn't bother with cures for werewolves, claiming that the only cure is death—and perhaps not even that, for the ghosts of werewolves still appeared as shapeshifters. There is doctrine among shifter groups that shifters cannot be cured. This doctrine was particularly prevalent in the earlier days of the movement, when it consisted almost entirely of hereditary shifters with very strong potential.

I believe that some shifters can be cured and some can't. Those who are born to it, who have a very high hereditary potential, cannot be cured at all. Many have tried, because they believed society's ideas that werewolves were evil, but the cures just didn't work. On the other hand, I've known cases of artificial shifters who stopped being shifters altogether. They relinquished their animal part that simmers on the surface of the subconscious, and no longer experienced mental shifts, or any other phenomena of shifting. This can happen in artificial shifters, either naturally or deliberately. Some artificial shifters, however, encounter considerable difficulty if they decide they no longer want to be shifters and try to "cure" themselves. What is once awakened is not always so easily put to sleep. In some cases, it even seems to be as difficult to cure a shifter as it is to become one.

When shifters try to "cure" themselves, one of two patterns is usually seen. In someone who can be cured, attempts to do so lead to an increasingly weakened animal side, until all shifting phenomena stop and the inner animal seems as quiet and asleep as it is in normal people. In someone who cannot be cured, attempts to do so lead to a great backlash of symptoms, such as an overly active and uncontrollable inner animal, deep depression and great anxiety, a great feeling of horrible crushing tension, a feeling of being deeply unsatisfied with life, and even physical illness. This incurable type of shifter remains healthy when accepting their inner animal and living in harmony with it, but comes to grief, mental instability, and problems when they try to reject or "kill" it.

If you are suffering because you are a shifter, or experiencing bad symptoms, it may well be that you are trying to cure yourself and can't be cured. Don't automatically decide that the problem is caused by excessively high shifting energy and try to reduce it. This will only make your problems worse, especially if the problems really stem from conscious or subconscious attempts to cure yourself of being a shifter.

Folk wisdom has various "recipes" for curing a werewolf, but many are ineffective. Sometimes they don't work at all, and sometimes the shapeshifter seems to be cured, and pretends to be cured, but later returns to shapeshifting. In few legends is the shapeshifter truly cured.

One traditional cure is to call the werewolf by its human name while it is in wolf form. However, as I discussed in chapter 5, this does not cure shapeshifters; it only returns them to human form. Another traditional cure is to perform a certain act of bravery, usually walking up to a shapeshifter who is in animal form and hitting it with a piece of clothing, wounding it just enough to draw a few (many legends say precisely three) drops of blood, or pulling out a whisker. Usually the person who does this must be a family member, friend, or lover.

I am doubtful of this cure. I think that what is really going here is that the friends or family are confronting the shifter, and showing that they mean it no harm, and that they can act without killing it, even in the most frightening circumstances. They are showing that the shifter is accepted, and will not be harmed. After this, the shifter's condition is no longer a problem. The shifter need not fear being killed by panicking friends or family, because the friends and family have confronted the worst and come out unscathed. It is not truly a "cure" of the shifter, but simply the defusing of a potentially dangerous situation.

Many cures mentioned in legends are really exorcisms, or ceremonies closely related to exorcism. Exorcism, however, is not an effective way of curing a shifter. A small minority of shifters are possessed by animal spirits, and so an exorcism might cure them. Exorcism is utterly useless, on the other hand, against the ordinary type of shifter. Modern teenage shifters have sometimes been forced to submit to exorcisms because the family happened to see extreme mental shifts that included paranormal effects, such as eye-color changes or supernatural strength. Exorcisms simply don't work at all. Unfortunately, parents who see any real evidence of the shifter nature in their children are likely to overreact and do everything in their power to suppress it. This can lead to nothing but more trouble in those truly born to be shifters. I have known shifters who underwent extreme abuse from parents, and who, even as adults, have strained relationships with their parents, or have disowned them entirely, as a result of this misunderstanding.

The most effective way to cure a shifter is to dampen the animal side. Shifters should be removed from any environment that stimulates the animal side. They should engage in human activities and surround themselves with humans. They should be separated from animals, and not spend time outdoors, especially at night. They should give up sports and physical exercise, and be closely supervised. You don't know whether they can be cured or not. If they start showing symptoms and side effects, they may be incurable. You should try to make their shifting less of a burden by having them learn integration and by smoothing their path. If, instead, their inner animal just quietly starts to fade away without a fight, you are probably well on your way to a cure.

Ancient esoteric cures for melancholy are sometimes effective for curing shifters. Wearing a turquoise at all times can help. If you have reason to believe that the shifter is truly possessed (remember, an ordinary mental shift can look like possession quite easily, so don't jump to conclusions!), an exorcism may be called for.

In most cases, cures are not really necessary, even if they are possible. Many people are meant to be shifters. It is part of their destiny, and wrong to impede them. By do so, you obstruct their personal path to enlightenment. Shifting is not evil. In fact, it can be a valuable power and blessing. Shifters—even artificial shifters—have received a great gift. Gifts like this are rare, and come our way for a reason. If you are encountering difficulties on the path of a shifter, the best solution is to smooth the path and forge forward as best you know how, not to try to get off the path altogether. Too many people are intent on "curing werewolves," once they find that they exist. This is an erroneous, outdated attitude from the Middle Ages. The energy is present in the world today, and we need to learn how to use it, or we will be used by it.

Epilogue

T he shifter movement, as I write this, is a fledgling movement. It exists largely as a subgroup within the furry movement, or as scattered, separated packs of three to five shifters who have found each other outside any larger movement. The "furry movement," whose members call themselves "furries," has several major conventions and countless minor gatherings every year, as well as publications and even communes. It consists of people who have joined together because they identify with all sorts of half-human, half-animal creatures.

Many furries (especially the faction who call themselves "lifestylers") feel that they have been "mis-incarnated." They feel that they are animals trapped in human bodies. The furry movement has many similarities with transgenderism, except that it relates to species instead of gender identity. Many furries are into "cross-dressing" as the animal self. Most have "personal furries," imaginary beings that represent what the furries might look like if their physical bodies truly reflected their souls. Much of furry culture is centered around efforts to connect with the personal furry.

Many shifter groups exist within furry culture, while others have severed their ties with furry culture altogether. To find proof of the existence of the shifter movement, one only has to look at furry culture to quickly stumble across shifters. One place to look is the Internet. The major furry newsgroups are news://alt.fan.furry and news://alt.lifestyle.furry. Try any major search engine, using terms such as "furry resources," "furry lifestyle," "furry conventions," "furry art," or "personal furries" as keywords. Shifters have also left traces on the Internet,[1] though these traces are fewer and farther between. Try entering keywords that relate very specifically to the shifter movement, such as "spiritual therianthropy," "wereside," "spiritual shapeshifting," "mental shifter," or "astral shifting." If you don't limit your search, you'll generate thousands of ordinary, non-shifter, werewolf pages. Be warned, however, that the portion of the shifter movement that exists on the Internet is very badly organized, has a dubious reputation, and is, sadly, often a "fishing ground" for all sorts of strange cults.

Today's shifter movement has no direct links to legendary werebeasts, although, in a sense, we do. Shifters have always been around. In cave paintings, half-human, half-animal figures appear quite frequently. *The Epic of Gilgamesh*, an ancient Sumerian document generally believed to be the earliest surviving literature, mentions a werewolf. Every culture has had legends of werebeasts. Even today, in places like the United States, where the wild has been driven out of the people and the land, shifters still crop up. The early shifter movement consisted almost entirely of those born with such strong shifter tendencies that they could not ignore or suppress them.

Hereditary shifters will always be with us, no matter how civilized we become and how much wilderness is destroyed. Some are truly destined to the path of being a shifter, and nothing can ever destroy that. Where will the future of the shifter movement go? Regardless of what anyone does, I believe it will continue to grow and become more organized. I hope that,

---

[1] Daniel Cohen has also spoken of the shifter movement and its traces on the Internet, though there are some inaccuracies in his account, probably attributable to the fact that he himself admits that he is inexperienced in computers and ignorant about the Internet. See *Werewolves* (New York: Penguin, 1996), pp. 101–107.

one day, our beliefs will be better understood and more protected. It would be nice if the world at large did not immediately think of shifting as a mental illness or as some kind of demonic influence. It is amazing how people retreat to small-minded and superstitious ideas as soon as they think that "werewolves," either mental or physical, may exist.

Lycanthropy is no more a mental illness than is the condition of those who feel they are women trapped in men's bodies. It is certainly not demonic, evil, or connected with violence in any way. Those concepts are outdated ideas from the Middle Ages. Wolves are not evil, and wolves don't eat people, so why would werewolves be evil or eat people? Werewolves are simply a blend of human and wolf. If they have any evil qualities, they come from the human part and have nothing to do with being a werewolf.

I believe this to be the most complete and useful book on the subject of "shapeshifters" in general, with the clearest, most detailed, and accurate descriptions of what a shifter truly is and how to become one. I hope it will help normal people understand us better and lose their fear of us. I hope it will be a valuable resource for shifters themselves. Many hereditary shifters don't really understand what is happening to them, especially at first. They misunderstand themselves, fear what they are, or don't know how to proceed properly along the path. The teachings of shifter gurus can help a lot, but to find good ones and spend a lot of time learning from them can be difficult. This book is a summary of all the most important teachings and beliefs in shifter culture. It is the end result of my having been immersed in shifter culture for some years and listening to a number of shifter gurus. I have taken pains to only include teachings and beliefs for which I've seen evidence, and which are common. Many of the things I write about are things I've experienced, or that friends of mine have experienced. I expect later shifter gurus to build on this material, discover new and better techniques, and do more research into the phenomena of shifting. I look forward to a brighter and better future for shifters everywhere. May this book be a help and resource, moving us closer to that goal.

Glossary

Ailurothropy: "Lycanthropy" pertaining to cats.

Alpha: When scientists first began studying wolves, they paid a lot of attention to the hierarchy of the pack. In wolf hierarchies, there are two wolves at the top, one male and one female. They are called the "alpha" wolves. They are usually mated to each other, but not always, and are often the mother and father of most of the other wolves in the pack. Shifters sometimes use the term "alpha" to refer to the two or three leaders who typically lead shifter packs.

Animal People: People with a strong soul-connection to animals, whether they shift or not.

Animal Side: Part of the inner self or subconscious that is animal in nature. Also referred to as "inner animal" or "animal self."

Animal Spirit Guide: Spirit guide ("guardian angel" is the term used by Christians) having the nature of a particular species of animal.

Apparition Shifting: Shifting in which the shifter engages in out-of-body travel while the spirit body assumes an animal form that is visible to others as a ghostly apparition.

Artificial: Short for "artificial shifter," a shifter who becomes a shifter "artificially," through meditation, trance work, vision quests, or magical rites—as opposed to a "natural shifter," born with a hereditary talent or inclination, who starts out with at least the ability to mental shift without deliberately seeking it.

Astral Body: One of the subtle bodies that are not made of physical substance, less "close" to being physical matter than the etheric body.

Astral Plane: The whole "universe" of astral matter. It overlaps the physical plane, and occupies the same space-time continuum. There are also areas of the astral plane that do not overlap any part of this world.

Astral Shifting: Shapeshifting of the astral body; most often takes place during sleep when it is spontaneous, and during meditation or trance when it is induced. Many believe that mental shifts (which happen while awake and do not involve astral travel) also involve astral-body shapeshifting. Throughout this book, I use the term for astral travel combined with shapeshifting of the astral body.

Astral Travel: A variety of what are collectively called OBEs (out-of-body experiences). Astral travel is the act of leaving your physical and etheric bodies behind, and traveling while occupying only the astral body.

Aura: Energy field of the human body, especially the shining inner layers that some psychics can see. Related to the magnetic field of the human body, it has a relationship to *chi*. Kirlian photography can actually photograph portions of the aura and the *chi* field.

Aura Shifting: A kind of mental shifting that involves the aura; also refers to mood shifts and very light mental shifts.

Awaken: Commonly used term in shifter packs to refer to the moment someone becomes a shifter. For natural shifters, this is the time, most likely in their teenage years, when they first start experiencing mental shifts. The term is used to refer to the process of turning a human into an artificial shifter. Awakening is visualized as a process of arousing the inner animal, which normally "slumbers" within the subconscious.

Awere: Slang term common in many shifter packs; a natural and facile pun or wordplay on the terms "aware" and "a were" (see **Were**). The moment you become "awere" is the moment when you first consciously realize that you are a shifter (or a "were").

Berserker: Ancient Norse word for mental shifters who use the strength and fury of the bear in battle, often linked with the use of "bear shirts." In modern shifter culture, "berserker" refers to mental shifters who sometimes manifest more-than-human strength, speed, agility, or senses during mental shifts, or experience other minor paranormal effects, such as eye-color changes. The powers of a berserker can be used for defense or fighting, but in most cases they are not.

Bilocation: Practice of engaging in etheric (out-of-body) travel, while making the etheric body more solid and substantial, until it is so close to being physical that it seems so in nearly every way (such as being able to eat, to leave footprints, and seem real to the touch). Normally, this materialized bilocation body is a carbon copy of the person's own physical body, and looks exactly like the person. Any wounds received by the materialized body immediately appear on the unconscious physical body as well.

Bilocation Shifting: Using bilocation to shapeshift into animal form; like regular bilocation except that the materialized body is not a carbon copy of the human's own body. Instead, it is an animal body.

Bitch Pack (also called "Dianic packs" and several other names): All-female pack of shifters. "Bitch" means a female dog or wolf, and is often used in shifter culture, without the slightest derogatory connotation.

Breaking Out: When physical shifters are injured in animal form, sometimes pieces of their human etheric bodies gather enough substance to be visible. They surface through the skin (break-out) like something surfacing from under water, drift around on the surface, then submerge again. When this piece is part of the human face, it sometimes allows people to recognize who the werewolf is in human form.

Catalyst: A person (usually a shifter, sometimes only a person with animal medicine, occasionally a mere psychic) who can manipulate the shifting energy of others. Usually, catalysts involuntarily increase the shifting energy of anyone they are near. Occasionally, they can manipulate it at will and in finer ways, building or draining it, and thereby guiding shifters through mental shifts. Some of them can cause involuntary mental shifts in others.

Chi: Type of other-plane energy involved in certain forms of magic, especially those that directly affect the physical plane. *Chi* has various alternate spellings, including *Qi.* In various cultures, it has had many different names—*prana, orgone, mana, odic force,* and *animal magnetism. Chi* has similar characteristics in the lore of cultures around the world, though some cultures do disagree about the minor details of how it works.

Classical Shifting: Physical shifting that happens more slowly, in a matter of minutes, instead of in a matter of seconds like in instantaneous shifting. This type of physical shifting is called many different things in many different packs, but "classical shifting" is one of the more common names.

Clinical: Shifter slang for "clinical lycanthrope" or "clinical lycanthropy," a delusional person who believes him- or herself to be a werewolf. This type sometimes becomes interested in shifter packs and tries to join them.

Coming Out of the Fur-Coat Closet: A term from the gay rights movement that refers to the act of divulging the fact that you are gay, now refers generically to the act of admitting to any secret lifestyle. Wiccans, Neo-Pagans, and others practicing magic or witchcraft often call it "coming out of the broom closet." "Coming out of the fur-coat closet" is shifter and furry slang for admitting secret lifestyle and beliefs.

Cultivation: Deliberately encouraging the characteristics of your species of animal, and acting like the species of animal that you are in order to strengthen your bond with it. This may occur in subtle ways worked into everyday life, such as being more concerned with your appearance if you are a cat shifter, or it may be in an episode in which you get down on all fours and meow. This is not a mental shift, though to the outside observer it may appear to be one. Cultivation may trigger a real mental shift on occasion.

Dream Shifting: The act of turning into an animal, or partially turning into an animal, during a dream; also, being in animal or quasi-animal form throughout a dream, even if no transformation takes place.

Ectoplasm: Partially solidified etheric matter, matter at some state between the etheric and the physical. Often it looks like thick white or grayish fog, sometimes it precipitates as a slime or powder, and sometimes it is a pastey or claylike white or grayish substance.

Etheric Body: A body closer to the physical than the astral body, it is more likely to directly affect physical reality, and more likely to be glimpsed as a ghostly phantom, even by those who are not psychic. Every shifter has two etheric bodies, a human etheric body and an animal etheric body.

Etheric Plane: The "world" of etheric matter that overlaps with the physical world. Unlike the astral plane, it is not so much a world unto itself, but is more like an extra dimension of the physical world. All living things, and even some nonliving things, have an etheric counterpart. Besides this, there are many "stray" etheric substances and structures in the etheric plane.

Etheric Shifting: Engaging in etheric travel with the animal etheric body, instead of the human body. This is like bilocation shifting, except that the animal etheric body is not solidified, but remains in etheric form. Normally, during etheric shifting, the animal etheric body is not visible to others. When it is visible as a ghostly apparition, this is the same as "apparition shifting." Etheric shifting is much more likely to produce a ghostly, visible body than astral shifting.

Etheric Travel: The act of leaving your physical body, while taking both the astral body and the etheric body with you; also called out-of-body travel. The inexperienced tend to confuse astral travel with etheric travel, but the two are distinct and different.

Familiar: A real animal who is a spiritual or magical helper for a witch or a shifter. In the case of shifters, a familiar is a real animal that shares a kind of soul kinship with the shifter, and who often acts as a channel for the animal spirit guide. It may also act as a channel for the shifter, as in sense shifting and possession shifting.

Fever: Term commonly used to refer to the mood swings, odd bodily feelings, cramps, nausea, or other symptoms that build up periodically in shifters who have high shifting energy.

FOL: Slang acronym for Friend of Lycanthrope, often used for those people who are "in the know" about shifters and like to hang out with shifters, but who are not shifters themselves. There seem to be a few of these in just about every pack.

Furry: A certain kind of animal person. The furry movement is much larger and better organized than the shifter movement, and has been around for a long time. It has just started to gain public attention in the past few years. Furries are people with a very strong connection to animals, especially anthropomorphized animals found in fiction. The furry movement is much more than just a fan club, however. Furries feel that they are somehow half animal and half human in their hearts. Their lifestyle centers around other furries and attempts to "get in touch" with this inner self. This often takes the form of collecting furry fan material, such as art of anthropomorphic animals, novels about fictional races of anthropomorphic animals, and costuming themselves as anthropomorphic animals.

Guardian: People who watch over groups of deeply mentally shifted packmates, while not mentally shifting themselves, to keep them from getting in trouble and to help guide the shifts for maximum result. Also called "watchers," and a number of other things in various packs. Guardians often have some ability to manipulate shifting energy, and they may also talk others through guided visualizations, taking them deeper or not, as they see fit.

Heightened Senses: Condition in which a shifter's senses become closer, to a greater or lesser degree, to what the senses of an animal are like.

Hereditary Shifter: Natural shifter who becomes a shifter because of hereditary influences.

Higher Powers: Those aspects of shifting that are miraculous or that involve the paranormal. These include more than human senses, strengths, or agility. They include minor physical changes such as eye-color changes, the growing of tiny patches of fur, possession shifting, apparition shifting, bilocation shifting, and physical shifting. For many shifters, part of the goal of the path of shifting is eventually to progress to the point of regularly experiencing one or more of the higher powers.

Howl: A gathering of shifters, usually held at night, often on the Full Moon. Most howls include the members of just one pack, but some, especially the less frequent, larger ones, include several packs, plus a number of "lone wolves."

Human Side: Part of the self that sees itself as human, usually allied to the conscious mind and the ego.

Hunger: Common term for the extremely large appetite that some shifters have, particularly common in shifters who have high shifting energy, hardly noticeable in shifters with very low shifting energy.

Instantaneous Shifting: Physical shifting that happens quickly—finished in seconds, rather than minutes, like the classical variety of physical shifting. This type of physical shifting is called by perhaps more different names, in different packs, than any other kind of shifting.

Integrated Shifter: Shifters whose human and animal sides are merged, so that they can think from both perspectives at once.

Kitsune: Fox shifter or werefox, sometimes used to refer to a fox spirit.

Leg Extensions: Devices that are like miniature crutches strapped to the arms. They add length to the arms and make it easier to run on the hands and feet.

Loup-Guru: Term common among shifter packs, a combination of *loup-garou* (French for "werewolf") and *guru,* used to refer to those shifters who set themselves up as gurus, and dispense teaching and advice to other shifters.

Lycanthropy: The power of becoming a wolf or of turning a human being into a wolf; the belief in werewolves. From the Greek: it is said that King Lycaon was the first werewolf.

Magic: Forces behind the paranormal. To "do" magic is to manipulate these forces.

Magical Shifting: Any type of shift, from mental to physical, that is triggered by a ritual act or an act of ceremonial magic, such as putting on a wolf belt, using shifting salve, or ceremonially swimming across a particular body of water. Most modern shifters consider this kind of shift to be entirely mythical, but I believe that it existed in the past, even though it is rare nowadays.

Magic Worker: Someone who works magic; a sorcerer, psychic, witch, or shaman.

Mental Shifting: What a shifter does when mentally transforming into an animal. In almost all cases, the shifter knows, while "transformed," that no physical transformation has happened. This term can refer to anything from "light" mental shifts, which may be no more than a wolfish mood, to "deep" mental shifts, in which the shifter cannot walk on two legs and virtually assumes the mental state of an animal.

Midform: Bodily form somewhere between human and animal, partially transformed form. There are a number of other terms found among shifter packs that mean the same thing, such as "half form" and "hybrid form." When shifters talk about "midform" they are often talking about the experience of assuming this form in a dream, the place it most commonly occurs, but they may also be talking about a classical physical shifter midway in transformation.

Pack: Term used to refer to groups of shifters, who commonly organize themselves much like a wolf pack, even when many members are nonwolf shifters. Sometimes cat-only "packs" will call themselves a "pride," as in a pride of lions.

Packmate: Fellow member of the same pack, more commonly called "packsister" or "packbrother," since packs of shifters often feel as if they are a family.

Personal Furry: Term used in furry culture to refer to an imaginary creature, sometimes a realistic animal, but more often a half-human, half-animal anthropomorphized form with human characteristics, such as walking upright and having hands. Personal furries represent what furries feel their real selves might look like if their outer forms truly reflected the reality of their inner selves.

Phantom Limb: Part of a phantom animal body that all shifters carry around with them, roughly superimposed over their human body. At certain times of high shifting energy or activity of the inner animal, these "phantom limbs" can be felt very clearly and vividly by the shifter. They are normally invisible and insubstantial, but occasionally they can be dimly seen (especially by psychics), or can have some small effect on physical reality.

Phenotype: A race or subspecies within a species. For example, the European wolf is a phenotype of the species called "wolf." Shifters often use "phenotype" to mean a species of shifter, as if "shifters" were one species, and cat shifters, bear shifters, were each phenotypes of the species called "shifters." If a shifter asks me, "What phenotype are you?" I reply, "wolf shifter."

Physical Shifting: Act of transforming the physical body into the body of an animal. The physical body actually flows and changes until it is indistinguishable from that of a real animal.

Polywere: Shifter with strong connections to multiple species. Shifting into multiple species is most common in astral shifting. It is practically unknown in physical shifting, though legends say that the wolf/bear physical shifter was common in ancient Scandinavia.

Possession Shifting: "Shifting" by leaving the human body (usually by astral rather than etheric travel) and possessing the body of an animal. While possessing the animal, possession shifters have no awareness of their human bodies.

Prowling: Wandering outside, usually at night and in some wild area, and releasing the animal nature.

Repercussion: Phenomenon of a shifter's animal body being wounded, and the wound remaining on the human form in a corresponding place.

Second Etheric Body: The animal etheric body that all shifters possess.

Selkie: Wereseal.

Sense Shifting: "Shifting" into a real animal, by perceiving one or more of its senses. Similar to possession shifting except that the shifter is still aware of and in the human body, and not in control of the animal body.

Shaman: Magic worker, usually one on a magical path oriented toward hermetic and nature magic.

Shifter: Modern substitute for the term "shapeshifter," more appropriate for modern shifters, because it does not imply physical shifting and includes all kinds and species of shifter (mental, physical, cat, wolf, bear, etc.). Along with "theriomorph," the most common term to describe all types of shifters.

Shifting Belt: Ritual item put on to trigger shifts, and taken off to end them.

Shifting Energy: Energy, similar to *chi*, that is intimately connected with shifters and shifting. High levels of it are necessary for berserker powers and for physical shifting.

Shifting Hour: Term used in shifter culture to refer to the hours of 10 P.M. to midnight, the time when the most shifts occur. Sometimes called "The Wolfing Hour."

Skinwalking: Using costuming, masks, or makeup, often in conjunction with "prowling," to get closer to the inner animal.

Spirit Guides: New Age terminology for those "guardian angels" that watch over all of us. Divine, guardian spirits (see Animal Spirit Guide).

Spiritual Therianthropy: Common term in shifter culture for the condition of being a shifter, referred to as "spiritual therianthropy" instead of just "therianthropy," because shifters want to stress that it is not (usually) a physical, but rather a spiritual thing.

Therianthropy: The condition of being both animal and human. Similar to "lycanthropy," except that it refers to any and all animals, and not just wolves.

Theriomorph: Shifter.

Theriophobia: "Fear of the beast," shifter slang for people who have phobias about animals. Theriophobia was especially rampant in the Middle Ages, and still crops up quite a lot. A fair proportion of people would be afraid of physical and mental shifting, if they thought it actually existed. Theriophobia is just as bad as homophobia, but, due to lack of information about shifterism, is more difficult to eradicate.

Totem: The animal species most similar to your personality. A totem is not your inner animal, although it is often of the same species. A totem is a guiding principle in your life, an influence or a tendency.

Totem Spirit: Common alternate term for the **Animal Spirit Guide**.

Totemic Shifting: A shift in which shifters are possessed by their animal spirit guides (or, rarely, some other kind of animal spirit). Many types of shift, from mental to physical, can be totemic, and most shifters who experience totemic shifts experience only totemic shifts. Very few other shifters experience totemic shifting.

Transspecies: Term used by animal people, including shifters, to describe themselves. Like transgender people, who are only one gender, but identify with both, transspecies people feel that their inner selves are both human and animal and refers to their inner identity.

Were: Short for "werewolf," "werecat," or any species of wereanimal, and including mental shifters as well as physical. Many packs start out using this term, but find it inadequate and switch to other terms such as "shifter" or "theriomorph."

Weredar: Sense by which many shifters can sense it when someone else is a shifter, derived from "gaydar," the sense that many gay people have that tells them when someone else is gay.

Wereshape: The animal form of a shifter, the shape assumed in a vision or dream. Sometimes this term is also used to refer to the animal etheric body of the shifter.

Wereside: Commonly used term meaning "animal side." Literally, "the side of one's personality that causes one to be a were."

Werewolf: Word used to mean so many things, in different packs or even in the same pack, that it has virtually lost all meaning. Many shifters consider it to be politically incorrect, because of its association with evil modern movie werewolves who bear little resemblance to either the physical shifters of legend, or to modern shifters. Many shifters will use just about any word, even awkward ones like "therianthrope," to avoid using the term "werewolf." Most do not want people to associate them with the term "werewolf."

Werewoof: Common shifter slang for a weredog, or dog shifter.

Wolf Shifter: Someone who shifts into a wolf in any type of "shift."

Wolf Spit: Shifter slang for the dry, gunky spit often found in the mouth when you first wake up in the morning. A hallmark of having reached a fairly deep trance state, this spit is often called "wolf spit."

Recommended Reading

The following books may be helpful to people who want to explore the possibility of becoming a shifter. These books can provide some of the necessary background for considering such study.

True Magic, by Amber K. A clear, concise, yet fairly detailed beginner's guide to magic, concentrates mostly on Wicca, but draws parallels to many other magical paths.

Between Heaven and Earth: A Guide to Chinese Medicine, by Harriet Beinfeld and Efrem Korngold. Perhaps the best guide to introduce Westerners to the basic Chinese concepts of medicine, including *chi*.

Ritual Book of Magic, by Clifford Bias. A beginner's book, but a well-known classic.

Natural Magic, by Doreen Valiente. Another classic beginner's book.

Real Magic, by Isaac Bonewits. A beginner's introduction to magic and esoteric phenomena.

The Spiral Dance, by Starhawk. A classic book on magic and the spirituality related to it.

The Training and Work of an Initiate, by Dion Fortune. A beginning magic-worker's book. Written by a famous and respected esotericist. Approaches magic from the viewpoint of Western-style ceremonial lodges and Christian mysticism.

Natural and Supernatural: A History of the Paranormal, by Brian Inglis. Probably the best and most understandable investigation into many kinds of paranormal phenomena. Very scholarly, covering an incredible number of the best-documented cases of supernatural phenomena. If you are looking for very scientific well-documented arguments to prove the existence of the phenomena associated with physical mediums, this is the book for you.

Psychic Discoveries Behind the Iron Curtain, by Lynn Schroeder and Sheila Ostrander. This book argues for the existence of the paranormal more convincingly, and in a more understandable way, than any other book.

Of Wolves and Men, by Barry Lopez. The best animal book for wolf shifters, approaching the subject from an accurate scientific viewpoint and a mystical one at the same time.

The Sacred Paw, by Paul Shepard and Barry Sanders. The best animal book for bear shifters.

Animal-Speak, by Ted Andrews. Probably the best New Age book on the subject of animal magic.

Animal Magic, by D. J. Conway. Contains useful visualizations and exercises.

The Way of the Animal Powers, by Joseph Campbell. Useful animal symbolism related to myth.

The Possible Human, by Jean Houston. A book version of a famous workshop on enhancing physical, mental, and especially creative abilities and intuition. Even though it is not considered a magic-oriented or New Age book, I especially recommend it, because the exercises contained in it are especially effective in strengthening your etheric body and training yourself to be more sensitive to it and manipulate it.

Spiritual Cleansing, by Draja Mickaharic. Many shifters with the high shifting energy necessary for the higher powers have problems at some point with psychic protection. Sometimes, high shifting energies can attract people and entities that "vampirize" supernatural energies. High shifting energy can also sometimes cause energy imbalances that cause "negative vibes" to build up. Both of these problems can form a significant block to progress on the shifter's path, unless they can be removed. Some people never have these problems, and some people instinctively protect themselves and cleanse their auras, without thinking about it or even knowing they are doing so. For the rest of us, *Spiritual Cleansing* is the best book on the subject of psychic protection and spiritual cleansing. It is very understandable and accessible to beginners.

Psychic Self-Defense, by Dion Fortune. This work covers the same subject as *Spiritual Cleansing,* but is less accessible to beginners. It is more effective for serious cases, for using advanced techniques, and for rarer types of "psychic attack" or build-up of psychic negativity. It is more for those who already know something of working with the paranormal than for rank beginners, though it does have some techniques available to beginners.

Women Who Run with the Wolves, by Clarissa Pinkola Estés. This is a very spiritual book about the wisdom contained in folklore and women's power—not a New Age book, and not about shifters, yet mystical. It is of interest to shifters, as it spends a lot of time discussing the inner wild woman, who is symbolized as part animal, especially part wolf. This is portrayed as similar to the way shifters view their own inner animal self. The mystical wisdom about the "inner wild self" that is contained in this book holds many valuable teachings that also apply to the shifter's inner wild animal.

Stop Sleeping Through Your Dreams, by Charles McPhee. A very accessible beginner's book on both dream interpretation and lucid dreaming.

Control Your Dreams, by Jayne Gackenback and Jane Bosveld. Exact, easy-to-use directions for lucid dreaming, along with detailed information about lucid dreaming.

Man and His Symbols, by Carl G. Jung. A classic and very useful work on symbolism, especially dream symbolism and interpretation.

There are also some fiction titles that are helpful to shifters. Remember, just as many myths are not literally true, yet can be full of wisdom, it is also true that teachings, intended and unintended, can be couched in the form of fiction and storytelling.

The Jungle Books, by Rudyard Kipling. About half of this collection of short stories concerns a different setting. The other half relate the evolving story of Mowgli, a boy raised by wolves. The Mowgli stories, taken together, form the chapters of a novel, and are sometimes published as one. *The Jungle Books* also include many deep and powerful "songs" that are more like poems, written in verse—songs about the law of the jungle, about hunting, about greeting the dawn, and other topics. This book is fiction, and animal life is not portrayed in a realistic way in these stories. Yet the book contains much deep wisdom about the ways of animal magic. Mowgli, the wolf boy, symbolizes a shapeshifter, and the stages he goes through in life are deeply symbolic of the stages that a shifter goes through. I have known more than one shifter who used this book as a kind of spiritual handbook, and some shifters also use the "songs" from this book as power chants or magical songs.

Never Cry Wolf, by Farley Mowat. This book is deeply mythic and spiritual, based on the author's experiences of wolves, plus Eskimo beliefs about wolves. Even though the events in it never happened, it represents a truth of a deeper kind, and is a valuable book for wolf shifters and those who work with wolf magic.

Many shifters look for novels that portray shifters in an accurate way that is meaningful to them. The sad truth is that almost all novels involving werewolves are absolute trash. Yet there are two novels that cut somewhat close to the truth about physical shifters. One is *Wilderness* by Dennis Danvers; the other is *The Adventures of a Two-Minute Werewolf,* by Gene DeWeese. Both of these are exaggerated, yet more accurate than anything else I've run across.

There are few novels that portray mental shifters. One is *Steppenwolf,* by Hermann Hesse. This is a portrayal of a mental shifter who is afraid of his own nature, the way many hereditary shifters are at first. It does not, therefore, present a role model to emulate. Yet many shifters have found it empowering and of spiritual value, and it does get an amazing number of the symptoms and feelings of what it is like to be a mental shifter exactly right.

Bibliography

Allen, Durward Leon. *Wolves of Minong*. Boston: Houghton Mifflin, 1979.

Amber, K. *True Magick*. St. Paul, MN: Llewellyn, 1990.

Andrews, Ted. *Animal-Speak*. St. Paul, MN: Llewellyn, 1993.

Baring-Gould, Rev. Sabine. *The Book of Were-Wolves*. London: Senate, 1995.

Beinfield, Harriet and Efrem Korngold. *Between Heaven and Earth: A Guide to Chinese Medicine*. New York: Ballantine, 1991.

Bernheimer, Richard. *Wild Men in the Middle Ages*. Cambridge: Harvard University Press, 1952.

Beza, Marcu. *Paganism in Roumanian Folklore*. New York: E. P. Dutton, 1928.

Bias, Clifford. *Ritual Book of Magic*. York Beach, ME: Samuel Weiser, 1990.

Bonewits, Isaac. *Real Magic*. York Beach, ME: Samuel Weiser, 1989.

Budge, E. A. Wallis. *Amulets and Talismans*. New York: University Books, 1961.

Burrows, Roger. *Wild Fox*. London: David & Charles, 1968.

Campbell, Joseph. *The Way of the Animal Powers*. San Francisco: HarperSanFrancisco, 1983.

Castaneda, Carlos. *Journey to Ixtlan*. New York: Simon and Schuster, 1972.

———. *The Second Ring of Power*. New York: Simon and Schuster, 1977.

———. *A Separate Reality*. New York: Simon and Schuster, 1971.

———. *The Teachings of Don Juan*. Berkeley: University of California Press, 1968.

Cohen, Daniel. *Werewolves*. New York: Penguin, 1996.

Conway, D. J. *Animal Magick*. St. Paul, MN: Llewellyn, 1995.

Cramond, Mike. *Of Bears and Man*. Norman: University of Oklahoma Press, 1986.

Crisler, Lois. *Captive Wild*. New York: Harper & Row, 1968.

Cumont, Franz Valery Marie. *Astrology and Religion Among the Greeks and Romans.* New York: Dover Publications, 1960.

Dale-Green, Patricia. *Lore of the Dog.* Boston: Houghton Mifflin, 1967.

Danvers, Dennis. *Wilderness.* New York: Simon and Schuster, 1991.

DeWeese, Gene. *The Adventures of a Two-Minute Werewolf.* New York: Doubleday, 1983.

Dömötör, Tekla. *Hungarian Folk Beliefs.* Bloomington: Indiana University Press, 1981.

Douglas, Adam. *The Beast Within.* London: Chapmans, 1992.

Eisler, Robert. *Man into Wolf: An Anthropological Interpretation of Sadism, Masochism, and Lycanthropy.* New York: Greenwood Press, 1951.

Elliot, Ralph Warren Victor. *Runes: An Introduction.* Manchester, England: Manchester University Press, 1980.

Estés, Clarissa Pinkola. *Women Who Run with the Wolves.* New York: Ballantine, 1992.

Fortune, Dion. *Psychic Self-Defense.* York Beach, ME: Samuel Weiser, 1992.

———. *The Training and Work of an Initiate.* York Beach, ME: Samuel Weiser, 2000.

Fowler, William Warde. *The Roman Festivals of the Period of the Republic.* London: Macmillian, 1933.

Gackenback, Jayne and Jane Bosveld. *Control Your Dreams.* New York: HarperCollins, 1989.

Goodman, Felicitas D. *Where the Spirits Ride the Wind.* Bloomington and Indianapolis: Indiana University Press, 1990.

Grant, Michael. *The Climax of Rome.* London: Weidenfeld & Nicolson, 1968.

Hamel, Frank. *Human Animals.* New York: University Books, 1969.

Heinrich, Institoris and Jakob Sprenger. *Malleus Maleficarum.* Rev. Montague Summers, ed. New York: B. Blom, 1970.

Hesse, Hermann. *Steppenwolf.* New York: Bantam Books, 1963.

Hill, Douglas and Pat Williams. *The Supernatural.* New York: Hawthorn, 1965.

Hittleman, Richard. *Richard Hittleman's Yoga.* New York: Wings Books, 1969.

Holmgren, Virginia C. *Cats in Fact and Folklore*. New York: Howell Book House, 1996.

Houston, Jean. *The Possible Human*. Los Angeles: J. P. Tarcher, 1982.

Inge, William Ralph. *Society in Rome Under the Caesars*. New York: C. Scribner's Sons, 1888.

Inglis, Brian. *Natural and Supernatural: A History of the Paranormal*. Dorset, England: Prism Press, 1992.

Jennings, Gary. *Black Magic, White Magic*. New York: Dial Press, 1964.

Jung, Carl G. *Man and His Symbols*. New York: Doubleday, 1972.

Katzeff, Paul. *Full Moons*. Secaucus, NJ: Citadel Press, 1981.

Kieckhefer, Richard. *Magic in the Middle Ages*. Cambridge: Cambridge University Press, 1990.

Kipling, Rudyard. *All the Mowgli Stories*. New York: Doubleday, 1954.

————. *The Jungle Books*. Oxford: Oxford University Press, 1992.

Lawrence, R. D. *In Praise of Wolves*. New York: H. Holt, 1986.

Lawson, John Cuthbert. *Modern Greek Folklore and Ancient Greek Religion*. New York: University Books, 1964.

LeShan, Lawrence. *How to Meditate*. New York: Bantam, 1974.

Lopez, Barry. *Of Wolves and Men*. New York: Scribner, 1978.

Macdonald, S. M., and C. F. Mason. *Otters: Ecology and Conservation*. Cambridge: Cambridge University Press, 1986.

Masters, Anthony. *The Natural History of the Vampire*. New York: G. P. Putnam's Sons, 1972.

McCracken, Harold. *The Beast that Walks Like a Man: The Story of the Grizzly Bear*. Garden City, NY: Hanover House, 1955.

McPhee, Charles. *Stop Sleeping Through Your Dreams*. New York: Henry Holt, 1995.

McPherson, J. M. *Primitive Beliefs in the North-East of Scotland*. New York: Longmans Green, 1929.

Mech, David L. *The Wolf: The Ecology and Behavior of an Endangered Species*. New York: Natural History Press, 1970.

Mickaharic, Draja. *Spiritual Cleansing*. York Beach, ME: Samuel Weiser, 1982.

Mowat, Farley. *Never Cry Wolf*. Toronto: McClelland & Stewart, 1963.

Neihardt, John G. *Black Elk Speaks*. Lincoln: University of Nebraska Press, 1979.

Newman, Paul. *The Hill of the Dragon*. Bath, England: Kingsmead Press, 1979.

O'Donnell, Elliot. *Werewolves*. Hertfordshire, England: Oracle Publishing, 1996.

Osborn, Harold. *South American Mythology*. New York: Peter Bedrick Books, 1983.

Ralston, W. R. S. *The Songs of the Russian People*. London: Ellis and Green, 1872.

Randolph, Vance. *The Ozarks: An American Survival of Primitive Society*. New York: Vanguard Press, 1931.

Richmond, Nigel. *Language of the Lines*. London: Wildwood House, 1977.

Russell, Jeffery Burton. *Witchcraft in the Middle Ages*. Ithaca: Cornell University Press, 1972.

Rutter, Russell J. *The World of the Wolf*. Philadelphia: Lippincott, 1968.

Schroeder, Lynn and Sheila Ostrander. *Psychic Discoveries Behind the Iron Curtain*. Englewood Cliffs, NJ: Prentice-Hall, 1970.

Scullard, Howard Hayes. *Festivals and Ceremonies of the Roman Republic*. London: Thames and Hudson, 1981.

Senn, Harry A. *Were-Wolf and Vampire in Romania*. New York: Columbia University Press, 1982.

Sharp, Henry S. and Roberta L. Hall, eds. *Wolf and Man: Evolution in Parallel*. New York: Academic Press, 1978.

Shepard, Paul. *The Sacred Paw: The Bear in Nature, Myth, and Literature*. New York: Viking, 1985.

Showerman, Grant. *Eternal Rome*. New Haven, CT: Yale University Press, 1924.

Simpson, Jacqueline. *The Folklore of Sussex*. London: B. T. Batsford, 1973.

Skeat, Walter Williams. *Malay Magic*. London: Frank Cass, 1973.

Slater, Candace. *Dance of the Dolphin*. Chicago: University of Chicago Press, 1994.

Smith, Richard J. *Fortune-Tellers and Philosophers*. San Francisco: Westview Press, 1991.

Smith, Susy. *The Enigma of Out-of-Body Travel.* New York: Helix Press; Garrett Publications, 1965.

Starhawk. *The Spiral Dance.* San Francisco: HarperSanFrancisco, 1989.

Summers, Rev. Montague. *The Geography of Witchcraft.* London: Routledge & Kegan Paul, 1978.

———. *The Vampire: His Kith and Kin.* New York: University Books, 1960.

———. *The Vampire in Europe.* New York: University Books, 1961.

———. *The Werewolf.* Secaucus, NJ: Citadel Press, 1973.

Thorsson, Edred. *Futhark: A Handbook of Rune Magic.* York Beach, ME: Samuel Weiser, 1984.

Toor, Frances. *A Treasury of Mexican Folkways.* New York: Crown Publishers, 1947.

Vacarescu, Elena. *Songs of the Valiant Voivode, and Other Strange Folklore.* New York: C. Scribner's Sons, 1905.

Walker, Benjamin. *Man and the Beasts Within.* New York: Stein and Day, 1977.

Wilson, Colin. *The Occult.* London: Hodder & Stoughton, 1971.

Wood-Martin, W. G. *Traces of the Elder Faiths of Ireland.* New York: Longmans, Green, 1902.

Woods, Barbara Allen. *The Devil in Dog Form.* Berkeley and Los Angeles: University of California Press, 1959.

Young, Stanley Paul. *The Wolves of North America.* Washington, DC: American Wildlife Institute, 1944.

Index

About the Author

ROSALYN GREENE is a highly gifted psychic whose shapeshifting experiences began at a very early age. Since there are few books available on this subject, she has written *The Magic of Shapeshifting* to share her experiences and thereby provide guidance, support, and deeper understanding to those interested in this fascinating area of psychic transformation.